NAZiK

The Politics Of Abortion

Janine Brodie

Shelley A.M. Gavigan

Jane Jenson

Toronto
OXFORD UNIVERSITY PRESS
1992

Oxford University Press, 70 Wynford Drive, Don Mills, Ontario M3C 1J9

Toronto Oxford New York
Delhi Bombay Calcutta Madras Karachi Petaling Jaya
Singapore Hong Kong Tokyo Nairobi Dar es Salaam
Cape Town Melbourne Auckland

and associated companies in
Berlin Ibadan

Canadian Cataloguing in Publication Data

Brodie, M. Janine, 1952-
The politics of abortion

Includes bibliographical references and index.
ISBN 0-19-540866-7

1. Abortion – Government policy – Canada.
2. Abortion – Law and legislation – Canada.
I. Gavigan, Shelley A.M. II. Jenson, Jane, 1946-
III. Title.

HQ767.5.C3B7 1992 363.4'6'0971 C92-093018-2

Design: Marie Bartholomew

1 2 3 4 – 95 94 93 92
Printed in Canada by Tri-Graphic

for
Judy Deverell and Amy Deverell
Lise Gotell
Bridget Jenson

Table of Contents

	Preface	1
Chapter 1	The Politics of Abortion	3
Chapter 2	Getting to *Morgentaler:* From One Representation to Another *Jane Jenson*	15
Chapter 3	Choice and No Choice in the House *Janine Brodie*	57
Chapter 4	Beyond *Morgentaler*: The Legal Regulation of Reproduction *Shelley A.M. Gavigan*	117
Appendix A	The Criminal Code	147
Appendix B	Speakers, 'Sense of the House' Debate, July 1988	151
	Notes	152
	Bibliography	186
	Index	199

Preface

This book had its beginnings in May 1988 when the three of us participated in a one-day colloquium at the Center for International Affairs (CFIA), Harvard University. Organized under the auspices of the Mackenzie King Chair in Canadian Studies, the colloquium brought together Canadian and American experts on the politics of abortion to consider the historic *Morgentaler* decision taken by the Supreme Court of Canada in January of that year. We are grateful to the CFIA and its staff for the support provided to the colloquium and for the opportunity for us to meet each other.

At the time of the colloquium, it was already becoming clear that the *Morgentaler* decision had not resolved the abortion issue in Canadian politics. In fact, on the very day of the colloquium the Mulroney government introduced its first—failed—attempt to reintroduce abortion into the Criminal Code of Canada. In the intervening years, the politics of abortion has taken a number of unanticipated and dramatic turns, all of which have ended in legislative stalemate.

During these years, work on this book has gone forward as a series of discussions among the three of us. Although Chapter One reflects our collective work and common understanding of the politics of abortion, the subsequent chapters are signed individually. This is because each of us has viewed the abortion issue from a slightly different angle of vision. Held together, however, we are confident that the essays provide a comprehensive overview of the politics of abortion in Canada during the past twenty-five years.

This collaborative process has been a joyful and fruitful one for all of us. We all have benefited from each other's comments, curiosities, and support. Many other persons contributed to this book, and we three will take this opportunity to thank them separately.

Jane Jenson's chapter benefited from a grant from the Carleton University Faculty of Graduate Studies and Research and from the research funds made available to her when she was the Mackenzie King Visiting Professor of Canadian Studies at Harvard University. Over the years of its life—which began well before 1988—this essay has evolved under the pressure of suggestions, comments and criticisms of many readers. Particular thanks go to E. Fuat Keyman for research assistance which included many suggestions for improvements, and to Greg Albo, Caroline Andrew, Hugh Armstrong, and Rianne Mahon for comments on the many earlier drafts.

Janine Brodie wishes to acknowledge the support provided by the York University Small Research Grants program, the York Institute for Social Research (and its Director, Valerie Preston) which provided a visiting fellowship during the writing of Chapter Three and the help of staff at York's Secretarial Services, especially Susan Rainey. Thanks also are owed to Chris Gabriel whose research, humour, and insights greatly improved this chapter. Appreciation for their comments and encouragement are owed to Isa Bakker, Lise Gotell, Meg Luxton, Thelma McCormack, Carol Smart and Reg Whitaker. Finally, a special thank you is extended to Nicole LaViolette who kindly provided the many documents which are necessary to this chapter.

Shelley Gavigan wishes to acknowledge with thanks Cynthia Trower, Didi Herman, Marcus Pratt and Chris Gabriel for their research assistance, Jill Maltby and Natalie Kirkwood for their technical assistance, and Karen Foti and Mary Anne Rogers, Librarians, Osgoode Hall Law School, York University, for both. Thanks as well to friends and colleagues who read parts of and commented on earlier versions of Chapter Four: Susan Boyd, Dorothy Chunn, Judy Deverell, Judy Fudge, Harry Glasbeek, Elizabeth Pickett, and Carol Smart.

Finally, we all wish to thank Olive Koyama of Oxford University Press for her patience and support in getting this book to press.

Chapter

1

The Politics of Abortion

On January 31, 1991 a tie vote in the Senate of Canada defeated Bill C-43, An Act Respecting Abortion. This unprecedented action on the part of the Upper Chamber ended the life of the highly controversial bill. Its defeat depended upon an implicit—albeit unacknowledged—coalition of pro-choice supporters who feared C-43 would result in even more limited access to abortion services and pro-life Senators who thought it went too far in permitting certain therapeutic abortions.[1] The unexpected decision marked the end of three years of bitter debate and intense political mobilization around the state's role in regulating abortion. Nevertheless, it did *not* settle the issue. Pro-life forces vowed to continue the fight, and pro-choice activists therefore prepared themselves for additional harassment, as well as legal initiatives to interfere with Canadian women's access to safe and state-supported abortion services.

This latest round in the politics of abortion was sparked by an action of the Supreme Court of Canada taken on 28 January 1988, almost exactly three years earlier. With its landmark decision in *Morgentaler v The Queen*, Canada's top court ruled that the existing federal legislation regulating access to legal abortions, which allowed doctors to provide women with therapeutic abortions under specified 'medical' indications and with the approval of a Therapeutic Abortion Committee (TAC), violated women's right to 'security of the person' and, therefore, was unconstitutional. The Court invited the federal government, if it so desired, to devise a new law which would strike a balance between the constitutional protection guaranteed to women under the *Charter of Rights and Freedoms* and the state's legitimate interest in protecting the foetus.

With one stroke of the judicial gavel, the Supreme Court had accomplished what almost twenty years of confrontation and intense political lobbying by pro-choice and pro-life groups in Canada had failed to achieve—the scrapping of Section 251 (now s.289) of the Criminal Code. This section, substantially amended in 1969 as part of an omnibus liberalization of the Code, effectively defined abortion as a medical matter. In so doing, it delegated decisions about the procedure to the medical profession and decisions about access to hospital boards. In the intervening years, this medicalized definition and institutionalization of abortion came under increasing fire from two bitterly opposed and increasingly articulate sectors of Canadian society. On one side, pro-choice groups decried state control over women's access to abortion, arguing instead that women should have the 'right to choose'. They founded their claim on the principle that reproductive freedom is integral to any realization of full gender equality. On the other side, pro-life groups countered with the claim that the right to life of the foetus takes legal and moral precedence over women's rights to self-determination.

Although claims and counterclaims about competing rights have increasingly characterized the politics of abortion in Canada, both Liberal and Conservative governments had attempted to contain the uneasy tension between the pro-choice and pro-life movements by keeping the divisive issue off the political agenda. Federal officials consistently maintained that abortion was a medical matter and that the 1969 legislation adequately addressed the health needs of Canadian women. The Supreme Court's decision in 1988, however, effectively destroyed this strategy of depoliticization; federal officials could no longer hide behind the 1969 legislation. The decision created political space for the pro-life and pro-choice forces to try to strip abortion of its medical and technical guises and recast the issue as a social and moral controversy over the respective rights of women and the foetus.

This book examines the politics of abortion in Canada leading up to and after the historic *Morgentaler* decision. Its three essays examine first, the twenty-year prelude to 1988; second, the political forces organizing the drive toward abortion legislation, which ultimately led to the stalemate of 1991; and third, the legal face of abortion politics. Abortion politics has changed dramatically in the past twenty-five years. We have witnessed the emergence of competing political claims, new social actors, innovative and intense organizational activity, and new sites of struggle. These manifest political changes, however, have been premised upon even more fundamental struggles over the social meanings ascribed to women's social roles, reproduction, and the foetus.

The Politics of Meaning

Traditionally, politics has been viewed as a process whereby competing social groups struggle around policy alternatives, one of which is then translated into law. In other words, politics is held to be synonymous with the public articulation of interests and their representation to society and the state by activists, social movements, parties, and other organizational entities. This way of thinking about politics assumes that society is comprised of social actors with more or less stable political identities whose interests are clearly defined, usually by their location in the social structure.

Our understanding of shifts in the politics of abortion, as well as initiatives to change the legislative and judicial regulation of women's reproductive capacity, reflect a more general approach to politics and the law. Numerous social scientists, many feminists among them, argue that political activity is always the result of socially constructed and historically variable meaning systems generated by political actors and defining the interests which they seek. Put differently, any expression of interest is the manifestation of a political process which also—and necessarily—involves a re-presentation of actors' identity. As social actors represent themselves as a collectivity to others, they simultaneously identify the goals of their political action. In this way they define their interests. Thus, interests are not 'given' once and for all. Rather, they emerge out of political action itself and are, moreover, variable, depending on how actors represent themselves both to themselves—how they develop their own collective identity—and to others. Such representations of identities are not given by social location, but are the result of the meaning collective actors attribute to the situation of being in that location.

This perspective on politics highlights the centrality of meaning as well as the outcomes of practice. Its focus is on the processes through which, first, new political actors come onto the scene. It also is a perspective in which questions of power are central, because it asks how new collective actors may develop sufficient resources to force their interpretation of the public interest onto the political agenda. One process is intricately related to the other. The meanings that social actors attach to themselves, to others, and to politics set the contours of political organization and mobilization, thereby informing the content of public policy.[2]

In this study of the politics of abortion in Canada, actors' definitions of themselves, the language of politics they use, the universe of political discourse[3] which they thereby create, is one starting point for analysing how social relations are constituted and understood, policy alternatives formulated, political coalitions forged and mobilized, and competing claims adjudicated by state institutions. It is our analytic proposition that ideas play a crucial role in defining how people come to understand their world, including who they are and what their interests are. Specific meaning systems, characterized by some as discourse and by others as ideology, weave together everyday statements, terms, categories, and beliefs.

In this book, we employ discourse and ideology as analytic tools. We neither collapse the concepts nor regard them as mutually exclusive. Each chapter illustrates how historically specific meaning systems give form to the social relations and political institutions within which power is both exercised and contested. Discursive construction is integral to the workings of any society's power relations because it defines our roles and our stakes in the political process.[4] Meaning systems serve to sustain power relations and inform the possibilities and limits of political struggle.

Nevertheless, the exercise of power cannot depend simply on ideas. All societies have a system of closure, based on economic, political, and social relations and practices, and this system of power organizes the hierarchy of meanings. Meaning systems are never completely autonomous of the unequal social relations which structure power in any society. At the same time, the hegemonic understanding of social relations is also a site of struggle. Although the unequal balance of power in any society ensures that some meaning systems will dominate by silencing and marginalizing other interpretations of social relations, alternative voices do emerge, especially in moments of crisis, to contest hegemonic understandings.

In many ways, then, political struggle is a struggle about meaning. Although particular social understandings are inherent in the institutionalization of subordination, not all social actors necessarily accede to the dominant representations of themselves, their interests or political issues. New social voices with different understandings may arise to contest the power structure and to represent themselves and their interests differently. The result is conflict about collective identities—about who we are and who has the right to make claims—as much as it is about who gets what, when and how. All meaning systems privilege certain social actors and viewpoints, making certain ideas and interests present and others absent.[5] They also generally prescribe where politics occurs. Whether social actors understand an issue to be 'public' or 'private', to be 'of the family' or 'of the state', or to be 'personal' or 'political' are all matters which are given to us through the power of social definitions.[6] More importantly, these matters have a profound impact on the character of political organization and struggle, the content of public policy, and the exercise of domination through the law. In this process state institutions—including the courts—are involved in organizing and reproducing relations of subordination; at the same time they may also create space for change.

The Discursive Construction of Reproduction

Feminist scholars have become increasingly sensitive to the power of language and discourse in the social construction of unequal gender relations. While women and men differ biologically, the social meanings attached to these differences have varied considerably across time and cultures. Pregnancy is a case in point. This condition singles women out as different from men, but how or even whether this difference is translated into law or politics is mediated through particular meaning systems. Most frequently, however, this biological difference has been used as a 'natural' justification for the differential treatment of women and men within and without the law.

State regulation and control of women's fertility has simultaneously sustained unequal social relations and constituted a site for feminist struggle. Modern states, whatever their form, have consistently constructed a so-called 'private sphere' in order to 'organize, rechannel, restrict or expand the fertility and sexual practices of ordinary people'.[7] State activity, however, has often led to contradictory results. The state and the law do reflect and enforce women's subordination in reproductive politics. The criminalization of abortion, for example, prohibits women's moral agency, autonomy, and choice. Yet the state may also contribute to and support shifts and modifications in social understandings and practices surrounding reproduction. Locating reproduction and more particularly abortion in medical discourse, for example, empowers certain social actors such as doctors, while formally excluding others, i.e., husbands or the church. Historically, the state has played a variety

NAZIK

of roles in the politics of reproduction, reflecting different and changing social definitions. Moreover, these definitions are always unstable, contradictory, and vulnerable to personal subversion and collective struggle. Within the universe of political discourse reproduction is an arena for contesting and resisting unequal gender relations.

The Politics of Abortion in Canada

In the history of abortion shifts in the meanings assigned to reproduction have resulted in complex interrelationships among discourses, political mobilization, and public policy. Historians remind us that women have *always* exercised choice, terminating their pregnancies as a means of fertility control.[8] Nevertheless, the meanings and legal prohibitions associated with this choice have varied significantly across time and cultures. Canadian practice, for example, has been strongly influenced by Christian tradition and by British law, both common law and statute.

The early legal history of abortion was inextricably bound up with theological doctrine. This is most clearly illustrated by the centuries-long entrenchment in English criminal law of the concept of quickening, a concept directly derived from an ecclesiastical concern to determine the first moment of vitality of the foetus. While the early Christian church stressed the sanctity of life from its very beginning, this 'moment' was not conception. Life was thought to commence only when the unborn infant first moved in the womb, that is, when it quickened. It was thought as well that only at quickening was the foetus infused with a soul. Abortion was thus initially regarded as an ecclesiastical offence, and, later, as a minor common-law offence if performed after quickening. In the early years of the nineteenth century, the significance of quickening as a momentous event in pregnancy was attacked by religious, medical, and legal authorities alike, not the least because the threshold determination of whether quickening had occurred was triggered by the word of the pregnant woman herself, and confirmed (or not) by a jury of matrons.[9]

The secular state's entry into the regulation of abortion has been relatively recent. In Britain, Lord Ellenborough's Act (1803) was an early example of such regulation. All abortions performed after quickening became punishable by death, while those performed before quickening were criminalized for the first time. Quickening as a significant distinction in abortion law was eliminated by an Act of 1837 which also dropped the death penalty for the offence. In 1861 the British House of Commons adopted the *Offences Against the Persons Act* which consolidated the offence as a felony punishable by three years imprisonment and for the first time explicitly extended criminal liability to a pregnant woman who attempted to obtain or self-induce an abortion. Abortion in Britain was governed by this Act until 1967. Nevertheless, in 1939 a British case opened space for the limited provision of legal abortions.[10] In the celebrated *Bourne* case, a jury acquitted a doctor who testified that he had performed an abortion on a fourteen-year-old who had been brutally gang-raped by three soldiers, because he had formed the opinion that the procedure was medically necessary to preserve the mental health of the young woman. Thereafter, medical practitioners who performed abortions, having formed a good faith opinion that the miscarriage was medically necessary, were reasonably secure that they would not be prosecuted. If prosecuted, they were of the view that an acquittal would surely follow. While the trial judge who charged the jury in *Bourne* did not make express reference to the defence of necessity, the case was taken to have rendered this defence available in abortion prosecutions.

Canada's legislative regime largely followed the British path. By the early 1840s, some of the colonies had legislation which imitated Lord Ellenborough's Act. The *Offences Against the Persons Act* was incorporated into Canada's Criminal Code enacted in 1892. It made abortion an indictable offence and those convicted were liable to imprisonment for life. It also made women who attempted to abort themselves liable to up to seven years imprisonment (see Appendix A). This general legal prohibition remained virtually unaltered until 1969.[11]

Canadian women, however, continued to resort to abortion as a means, albeit illegal and often dangerous, of fertility control. The practice was usually carried out in secrecy either by women themselves or with the aid of an illegal abortionist. Historical evidence suggests that abortion services were also offered overtly, but in a disguised form. Newspapers at the turn of the century and later, for example, openly advertised services and products for women designed to make their periods 'regular'.[12] This extra-legal abortion regime, however, was not without its costs: many Canadian women died and many more became infertile as the result of desperate last resorts to gain control over their reproductive capacities.

Canada finally moved to change the regulation of abortion in the late 1960s. The new law, Section 251 of the Criminal Code, maintained a general ban on abortions, but allowed a 'therapeutic exception' for a doctor who received certification from a Therapeutic Abortion Committee (TAC) in an accredited hospital that the continuation of the pregnancy 'would or would be likely to' endanger the life or health of the pregnant woman. (See Appendix A.) In effect, this reform of the law replaced judicial control after the fact for medical control before the fact.[13]

As Jane Jenson describes in Chapter Two, the 1969 reform was framed and achieved within a discourse of medicalization. Reproductive decisions—especially those related to contraception and abortion — were designated as medical ones; the moral or political content was downplayed. As a result doctors were assigned control over women's reproductive decisions. This change had been motivated by the concerns of some doctors who had been performing abortions but who were becoming increasingly concerned about their criminal liability in the face of mounting demand. The principal motivation for the new legislation was to clarify the doctors' legal liabilities and define the state's interest in regulating the procedure. During these years, the voices of women as collective actors with different interests in the abortion issue were largely marginalized and muffled. To the extent that women figured in the debate, they were seen as objects—the victims of 'the backstreet abortionist'—and in need of protective legislation. As Jenson points out, this medicalized definition made abortion reform possible, but it was soon challenged by the emergence of new actors with new definitions of their interests and the issue. Feminists immediately began to make claims for women's control over reproduction. By the mid-1970s, pro-choice groups began to challenge the prevailing medical definition, using instead a language of rights. By the 1980s the politics of abortion encompassed forces advancing either the rights of women or the rights of the foetus.

The struggle over competing definitions of abortion was propelled with full force into the political arena by the Supreme

Court's judgement in the 1988 *Morgentaler* case. Pro-choice groups celebrated the decision because the court appeared to embrace and legitimize key themes of their rights-based discourse. The majority ruled that the Criminal Code's provisions infringed upon a woman's right to security of the person and that the requirement of approval by a TAC was inconsistent with the principles of fundamental justice. Nevertheless, as Shelley Gavigan observes in the last chapter of this book, the *Morgentaler* decision, like many other apparent victories, was contradictory, fragile, and incomplete. The Court continued to insist that abortion was a medical matter, and that the growing struggle between pro-choice and pro-life forces about the respective rights of women and the foetus had to be settled through political rather than legal mechanisms.

In Chapter Three Janine Brodie traces the politics of abortion after the *Morgentaler* decision until the Senate's defeat of Bill C-43 in January 1991. The chapter examines the failed attempts of the federal government to depoliticize the abortion issue and then to locate a compromise position on this deeply divisive issue. After the *Morgentaler* decision both pro-choice and pro-life groups attempted to seize the opportunity to displace once and for all the medicalized language of abortion and replace it with their respective discourses around rights. At stake was the content of the new state regulatory regime. The ensuing struggle reflected the dual nature of politics. It took the form of conventional politics—lobbying, mobilizing, and demonstrating. At another level, however, it was a struggle over vocabulary and meaning because the content of any new policy was premised upon particular understandings of the objects of regulation—in this case women's fertility and access to self-determination. While both the pro-choice and pro-life arguments centred on the issue of abortion *per se*, each promoted very different understandings of women, their place in society, and their rights. Unlike the 1969 parliamentary moment, when the collective interests of women were obscured within the discourse of medicalization, this time their interests were pitted against a relatively new actor in the politics of abortion—the foetus.

The foetus, much like the body of the pregnant woman, is a technical term which pro-life discourse has very powerfully imbued with social meaning. According to medical parlance, an embryo becomes a foetus when it completes its basic organ development, approximately eight weeks after fertilization.[14] At this stage, it is roughly an inch in length and can only be categorized as 'human' by reference to its genetic structure. The development of the foetus is a biological process, but the point at which we elect to represent the foetus as a human and assign human qualities to it is very much an issue of interpretation and social construction.[15]

Historically, western societies have not defined the foetus as a person and certainly not a person with rights which take precedence over those of the living. To the extent that it was valued, it was valued as a father's property.[16] As Shelley Gavigan explains in Chapter Four, the discursive construction of the foetus as a person is a relatively recent innovation in Canadian legal practice and a critical victory for pro-life forces. Although the courts have not, as yet, granted constitutional protection to the foetus, they have moved in ways to 'protect' the foetus from the threat supposedly posed by pregnant women. Again, the real targets of this pro-life campaign are women who wish to retain their status as autonomous individuals.

As Chapter Four shows, the law, like legislative politics, constitutes a site for struggles over meanings — meanings which feminists have attempted to influence but do not control. The power of law is to reflect and reinforce particular meaning systems over others. Feminists have sought to focus judicial treatment of abortion on the matter of women's rights, but their reliance on rights-based claims also has given rise to counterclaims about the rights of the foetus and of fathers. Nevertheless, Canadian courts' continued adherence to a medicalized definition of abortion may paradoxically protect Canadian women from many of the setbacks suffered by women in countries such as the United States, where abortion has been subsumed under the constitutional protection of individual privacy.

This book recounts the story of abortion politics in Canada over the past twenty years and how this politics has been practised in public, the legislatures, and the courts. Although each author takes a somewhat different approach, all three demonstrate the centrality of analysing both meaning systems and practices in order to understand the dramatic changes which have characterized the politics of abortion. Even more broadly, we must comprehend such meanings and practices if we are to understand the regulation and construction of the female body and subject, the emergence and politics of social movements, and the role of the state and law in the reproduction of patriarchal gender relations. The book has taken the *Morgentaler* decision as its point of departure but, as the following chapters will make clear, that decision, as historic as it was, did not settle the issue. It simply moved the debate to new terrain. Now more than ever the politics of abortion contest the social meanings attached to gender and representation as well as women's access to social equality and self-determination. We ignore this crucial dimension of the abortion debate only at great costs to ourselves and our daughters.

Chapter

2

Getting to *Morgentaler*: From One Representation To Another

Jane Jenson

The Supreme Court decision of 28 January 1988 which found Section 251 of the Criminal Code unconstitutional came as a shock to most of the people who had been actively following the abortion controversy. Those who had struggled for years for an extension of women's reproductive rights and who had defended Dr Morgentaler's clinics lauded the decision but were nevertheless surprised by how far-reaching it was. Previous state action on this matter had not prepared them for the Court's removal of all restrictions on doctors performing abortions. For the pro-life forces the decision seemed an immense setback to their efforts to restrict, even eliminate, access to abortion, in the name of religious morality and/or competing foetal rights.

The Court's decision was a complicated one. It struck down the restrictions on abortion inscribed in the Criminal Code in 1969, on the grounds that they unduly limited women's access to a medical procedure guaranteed by the 'security of the person' provision of Section 7 of the Canadian *Charter of Rights and Freedoms*. In other words, the majority of the Court decided that an individual's Charter-guaranteed rights included access to medical care and procedures. The majority decision did not address the question of whether women had reproductive rights, nor did it make any attempt to reconcile women's rights with those of the foetus.[1]

Since the mid-1980s, the issues of conflicting rights has polarized public debate about abortion into two militant camps of pro-choice and pro-life supporters. The Supreme Court refused to engage in *this* controversy, insisting that legislators must decide. The decision may have come as a bolt from the blue, but the terms within which the Court confined its decision were much less surprising. It was a continuation of a discourse about abortion employed by the Canadian state for over twenty years. Before 1988 the state had never treated abortion as a 'women's issue'. Very often earlier debates about state regulation of abortion occurred as if the pregnant women had little interest and few rights in the matter. Controversy raged about the rights and responsibilities of doctors and the social consequences of abortion or compulsory pregnancy. The voices raised were often those of humanists, doctors, social reformers, judges, religious leaders, and state officials. Feminist voices, expressing a clear pro-choice position, had had a much harder time being heard.

The constitutional entrenchment of new individual rights via the *Charter of Rights and Freedoms* in 1982 provided an important potential for change in the meaning attached to abortion by state institutions, and therefore in the way that the state would regulate reproduction in the future. The Charter clearly re-oriented political discourse in Canada towards greater attention to rights, both individual and collective. The Supreme Court began to reinterpret the abortion issue in terms of rights, but it did so by continuing to insist that it was dealing with a medical matter.

This chapter will describe the ways that the courts and other institutions dealt with the abortion question before the *Morgenthaler* decision. In doing so, it will highlight the important differences between the discourses of liberalization and medicalization with which the state bounded the issue before *Morgentaler* and the terms of the prevailing public discourse evident in the parliamentary controversies recounted in the next chapter.

This shift in political language occurred in large part because of the manner in which the Supreme Court decided to deal with abortion in 1988. By refusing to modify Section 251 of the Criminal Code and striking it down instead, the Court threw the ball back to Parliament and/or the provincial legislatures. In so doing, the Court contributed to an undermining of the idea that abortion was a medical matter, which was how it had decided *Morgentaler* and similar cases. Public debate was no longer bounded by the terms of the medicalization discourse, and throwing the issue into the legislative arena meant that new positions would reorient the discussion. Thus, the Court's decision, despite reflecting its traditional preference for medicalizing the abortion question, opened space for subsequent public controversy between pro-life groups championing the right-to-life of the foetus and pro-choice supporters claiming women's right to control their own reproduction.

Before 1988 this confrontation had never totally manifested itself within the state, despite the growing political power of the two opposed movements. The definition of abortion as a medical matter had effectively limited the power of both pro-choice and pro-life groups. It limited the pro-choice movement's ability to wrest control over decisions about reproduction from doctors and hospitals, to which Section 251 had assigned it. But it also limited the pro-life group's ability to make the question simply one of morality and foetal rights.

These limits effectively created a stand-off in the abortion debate.[2] By the late 1980s that situation could not continue. Each side had gained sufficient strength to impose itself on the other. As pro-life groups captured control of hospital boards and closed Therapeutic Abortion Committees (TACs), pro-choice groups saw women's access to legal abortion services virtually disappear in many places. As free-standing abortion clinics supported by pro-choice groups opened in several provinces, flouting the existing law by performing 'illegal' abortions, pro-lifers gained public visibility and even support for their argument that 'social stability' depended on severely restricting abortion. Therefore, it is not surprising that the consequence of the *Morgentaler* case was further difficult, even bitter, confrontation between two sides with often diametrically opposed views of what abortion represents for women, for families, and for society.

The Politics of Representation

The history of the abortion issue in Canada provides an excellent example of the power of representation. In Chapter One we explored theoretically the politics of representation. There we argued that one way to think about politics is to focus on the processes by which new actors come onto the scene and develop sufficient resources to force their interpretation of their own interests and those of others onto the political agenda.

This chapter traces the emergence of new actors and their redefinition of the very meaning of the abortion issue. But before such actors, and especially the pro-choice movement, could contest long-dominant representations of the interests of women and society, they had to challenge the power of earlier organizers of the representation of the issue. The power of other collective actors to shape the abortion issue around their own definition of interests was a major block to new representations and the actors promoting them.

In general terms, the history of the abortion issue both reveals the extent to which the Canadian state continued to exercise an inordinate amount of influence over women's reproductive lives and explains why the access to abortion which was established in the late 1960s proved so vulnerable to attack by those who would limit it further. The history of legal abortions in Canada teaches us that politics maintains relations of domination over women in part by defining the very meaning of those relations, as well as by institutionalizing practices which restrain women.[3]

Particular meaning systems sustain institutions within which specific practices take place. Through these institutions relations of subordination are organized and reproduced, and in this way ideas take on a material existence which continues over time. While analysis of the social construction of meaning is necessary to understand policy outcomes, meaning systems are never completely autonomous of the unequal social relations which inevitably exist in a society in which the relations of production, in the family, and between women and men—among others—structure power. In any social formation, basic social arrangements provide the limiting conditions for the specific content of the universe of political discourse. Only an examination of a society's politics can make visible the concrete historical power struggles over its ideas and practices.

This understanding of representation clearly implies that a power relationship is at the root of all political discourse. All actors do not exercise the same power over the meaning systems which organize political debate. So, while contestation may exist, as in any contest there are winners and losers. Some actors manage to make their voices heard loudly within the universe of political discourse while others are silenced, speaking among themselves in a language that only they can understand.

This play of sound and silence, of the power to represent, provides a crucial focus of this chapter. The dominant representations of the abortion issue up until the mid-1980s were promoted by actors other than pro-choice feminists concerned about women's need for access to legal and safe abortions, or other than the pro-life movement demanding recognition of foetal rights. Abortion reform in 1969 was understood primarily within a discourse of medicalization and this particular representation of the issue dominated state interventions on the matter until 1988. Many actors consistently represented abortion as a medical practice, one which was within the realm of doctors' control because it involved issues of health. Most simply, if doctors saw any pregnancy as 'unhealthy', they could legally abort it. A second facet of the representation of abortion, which had been initially important but then almost disappeared, was a discourse of liberalization, employed by some actors to discuss sexuality. Because abortion was indirectly related to sexual practice, some reformers linked changes in Section 251 to a more general liberalization of social mores and an expanding space for sexuality free from state interference.

In neither of these meaning systems did abortion address women's situation or their needs. Only if women themselves had gained more influence over the decision would the discourses of medicalization and liberalization have been successfully contested, and only in that way might state action have been differently constituted. The almost total absence of feminists' pro-choice voices in the universe of political discourse in 1969 set the politics of abortion in Canada off down a road to 1988 via the path of medical definition in an uneasy silence about the moral dimensions of the issue, as well as about whose interests were implicated by this issue. This trajectory had both positive and negative consequences for women in the intervening years.

In the 1970s and 1980s, however, new loud voices emerged in the universe of political discourse—those of pro-choice and pro-life—and they began to represent the issue differently. Gaining political power through their ability to challenge the state and influence partisan politics, their representations competed with that of the state and doctors. Finally, then, the 1988 *Morgentaler* decision opened the way for this new discourse to dominate the terrain of dispute as it moved back into the realm of Parliament and political parties.

Reform of the Criminal Code—1969

In 1969, as part of an omnibus reform of the Criminal Code, the Canadian state altered its regulation of women's reproductive lives. That bill brought a number of important revisions in the state's monitoring of individuals' sexual, reproductive, and family activities. Divorce, birth control, and abortion became more accessible at the same time as homosexual relations between consenting adults were de-criminalized. In 1969 the realms were all inscribed in a single meaning system. The discourse of liberalization would have the state withdraw from areas of moral controversy rather than 'impose' any particular values. The reformers' intent was to save the state from the threat to its legitimacy presented by unenforceable laws—like those on contraception and abortion—as the public became more sexually broad-minded in the 1960s.

In the case of abortion, however, the considerations of liberalization were coupled with a discourse of medicalization, which focused on the practical needs of doctors. The state continued to regulate abortion primarily by controlling the behaviour of doctors. The 1969 reform of the Criminal Code clarified some ambiguities of wording and specified the procedures that doctors must follow in terminating a pregnancy. After 1969 a woman might ask for an abortion but it was the doctor who decided whether to grant that request. Doctors could perform abortions only in approved or accredited hospitals and only after a Therapeutic Abortion Committee (TAC) established for that purpose gave its approval.[4] The only condition such Committees could consider was a threat to the woman's life or health following from the continuation of the pregnancy.

This reform did not fundamentally alter the existing meaning of abortion for doctors. For years, some doctors had been performing abortions when they considered women's health threatened, and the 1969 reform merely cleared up the grey areas in such practices. Abortion remained out of women's control because it was still a medical practice in the hands of doctors. The state considered that it had merely clarified a medical practice, albeit one which was not quite like all others since the Criminal Code regulated it.

Women's voices were diffused and weak during the development of the discursive compromise establishing the institutions within which the practices of abortion politics would occur for the next two decades. The second wave of feminism had not yet made itself felt in Canadian society. Women had not yet developed the powerful collective identity with which they could name themselves as women and act on a gender-based solidarity. Therefore, the compromise embedded in the Criminal Code in 1969 was derived from the dominant voices of professional men and some Protestant church leaders.[5]

The Coalition for Reform

By the late 1960s in many countries pressure was mounting for changes in the restrictions on abortion and the Canadian case can be seen as part of this postwar movement.[6] Moreover, in these years actors' representation of the issue was often very similar: an alliance of social reformers and doctors advocating expanded access to contraception and the easing of abortion restrictions.[7] In the interwar years effective methods of contraception had finally been developed and publicized and by the early 1960s the birth-control pill began to be marketed. Promoting the benefits of these technological changes was a social movement for birth-control reform, the family planning movement. This international movement, institutionalized after World War Two in the International Planned Parenthood Federation (IPPF), sought legalized contraception in order to allow families to achieve control over family size and the timing of their children, so as to improve the quality of life of both parents and children. As an international body, IPPF was also involved in the campaign to limit world population growth, as part of postwar planning for development of non-Western countries.[8] Doctors and other health professionals were important leaders of the family planning movement, and some Protestant churches provided much needed legitimation of the new representation of contraception as a desirable practice.[9]

Supporters of the family planning movement addressed the issue of abortion as well because, in their discourse, lack of access to reliable methods of contraception was the root cause of the problem of illegal abortion. In every country the rate of illegal abortion was very high; one Canadian estimate was 33,000 in 1959 alone.[10] Such abortions were extremely dangerous, often resulting in deaths and even more frequently in permanent damage to women's reproductive capacities. Technical improvements in medical care occurring through the interwar years and after 1945 substantially lowered maternal mortality, and made starkly visible the contribution of abortion to childbirth-related deaths. From the 1930s to the 1950s, maternal deaths declined dramatically and abortion-related deaths rose in both relative and absolute terms.[11] Thus, there were substantial grounds for reformers to begin to represent the issue as an 'abortion epidemic'.

The family planning movement linked contraception and abortion by advocating legal contraception in order to eliminate resort to illegal and dangerous 'backstreet abortions'. Many reformers recognized, however, that all methods to control conception were not 100% reliable and contraceptive failure, as well as ignorance, rape, and incest, still made unwanted pregnancy a real possibility. Therefore, they often simultaneously sought legalization of abortion in order to guarantee safe procedures in such unfortunate situations.[12]

This kind of reasoning for reform of both contraceptive practices and abortion appeared in one of the first salvoes of the abortion-reform campaign. In 1959 an article in *Chatelaine* made a series of arguments for reform of the abortion legislation. It was a quite classic version of an internationally familiar genre.[13] It began with an example of an uncomplicated case, that of a fourteen-year-old pregnant as the result of a gang-rape who could not abort even after such an awful experience. It went on to argue that unwanted pregnancies of this dramatic sort, or even those of poor women with several living children, would lead to dire social consequences. Sociopaths were likely to begin as 'unwanted children'. Moreover, important to the argument was the notion that quality of life, for the mother and other members of the family, counted more than that of the foetus.

Such emphases on social arguments, representing the needs of both society as a whole and of the 'under-privileged', were common to campaigns for abortion reform in most countries. They were evocative in many cases because they could be linked to the prevailing postwar discourse of Keynesianism and state welfare, in which societal well-being and development depended on state provision of economic and social conditions benefiting all citizens. This was a discourse of social equality. Therefore, the representation of abortion restrictions as affecting the poor more than the rich—who could afford contraception and travel to jurisdictions where abortion was legal—and as generally unfair fitted well within it.

In Canada, however, such a discourse of social and economic justice was less powerful and the *Chatelaine* article was one of the few of this genre. The dissemination of this discourse depended in most countries upon its use by left-wing parties and other reforming organizations, the initial promoters of Keynesian state welfare. The Canadian Keynesian discourse was much weaker.[14] The state's commitment to Keynesian state welfare was mild in the postwar years and the New Democratic Party (NDP) had a marginal influence (especially in the early 1960s when it had just been founded) in the universe of political discourse. Thus, abortion reform as a means of achieving social justice for mothers and for families was a theme present in debate but without much power to shape the representation of the abortion issue.[15]

As a result, the issue of abortion reform, the actors involved, and the interests evoked were constituted in Canada primarily in medical terms. Pressure for reform came from a combination of lawyers, clergymen, and doctors.[16] All three groups had wide-ranging political influence, especially within Parliament which looked to socially powerful 'experts' for a rationale for the reforms. After some jostling, a compromise resulted which combined the lawyers' and religious leaders' enthusiasm for liberalization of state enforcement of moral codes and the doctors' concerns about the legality of their actions when they terminated pregancies.

The roots of this compromise lay in doctors' confusing and inconsistent experiences with respect to abortion in the early 1960s. When the Canadian Criminal Code was consolidated in 1892 it incorporated the existing law on abortion, modelled on the British *Offences Against the Person Act*. The relevant sections were Sections 271-274 of the Criminal Code which made it illegal and punishable by life imprisonment for someone to procure a woman's miscarriage and made self-inducement of abortion subject to seven years in prison (see Appendix A). But there was a clear 'saving' provision in the Code which absolved doctors who acted to preserve a woman's life and thereby killed the foetus.[17]

In subsequent years, and taking the lead from developments in British law, many Canadian doctors considered the Criminal Code's injunction against 'procuring a miscarriage' inapplicable to abortions performed to save the life of a woman. Such exceptions depended, of course, on their peers and the courts accepting their professional judgement about what was necessary for their patients. The stress on judgement, which was central to interpretation of the Criminal Code's provisions, was the problem in the doctors' eyes and became more so as the law evolved.

The important 1939 *Bourne* case in the UK—in which an abortion performed on a young woman whose pregnancy was judged to threaten her mental stability was ruled medically necessary—provided a precedent for the existence of 'legal' abortions in Canada, even in circumstances in which the threat to life was indirect. The *Bourne* case captures, in fact, all of the confusion plaguing the medical establishment.[18] According to the court deciding the case, abortion was possible if the pregnancy threatened the life or health—even the mental health—of the woman. This language of possibility contained a major ambiguity, however. There was no adequate definition of 'health', although any decision depended on its meaning. Doctors were assigned responsibility, granted by their professional qualifications, for determining whether a woman's 'health' was at risk.

Not surprisingly, Canadian doctors tried to clarify the ambiguity. Most doctors who contemplated terminating a pregnancy consulted at least one colleague, so that a second opinion on the case existed. Sometimes hospitals formalized this procedure by setting up a committee of doctors to hear the details of such cases.[19] Indeed, by the early 1960s therapeutic abortion committees, whether so labelled or not, existed in many non-Catholic hospitals. Nevertheless, even when doctors felt their procedures stood up to professional scrutiny, they still feared prosecution under the Criminal Code because of the ambiguities inherent in the existing judicial language and procedures. Therefore, in the early 1960s most doctors did not perform abortions. People who did not think they were undertaking a legal medical practice and who therefore carried out abortions secretly and in less than optimal facilities—that is, performed 'backstreet' abortions—did most of the estimated 20,000 to 120,000 a year.[20]

Doctors who did admit doing abortions but who feared the legal ambiguity of their situation led the reform campaign which began in the mid-1960s. By 1963 professional associations of doctors, the Canadian Medical Association (CMA)—and of lawyers—the Canadian Bar Association (CBA)—began at their annual meetings to question the Criminal Code's regulation of abortion. The intra- and inter-professional discussion continued until 1969, paying little attention to the needs of anyone but doctors or lawyers.[21] As a result of this process, the voices of women who were the recipients of the most common type of abortion—the 'backstreet' ones—were marginalized in the debate. Indeed, the silence extended to all women, despite the fact that they were the objects of the practice, if not the perceived subject of the law.

Women, organized as women demanding specific and particular gender rights, had as yet no status as political actors. Women in the mid-sixties did not have the political resources to press their positions or even a language in which they could express them. Second-wave feminism did not yet occupy any significant space in the universe of political discourse. The women's voices which were heard, then, tended to reflect the discomfort which the heirs of first-wave maternal feminism had in dealing with reproduction and sexuality. Moreover, existing organizations of women were either weak or non-confrontational—or both. Few as yet had a critique of the system of gender relations which subordinated women to men and silenced female voices in public debates.

Arguments for Reform

The amendments to the Criminal Code which did emerge, promoted by traditionally dominant intellectuals—doctors, lawyers, and clergymen—reflected the power relations then existing in Canadian society and represented in the universe of political discourse. Unequal power relations—in which neither women nor a progressive Left spoke very loudly—were reproduced in the debates about reform of the Criminal Code. The discourse of neither medicalization nor liberalization incorporated the idea that access to abortion was a basic right of women—as the American Supreme Court decision on *Roe v Wade* established in 1973 after substantial mobilization of the women's movement around a rights-based discourse.[22] Nor were these discourses utilized to discuss abortion as a way of preventing unwanted pregnancy from bringing about a deterioration in women's economic and social conditions, as was argued by many European Left political parties and social democratic governments.

The description of the Canadian Medical Association's (CMA) delegation to a House of Commons hearing in 1967 clearly reveals the structure of the situation:

> Dr Aitken acted as spokeman for the CMA delegation, which included . . . three distinguished practitioners and teachers of obstetrics and gynecology, and Dr Kenneth Gray of the Clarke Institute of Psychiatry. Dr Lewis Brand (PC, Saskatoon) referred to them as 'distinguished lawbreakers' and Robert Stanbury (L, York-Scarborough) as 'the biggest gathering of abortionists ever held in Canada'—a bantering reaction to Dr Cannell's admission that 'I and my colleagues have been breaking the law now for a long time', both in performing therapeutic abortions and in advising patients on methods of contraception.[23]

This scenario is worth examining in detail. The CMA group were all male, successful obstetricians and gynaecologists who had encountered enough potential and actual abortion cases to cause them to push for reform. Their disingenuous appeal to being 'law-breakers', despite their professional status and success, could only effectively point out the impossibility of prolonging the current ambiguity. Indeed, there was a clear notion that the existing law was discredited, if persons of this stature had to break it. They stressed, as well, the relatively minor nature of the proposed change. In fact, the briefs from the CMA and provincial associations of doctors proposed 'tidying up' the situation so that the law and common practices would again coincide. The following exchange between Dr Cannell and Liberal MP Robert Stanbury, an enthusiastic supporter of the doctors, demonstrates this clearly:

> Mr Stanbury: Is it then fair to say that . . . Canadian doctors have indeed, on compassionate grounds, been performing abortions for some years?
> Dr Cannell: I think that is a fair statement.
> Mr Stanbury: I am glad that they have but it is unfortunate that you have been exposed to criminal prosecution by so doing. I gather the main purpose of your resolution is to try to clarify the fact that it is permissible for doctors to do what they have indeed been doing and to encourage the availability of such treatment on a more equal basis in all hospitals across Canada rather than just in some, as has been the case.
> Dr Cannell: I would say that is correct.[24]

The CMA's resolution set out three conditions under which a legal abortion might be performed: if the woman's life or health was threatened, if the foetus was defective in some way, or if the pregnancy resulted from a sexual crime. In the first two cases such abortions were clearly 'therapeutic'. Therefore, all abortions were to be approved by a hospital Therapeutic Abortion Committee.

In the hearings before the parliamentary committee the representatives of the CMA were not willing to engage in any debate about the 'philosophical' or 'moral' issues which abortion might raise. They declared themselves unable to discuss questions of social justice. Indeed, such a notion made the assembled doctors very nervous because, as they clearly testified, the resolution they presented had been arrived at only after hard negotiations within the CMA. It worked as a compromise precisely because it kept control in the hands of the doctors. The doctors testifying were adamantly opposed to 'abortion on request', and looked askance at the Humanist Fellowship of Canada's proposal for just that in the first three months of pregnancy.[25]

The CMA did suggest, however, extending the power of doctors quite substantially. Its resolution proposed legalizing abortion not only when the life or health of the 'pregnant female' was threatened but also when a TAC judged there was a reasonable chance that the foetus would be deformed or when the pregnancy was the result of a sexual crime. In the days before amniocentesis, judgements of foetal deformities were haphazard at best. German measles (rubella), contracted during the early weeks of pregnancy and sometimes causing deafness, blindness, etc., was the primary example of a condition that the doctors pointed to as making abortion for 'deformity' necessary. Yet, in this testimony the doctors revealed that they had only imprecise probabilistic ways of anticipating the foetus had been harmed. Therefore, there was always a relatively high chance that a healthy foetus might be aborted.[26]

While the spokesmen for the CMA strongly defended their professional ability to make such predictions—and to assess the burden to mothers of bearing such children—the parliamentarians were much less convinced that such power should reside in their hands. This element of the CMA's proposal, then, disappeared from the final amendment.

The verbatim report of the Parliamentary Committee clearly reveals the stranglehold that a discourse of medicalization could create. Abortion itself was hardly mentioned in an active sense. It appeared as an adjective in 'therapeutic abortion committee' but beyond that the actual act was referred to as a 'procedure' and the need for abortion as a 'situation', always one to be avoided. Illegal abortions were frequently mentioned, again as an evil. Of more interest—and importance for the future—were the ways the objects of 'the procedure' were consistently labelled either 'pregnant females' (as in the CMA's resolution), 'people', or 'mothers'. The head of the Medical Association's delegation—finally provoked by incessant demands by the MPs that they address matters of morality—finally said the following:

> Dr Aitken: Our position really is sort of summed up in the fact that we feel the rights of the living, the actual human being at the moment—basically the mother—override consideration of the rights of a potential human being, the embryo, which will develop into a human being.[27]

Thus, in the representations of the CMA, the mother—their patient—had greater rights than those of the unknown, carefully referred to by the technical medical name used for the foetus for the first weeks of pregnancy.

Who were the doctors speaking of, then? Beside the somewhat stick figure of the 'pregnant female' they clearly saw patients, who had oftentimes no gender, being simply 'people'. More commonly, however, doctors saw 'mothers'. These mothers came in several varieties, being ones who already had too many children, or who were forced-to-be-mothers, or who were not healthy enough to be mothers, or who were too young to be mothers. For these obstetricians and gynaecologists who dealt all their working lives with women seeking to be or about to be mothers, their patients were always potentially maternal and could never be represented by other than that status.

But in the discussions of the Parliamentary Committee there was—only rarely to be sure but she was there—another figure, a much less appreciated one.[28] The Committee had heard the brief, presented by Dr Henry Morgentaler, of the Humanist Fellowship before that of the CMA, and the MPs were anxious to discuss 'abortion on request'. In those discussions, however, this new figure—the woman who wanted simply to ask for an abortion from her doctor—suddenly appeared. Gone were the anonymous pregnant females and the mothers; 'women' were hovering on the edge of the universe of political discourse of even this Parliamentary Committee in 1967. Their full appearance in subsequent years would challenge the medicalized representation of abortion.

Another major entrant in the campaign for reform was the Canadian Bar Association (CBA), which proposed that hospitals establish Termination Boards and that these permit abortion under three circumstances—when the pregnancy constituted a danger to the 'mother's life or health', resulted from rape or incest, or was likely to produce a mentally or physically disabled child.[29] The lawyers also advocated this change to improve the condition of 'the pregnant female'. But the needs of doctors—the potential clients of the lawyers—were most important to the members of the CBA who debated these issues at their conventions. For example, in the words of one speaker at the 1966 meeting of the CBA, 'there can be nothing more immoral, nothing more irreligious than turning medical practitioners and decent people into criminals in the way our present legislation does'.[30] The CBA also weighed the predicament of the police and the courts, both of which lost legitimacy before an essentially unenforceable law.

For the CBA, more than for the CMA, discussions of abortion reform also arose in the context of proposals for wide-ranging alterations in the state's regulation of sexual practices. In the mid-1960s the Bar Association focused on many parts of the Criminal Code, seeking reforms which would better match state regulation with contemporary mores. Parliament often called on the CBA for suggestions and the lawyers couched them in a discourse of liberalization.

> When we check the arguments used in 1968 and 1969 we find that the most frequently quoted phrases and most commonly expressed sentiments were that 'sin is not the same as a crime' and that morality ought to have nothing to do with civil law.[31]

The CMA, in contrast, continued to insist that all it wanted was a clarification of existing medical practice.

Other major interventions in the discussion of abortion reform came from several Protestant churches. By 1960 the United Church had adopted an official position which deferred to medical opinion. It refused to accept abortion on social grounds—for poor women or unmarried women for whom an unwanted pregnancy would fundamentally restrict their life chances—or as a form of contraception, but it was willing to allow doctors to decide on abortion for health reasons.[32] The official Anglican position followed the lead of the Church of England, which had proposed legislation substantially extending the conditions under which doctors could perform abortions.[33] While both churches were more likely than the professional associations to see abortion reform in the light of moral strictures, they also used a discourse of medicalization, claiming that the state should defer to the professional judgement of doctors.

The major group which explicitly addressed women's interests in abortion reform was the National Council of Women, the first national organization to go on record favouring more widely available abortions. From 1963 to 1966 it presented annual resolutions to the government arguing that the existing situation was 'confused, conflicting, outdated, and in certain instances, cruel and unjust'.[34] In other words, the law hurt *women*, in large part because it led to inequities. Women who could find doctors willing to perform abortions in the hazy area of *Bourne*, could save themselves from an unwanted pregnancy. Others were forced to carry to term or risk a backstreet abortion. Obviously, the chance of finding a doctor willing to perform a 'legal' abortion was higher in some places or for women wealthy enough to make feasible a wide-ranging search, even involving travel. Therefore, according to the National Council of Women, the state should make the law more just by recognizing that all women might at some time require an abortion. This was not an argument based on the 'right to choose' but rather on the injustice of uneven access.

The National Council of Women was the largest and most accepted representative of Canadian women at that time. Founded in 1893, it had committed itself to serving 'the highest good of the family and the State and application of the Golden Rule'.[35] Within these terms of reference, any advocacy of women's right to control their own bodies or expression of the anger and anguish of women who had been forced to seek backstreet abortions was difficult. Either would have gone against the traditionally restrained behaviour of the Council and its fear of rocking the very delicate political boat in which it found itself.[36] The most it could do was to argue that current practices were unjust and inequitable and demand reform in the direction of greater social justice. The Canadian Committee on the Status of Women and the Women's Liberation Group also presented briefs to the parliamentary hearings. The Toronto Women's Liberation Group was the only one to articulate a position of reproductive control.[37]

None of these groups of women ever gained recognition as major actors in the debate. While they did present briefs to the government both before and during Parliamentary hearings on the proposed reform, public symposia rarely included any representatives of women. For example, when *The Globe and Mail* began to campaign for abortion reform and ran a series of articles in 1961 it claimed to cover all interested parties by inviting only religious and medical men to participate. It seems that for *The Globe and Mail*, abortion was a 'man's problem', being about law, medical practices, and morality.

Opposition to reform came primarily from the Roman Catholic Church, but it was restrained. At the time the Church itself was experiencing social and doctrinal upheaval associated with the Vatican Council and the papacy of John XXIII. While Catholics themselves were debating doctrinal and social questions, their interventions in the public and Parliamentary discussions tended to reflect a certain hesitancy to promote traditional positions with complete enthusiasm.[38] By 1968 the publication of a papal encyclical against contraception and abortion began to rally some Catholics to oppose reform. Nevertheless, the papal pronouncement provoked so much initial opposition *within* the Catholic community that the Church remained inward-looking for a while.

Doctors and lawyers concerned for their medical clients, then, organized the movement toward reform. The proposals with the greatest impact on the deliberations of the Parliamentary Committee came from the CBA and CMA.[39] Because of the perception that doctors and lawyers were the experts on the topic and because of the privileged access they had to the legislative process, their testimony was received with deference and their preferred discourses of medicalization and liberalization shaped the reform. As a result, the reform was interpreted at the time to be one addressing *doctors'* difficulties with an ambiguous law. Women's needs and women's voices counted for little and the themes their groups expressed about fairness, equity, and social justice were taken up by very few.

The Parliamentary Moment

Prior to the proposal to present an omnibus reform of the Criminal Code, in order to liberalize it and supposedly make it better conform to current standards of morality and social practice, abortion reform had been dealt with separately by Parliament. Three private members' bills were considered by the Standing Committee on Health and Welfare in 1967, and it is the deliberations about those bills that provoked the representations of most of the actors decribed above.[40]

Two of the three bills—proposed by NDP MPs Grace MacInnis

(C-122) and H.W. Herridge (C-136)—would have made substantial alterations in the conditions under which women could terminate their pregnancies. The MacInnis bill was very similar to the resolution of the CMA, calling for therapeutic abortions in the case of grave danger to the physical or mental health of the woman, a substantial risk that the foetus would be born disabled, or a pregnancy resulting from a sexual crime.[41] Herridge's bill was more ambitious. Modelled on the recent British legislation, it would have allowed theraputic abortion when the woman's health and well-being, or those of her child or already living children, were threatened. In determining such situations, C-136 instructed the two deciding doctors to consider the patient's 'total environment, actual or reasonably foreseeable'. The third Private Member's Bill, that of Liberal Ian Wahn, was a straightforward proposal to use TACs to determine whether a woman's life or health was threatened. It was simply intended to clarify wording, to remove confusions arising from different sections of the existing Criminal Code.

The Herridge bill was a non-starter. Speaking of social justice and linking reproductive decisions to social needs, it was far too radical and too 'social' for Canadian political discourse at that time.[42] Committee members who bothered to address the bill and oppose it, set out to tar it with the brush of eugenicism as well as claiming it opened the door to abortions-of-convenience.

More difficult was the MacInnis bill, because it was much less radical and it did conform rather closely to what the CMA was proposing. While the intent of the bill was to lighten the burden of families faced with severely handicapped children, the MPs were nervous that the provision for aborting 'defective' foetuses would involve too much risk for healthy ones. Moreover, since German measles was the major cause of deformities discussed at that time, some MPs were reluctant to accept that the possibility of deafness or blindness was sufficient reason for terminating a pregnancy. Therefore, the Parliamentary committee dropped both this bill's proposal and that of the CMA when it made an interim report in December 1967 recommending that therapeutic abortions be permitted when the woman's life or health was seriously endangered.

Events moved quickly, however, and simultaneously with this interim report, the government announced its omnibus bill, including virtually the same wording for the abortion section, dropping only the insistence that the threat must be 'serious'. By inserting the reform of Section 251 into the omnibus reform of the Criminal Code the government stressed the fact that the demand for abortion resulted from pregnancy and pregnancy was a consequence of sexual practices. Attitudes towards such sexual practices, moreover, appeared to the government to be a matter of private conscience rather than state regulation. As Mark MacGuigan, Liberal MP for Windsor-Walkerville, said in the House of Commons debates on 24 January 1969:

> I believe the omnibus bill reflects an entirely new governmental approach to the criminal law. . . . The bill would bring about a change not in criminal legislation but also in the philosophy behind it, for it apparently indicates a determination that law shall no longer be thought of as a mirror of morals, and that from now on crime and sin, law and morals, must be distinguished.[43]

In this way, liberalization of sexual behaviour—both heterosexual and homosexual—implied the necessity of changing state regulation of its processes. For heterosexual women, this meant legalizing the possibility of sex without procreation (contraception) and failed contraception (abortion). It also meant unlinking the centuries-old relationship between sexuality and illegality; many parliamentarians were concerned to reduce substantially the prevalence of illegal abortions.

Within such a discourse of liberalization, then, abortion was 'about' sex, and changing mores meant making it easier and safer for people to practise their sexuality. But there were, of course, other ways to represent the reform of abortion and these alternatives actually overwhelmed, in sheer volume, the voices speaking of liberalization. Most important, of course, was the discourse of medicalization. Fears of the deaths and mutilations of illegal abortion, hopes of clarifying doctors' legal position, notions of the awful effects of both incestuous sexuality and the lives of 'defective' children pushed legislators to advocate the legalization of abortion.

It was in terms of the latter representations that the NDP launched its criticisms of the abortion provisions of the omnibus bill. MP Grace MacInnis continued to argue that the best way to solve the health problems created by illegal abortions, as well as to guarantee mothers the right to healthy, 'wanted' children, was to take abortion out of the Criminal Code. Her definition, shared by colleagues in her party, was that abortion was simply a medical matter, to be decided by the woman and her doctor, after consultations with other persons — husbands, parents, social workers, etc. — as appropriate.[44] Thus, abortion was a medical, not a criminal, matter but it was not a 'right'. Other people could, and should, be involved in a woman's decision, because medical matters, within this discourse, were as much social as they were individual. Society had an interest in healthy women, children, and family situations. Nevertheless, while the medical aspects of the matter were taken up by many other debaters in the House of Commons, the NDP's concerns with the social consequences of unwanted pregnancy, especially among the poor, and with women's health remained marginalized in the debate. Indeed, John Turner, speaking as Minister of Justice, explicitly rejected what he called 'sociological' reasons for abortion.[45]

Even more marginalized, although loudly and frequently present, was the anti-abortion discourse which existed at that time. Spoken primarily by Créditiste members from Quebec, these criticisms of abortion as 'murder' and as against the values of Western society, found few adherents in other parties, with the exception of a few backbench Tory MPs. This language, which had been much tamed in the Committee deliberations by the deference to doctors' control over scientific knowledge, burst out in long speeches in the House. Asserting that life begins at conception, Créditiste MPs pounded home their arguments with detailed citations to historical fact and, especially, to 'scientific evidence'. That the science often emanated from Roman Catholic sources was irrelevant to the speakers of these hermetic texts.

Their problem was that no one, including the Catholics in the Liberal party, would accept their representation of the issue. For example, speaking in extreme frustation Créditiste MP Matté said:

> Mr Speaker, I have been in this house fourteen months, and I am still at a loss to find a way to have our arguments taken into consideration.
> . . . Nothing is more depressing for us than to realize that all we do is bring forward, for posterity, arguments which we did

> not make up ourselves, but found by reference to appropriate sources.
>
> Since this matter deals first of all with medicine and the first signs of life, we consulted scientists and gynaecologists who explained to us what is a human being and at what time it appears in the human foetus.
>
> . . . We did not invent our arguments.[46]

But the scientific status of this position could not, in 1969, successfully compete with the science of the CMA which argued that there were times in which legal abortions were needed, and doctors had the professional skill to determine such needs.

In this way, linked to other efforts to recognize a supposed new consensus about sexual mores and other moral issues, regulation of abortion was maintained in the Criminal Code. Efforts both to excise it and to debate it separately—which might have led to greater restrictions—were defeated. Abortion was buried in the omnibus bill, and there was little support for extracting it from that location. Fears of 'abortion on request' were high among much of the House and there was little enthusiasm outside the minority NDP for a discussion of abortion as a social rather than an individual, medical issue. The House treated the reform as one intended to define the boundaries of the legal and the illegal, not to give anyone new rights or to find a consensus about the appropriate balance between the state's responsibility for family life, through social programs, and women's need to control their own lives.

The Consequences of Medicalization and Liberalization

There were both immediate and long-term consequences of representing state regulation of abortion through the linked discourses of liberalization and medicalization. The first, and most obvious, result was that women acquired no new individual or collective rights as a result of the reform process. 'Choice' was not part of Canadian political debate prior to 1969 and the interpretative professionalism of doctors always mediated women's needs. This result contrasted sharply with the situation elsewhere. In some countries abortion was treated as a medical procedure, but a simple one which women might select for themselves in the early weeks of their pregnancies.[47]

In France in 1974, for example, the state relabelled abortion 'the voluntary interruption of pregnancy' and, while regulating the procedure somewhat more than other voluntary ones, it left the essential decision up to women themselves.[48] Moreover, in those countries where reform came in the 1970s, women themselves gained control over the decision to have an abortion. In the United States, for example, the Supreme Court in the 1973 *Roe v Wade* decision determined that first- and second-trimester abortion fell under women's constitutional right to privacy and, therefore, the state could intervene to regulate the procedure only if a compelling state interest could be demonstrated.

The consequences of the Canadian reform were mixed; not all were negative for women. Access to safe abortions did exist for many more women than ever in the past. Nevertheless, in general, the new law still denied women control over their own reproductive decisions. These remained in others' hands and subjected women to the vagaries of doctors' and hospitals' judgement of the morality and politics of abortion. In other words, questions of women's rights and equity were subordinate to the legal rights and moral scruples of doctors and hospitals, to whom the state had delegated responsibility.

A concrete effect of the medicalization discourse and the lack of any guaranteed rights for women was that hospitals could *choose not* to provide abortion services, simply by refusing to establish a Therapeutic Abortion Committee.[49] Without a TAC doctors could not terminate pregnancies; restrictive TACs substantially limited them. The real results of leaving the decision to provide service to doctors and hospitals were clear in the 1977 *Report of the Committee on the Operation of the Abortion Law* (*The Badgley Report*) commissioned by the federal government. The Committee's major finding was that access to service was extremely uneven across the country and that, in sum, 'the procedure provided in the Criminal Code for obtaining therapeutic abortions is in practice illusory for many Canadian women'.[50]

A second consequence of institutionalizing a medicalized representation of abortion has been that subsequent disputes have often taken the form of debates among doctors over their professional actions. A first controversy involved the definition of 'health'. Since a legal abortion required a determination that the life or 'health' of the woman was threatened, obviously the definition of 'health' became central. In the Parliamentary Committee which recommended the 1969 reform there was consensus that the concept of 'health' included mental health but did not incorporate consideration of social and economic conditions threatening the long-term health of the woman or her living children. Vagueness in the actual wording of the bill, however, meant confusion continued to exist.

The controversy over definitions quickly surfaced in the 1970s, once again following expressions of concern by doctors and their lawyers. While John Turner, as Minister of Justice in 1969, had implied health had a broad definition, his successor, Otto Lang, who was a devout Roman Catholic and personally strongly opposed to abortion, attempted to make the meaning much more restrictive. He claimed that hospitals were using social and economic criteria to approve abortions and this was causing 'too many' to be performed. Lang instructed TACs to be much more restrictive in their interpretation of threats to health. This heavy-handed interference in a 'medical' issue provoked a response from doctors.

The CBA also objected to the lack of legal standards within the TACs. The Committees were delegated responsibility for making decisions about what was legal or illegal, yet no criteria or procedures for due process were set out in the legislation. Therefore, the lawyers' association feared that their doctor clients might be subjected to lawsuits contesting the procedures used by a TAC.

As a result, the CMA and CBA called for a review and greater liberalization of the abortion law.[51] Under pressure from both professional associations, Lang finally retracted his instruction and established the Badgley Committee to investigate the working of the abortion law.[52] Not surprisingly, given this lineage, the Badgley Committee investigated only the machinery of the law, not the fundamental question of women's rights (or foetal rights or state interests, for that matter).

The Badgley Committee found that the variable definition of health led to 'considerable inequity in the distribution and the accessibility of the abortion procedure'.[53] Moreover, the administrative restrictions which hospitals imposed for their convenience also interfered with equity.[54] This Committee, constituted by the Minister of Health and reporting on a supposedly medical matter, operated within the discourse of health care which by the mid-1970s in Canada was shaped by the existence of medicare. Equity was one of the central pillars of the nation-wide health care system established in the late 1960s, and so the examination of this particular medical procedure was very susceptible to criticisms of inequities in access to care.

Because of its terms of reference, the Badgley Committee could only operate within the very restricted terms of post-1969 medicalization of abortion, as materialized in the procedures of the various TACs. Doctors objected to having such uncertainty in an arena where they were assigned responsibility as gate-keepers or judges. Some doctors found these tasks repugnant, and they wanted to make the decision process more open. Others found them compromising in their present form, and they demanded clarification.[55] Little was actually accomplished in the direction of greater equity and the representation of actors and interests involved did not alter.

A second area in which doctors' professional needs provided a focus for discussion also related to the matter of professional judgement. Without a doubt the most prominent struggles around abortion since 1969 have been those of Dr Henry Morgentaler and his supporters. Specifically, his challenge was to the law's requirement of approval by a hospital board. Morgentaler defied that regulation by establishing free-standing clinics, first in Quebec and then in Manitoba and Ontario.[56]

Since such clinics were not part of any hospital and he performed abortions without the approval of a TAC, Morgentaler was clearly breaking the law as set out Section 251. His defence depended, then, on whether there were other parts of the law which might override Section 251. Morgentaler justified his actions by combining 'secular humanism' with a language of medicalization; and in his legal cases he claimed that, as a doctor, he had to respond to women's need for abortion and he alone could make the judgement of such need.[57]

In his early legal battles, Morgentaler used the defence of 'necessity', making use of traditional common law. He argued that the Criminal Code established an unwieldy bureaucratic apparatus that prevented women from obtaining the medical care which he, as their doctor, considered they needed. The so-called 'Morgentaler defence', accepted by the Supreme Court in 1975, argued that doctors might by-pass the TAC when they could show the abortion was necessary and it was impossible to comply with the requirements of the Criminal Code.[58] As Gavigan wrote at the time, 'in advancing the defence of necessity, Dr Morgentaler has opened up a hole in the legislation; however, it is important to remember that the decision is still a medical one'.[59] In the battles of the mid-1980s, Morgentaler and his allies among doctors and pro-choice activists stressed the community consequences of an unenforceable law. An important component of their argument was that a law which cannot be enforced is a bad law. The potential damage to state legitimacy coming from continued law-breaking was the threat which the coalition held over the state. In this way they stressed the needs of the state more than the needs and rights of women.

Before the legal conflicts moved in this direction, however, Morgentaler was subjected to unusual legal procedures, which many observers considered a miscarriage of justice.[60] His situation thereby became a legal *cause célèbre*, in which his civil rights and professional credentials became major topics of dispute. The title of the movie made about these cases—*Democracy on Trial*—indicates how far Dr Morgentaler's struggles with the state failed to place the claims of Canadian women at its centre. As an editorial in *The Globe and Mail* said in 1975, 'the Morgentaler case has no more to do with abortion than it has to do with allegations of mistreatment visited upon the Montreal doctor in a Quebec jail. The issue is about juries . . . '.[61]

This displacement of the problem from women to another issue is a clear echo of the description of the 'immorality' of the law which the CBA represented in 1966, when it claimed that doctors were the major victims of the abortion law. In other words, Morgentaler's courageous and costly struggle did not—nor could it have ever alone—transform the situation of Canadian women, who remained confined by an abortion law that required them to demonstrate that their pregnancy made them 'unhealthy' and that subjected them to the decisions of medical men.

An important additional result of relying on representing abortion interests in terms of medicalization and liberalization was that neither the state nor other major actors engaged a particular moral position as they reformed the abortion law. As Prime Minister Trudeau put it in the famous debate on the omnibus bill to reform the Criminal Code, 'the state has no business in the bedrooms of the nation'.[62] While it is obvious that the implications of pregnancy and the need for abortions are usually quite a distance from the 'bedroom', the fact that no stand was taken either for or against abortion meant that future debates would remain morally open. While the state was not engaged on a pro-choice or pro-women's rights position, neither had it addressed any other moral position. Rather, the state delegated—and the courts confirmed this delegation—the decision about terminating a pregnancy to the medical profession, and the 1969 reform made it very difficult for courts or a jury to intervene in what was defined as a medical decision. As the Ontario High Court said in 1984 in *Medhurst v Medhurst*, 'Parliament, in its wisdom, has required such decisions be made by persons it considers better qualified than the courts'.[63]

In this regard there is a clear difference between the position of the Canadian state and that of the American state. When *Roe v Wade* permitted women to choose abortions, under their constitutional right to privacy, the decision also established that there were areas where the state had an interest. Its first interest was in protecting the foetus when it was deemed potentially viable, but other state interests could also compete with women's right to privacy. A consequence of this reliance on the language of civil rights has been that anti-choice militants have been able to conduct their struggle precisely at the intersection between the right of the individual to seek an abortion and the interest of the state not only in protecting the foetus but also in promoting a particular kind of national morality. Therefore, 'pro-family' themes have been successfully mobilized in campaigns to cut off federal and state funding of abortions and to require parental or spousal consent. The argument made is that the American state has a 'compelling interest' in maintaining and promoting a particular kind of family and a specific morality, and that this interest can override the right of the individual to privacy.[64]

In Canada, because the abortion law regulated doctors, this particular formulation of the controversy made little headway before 1988. Since abortion was considered a medical procedure, albeit an extraordinary one, the state did not recognize an area of individual privacy. Given the institutionalization of the discourse of medicalization in the procedures of the TACs and the courts, challenges to the boundaries of the 'private' and the 'public' were less successful in Canada. The result was that efforts to restrict abortion on the basis of specific social or moral strictures failed.

For example, promoters of a 'pro-family' discourse insisted that women formed part of a family unit, and they opposed abortion not simply because they wished to protect the foetus but also because acceptance of abortion implied acceptance of a form of reasoning which stressed the individuality of women rather than their family-centredness.[65] This ideological position found little support in court cases in which men tried to restrict their wives' access to abortion. In Canadian law all adults are considered individuals for purposes of medical treatment and, therefore, family members do not have control over medical decisions made by adults. The courts confirmed that this principle applied to abortion as well. Thus in a 1981 case the British Columbia Supreme Court found that the therapeutic abortion provisions of the Criminal Code did not give husbands a veto. Then in 1984 the Ontario High Court found that a husband had no right to be consulted on his wife's decision to seek an abortion. In Saskatchewan in 1986 the Court of Appeal struck down Bill 53 (The Freedom of Informed Choice in Abortion Act) on the grounds that this effort over-reached legislative authority.[66]

These cases constitute a recognition that the medical profession alone had the right to decide to terminate a pregnancy, after considering the needs of only the woman. The British Columbia case in particular emphasized that the hospital board had priority in making the decision. Therefore, while such a representation clearly denied women control over their own bodies, it also prevented other members of their family and even the state from staking claims to the same territory.

This particular interpretation provided some protection to women as the 'New Right' tried to reduce access to therapeutic abortions. At the same time, however, deference to the medical profession was destructive of real access to abortion. Because the law delegated decisions to local hospital boards, the abortion controversy was subject to the vagaries of local public opinion.[67] Passing responsibility 'down' meant that activists were able to mount attacks against individual hospitals. Targeted hospitals found themselves subjected to unusually intense and often unprecedented campaigns to place pro-life activists on hospital governing bodies, in order to abolish the TACs.[68] Other hospitals, hoping to avoid the messiness of such public campaigns, either reduced their 'service', making it more difficult to obtain an abortion, or disbanded their Committee altogether. Thus, the ultimate effect of the law was that each community could settle the issue and the decision could be re-opened whenever a militant minority chose to act.

This was the situation the Supreme Court observed when in 1987 it sat to hear the Morgentaler case. In 1982 only 261 of 861 public hospitals had Therapeutic Abortion Committees and could therefore perform legal abortions, although 47 of the 261 did none in 1982. By 1983, the number of hospitals with Committees had dropped to 249. Even more indicative of the reduction of access to legal abortions was the fact that only 43 hospitals performed 70% of the country's abortions.[69] By 1987 abortions were reliably available in only two provinces and even there often only for women willing to risk seeking them in clinics operating outside the letter of the law.[70] There were *no* hospitals in Prince Edward Island performing abortions, while women in Newfoundland lost their access completely for a time because the one doctor still willing to perform abortions became ill.

The Women's Movement, the State, and Abortion

As the previous pages have demonstrated, it is possible to recount the history of abortion politics in Canada without making much reference to the actions of the women's movement; state actions regulating the termination of pregnancy have been constituted by a variety of other actors. The effect was overwhelming enough for one pro-choice activist to declare in 1981 that 'abortion is the forgotten issue of the women's movement in Canada'.[71] Our argument is that abortion reform was less 'forgotten' than overwhelmed by other discourses, other concerns, and other politics until mobilization by the pro-life movement forced feminists to take it up again.

The Canadian women's movement, like those in other advanced capitalist societies, rose in the late 1960s as part of a critique of the effects of existing social and political practices on women. Thus, the student movement of the late sixties produced a number of feminist groups that provided birth control and abortion counselling as an important out-reach activity.[72] For example, the Student Union for Peace Action (SUPA) took up abortion reform as both a working-class demand and one which could forge cross-class links for the Left.[73] In addition, as existing women's groups—like the National Council of Women and the Fédération des Femmes du Québec—radicalized, pro-choice discourse formed a growing part of their rhetoric and practice, linking them to other groups promoting a new collective identity for women.[74] By the first years of the 1970s women supporting a variety of feminisms claimed greater control over reproduction as a prerequisite for improving women's condition. Yet, while the recognizing of the importance of the issue was a foundation of their analysis, some feminists were reluctant to place it high on their agenda of demands, while the politics of abortion reform provided a focus for conflict among the various wings of the movement.

Feminists were immediately critical of the 1969 law, claiming that too little had been done. One of their first responses was a spectacular, nation-wide action to publicize the demand that abortion be removed from the Criminal Code altogether.[75] The Abortion Caravan of 1970 had the effect of both mobilizing support for abortion rights and providing a dramatic public announcement that a women's movement prepared for radical action had arrived on the scene, with abortion on demand as a key claim.

The Caravan—modelled on the On-to-Ottawa trek of the unemployed in the 1930s—was initially proposed by the Vancouver Women's Caucus and then taken up by feminists across the country. Indeed, some feminist groups came into existence in order to participate in the Caravan.[76] Departing from Vancouver in May 1970, the Caravan visited many cities before arriving in Ottawa. There a group of feminists chained themselves to the Public Gallery in the House of Commons and pelted the MPs with their slogan of 'abortion on demand'.

Despite the solidarity and publicity generated by this spectacular event, even the Caravan demonstrated that the meaning of abortion divided the several tendencies within the women's movement. These divisions continued; other issues, too, marked out the differences among ways of being feminist. Abortion reform, while never disappearing from the agenda of demands of all feminist groups, declined in importance as other issues and interests emerged to define the collective identity of the emergent social movement. Throughout the 1970s, beginning immediately after the Abortion Caravan, it became more difficult to talk about abortion reform within the political categories used by some parts of the women's movement, and for others it became a controversial issue.

A first division, which went to the heart of the identity of the radical feminist movement, was whether abortion law reform should provide the major—indeed sole—focus of mobilization of women *qua* women or whether abortion on demand should be represented as only one of several major changes in law and social practices necessary for women's liberation.

The first position was advocated by women close to far left, especially Trotskyist groups and parties. For these activists, abortion was an issue with great mobilizational potential. However, since their existing analyses of capitalist oppression and exploitation provided the explanation for women's situation, abortion was characterized primarily as a useful issue to bring people into contact with left-wing analyses of capitalism.

The second position was argued primarily by non-aligned feminists who were less tightly tied to existing political groupings and tried to undertake autonomous women's politics. They sought to develop a new analysis of women's oppression either by merging analyses of class and patriarchal relations, or by deducing it from a theory of patriarchy alone. No matter the theoretical differences among these non-aligned feminists, they all agreed that, while access to abortion was a basic need for women's liberation, it was inappropriate to focus all politics on it. Women should be mobilized on other issues as well. Only with broad-based analyses and actions would feminism create solidarity across the existing divisions among women.

Thus, in the very first strategic debates among feminists—debates which engaged the basic questions of identity and affiliation—the abortion issue was important and contentious. Controversy divided the first national conference of the women's movement held in Saskatoon in November 1970. There Marlene Dixon, who taught Sociology at McGill University and was active in a far left group, advocated the single-issue approach. She argued that women divided by race and class could never imagine uniting under a single movement label; the goal of feminists for such solidarity was chimerical. The consequence of such reasoning, promoted most by the Young Socialist/League for Socialist Action, was to press for a national day of protest around the abortion laws. For others, concerned to expand their feminism beyond the universities and to develop a broad strategy for the movement, downplaying the centrality of abortion reform seemed more promising.[77]

A book published in 1972 by the Canadian Women's Educational Press, entitled *Women Unite!*, presents both the outline of the controversy and an assessment from the perspective of non-aligned feminism:

> Those concerned with a single-issue orientation began coalitions for a national movement for repeal of the abortion laws. This group has become synonymous with women's liberation for many sectors of the Canadian population. This is unfortunate as it demonstrates the failure of the Canadian movement to develop a comprehensive strategy. While the control of our bodies is fundamental to the liberation of women, taken in isolation and within the context of the existing political structure, the demand for repeal of abortion laws will do little to change the general situation of women.[78]

Such debates were never simply about words or theory. One real consequence was splits in groups, as factions were expelled for their opposition to the dominant line or departed with their criticisms intact to form new small groups doing different kinds of work.[79] Another consequence was to provide the orientation of feminist work through the 1970s. As described by Adamson, Briskin, and McPhail, non-aligned feminism in anglophone Canada, looking beyond the issue of abortion, divided relatively peacefully into two tendencies. Socialist feminism turned its attention to theory and workplace issues while radical feminism concentrated on struggling against violence against women and other manifestations of misogyny as well as the creation of cultural alternatives.[80]

With these shifts in strategy and practical work, abortion reform became the primary responsibility of a broad-based coalition of reformers organized in the Canadian Alliance for the Repeal of the Abortion Law (CARAL) and other groups supporting Dr Morgentaler through his encounters with the justice system.[81] In Quebec, where the first Morgentaler trials were held, the left-leaning feminists who had founded Montreal's Centre des femmes quit the Morgentaler Defence Committee in 1972. Explicitly rejecting the Committee's focus on the rights of doctors, they set out as feminists to articulate their stance toward the abortion issue. While developing this analysis, eventually published in 1974 as the manifesto, 'Nous aurons les enfants que nous voulons', the Centre continued to provide abortion referral services. Nevertheless, the analysis of this marginalized group did not have much public success until later in the decade, when the *Comité de lutte pour l'avortement et la contraception libres et gratuits* emerged as an an important actor in post-1976 Quebec.[82] The Morgentaler Defence Committee, composed of a broad-based coalition of doctors, members of family-planning associations, CARAL, Trotskyists, anglophone feminists, and the women's commission of the Quebec teachers' union, lobbied the federal government for abortion law reform and publicized the Morgentaler cases.[83]

These internal and strategic conflicts among radical and socialist feminists as well as between non-aligned socialist feminists and those linked to far left groups drew energy inward, away from large public events like the Abortion Caravan.[84] The absence of such massive outreach activities left the stage open for those who continued to discuss abortion in the prevailing terms of a medicalized discourse. One result was that within the several organizations demanding repeal of the law, voices calling for abortion on demand were weakened, while those taking up the new equity discourse unveiled around the Badgley Committee report strengthened. It was left to liberal feminism to speak most clearly in public for women's abortion rights.

The Canadian women's movement is not only divided but also heavily weighted towards liberal feminism.[85] Equal opportunity and individual rights claims have dominated the agenda of this wing of the movement since the middle 1960s, affecting the representation of abortion by this wing of the movement.[86] For example, since its founding the Canadian Advisory Council on the Status of Women has demanded the removal of abortion from the Criminal Code. Nevertheless, in its assessment of the ten years after the Report of the Royal Commission on the Status of Women (RCSW) the Advisory Council placed more stress on the 'new issues' to arise in the 1980s—women's special needs in the labour market, equality in social programs, overcoming sexist attitudes, etc., than on reproductive rights.[87] The National Council of Women, the oldest and largest women's rights group in the country, did not present a resolution on reproductive rights or abortion to its 1983 Annual Meeting, although the list of resolutions 'reflects a commitment to broad social goals beyond the status of women'.[88] In a very wide-ranging list of concerns of the 1980s women's movement —reflected in the recommendations made to the Macdonald Commission by women's organizations—references to reproductive freedom, to reform of the abortion law, or to any version of the demand for women's control over their bodies were absent.

Such groups are the largest and most visible parts of the Canadian women's movement. Some organisations existed long before the RCSW was established in 1967 and others were created in the years immediately following its 1970 Report. For example, the government established the Canadian Advisory Council on the Status of Women as part of its reaction to the recommendations of the Royal Commission. While funded by the government, the Advisory Council maintains a position of semi-autonomy from the Department of State and the Minister Responsible for the Status of Women. The National Action Committee on the Status of Women, founded in the early 1970s, is a federation of groups which wishes to remain autonomous of the government, in order to monitor its programs affecting women.

No matter the time of their founding, however, the agenda of reform which the state itself established, through the RCSW, deeply influenced the agenda of liberal feminism. For Sandra Burt, 'the establishment of the Royal Commission on the Status of Women in 1967 helped to legitimize the concept of equal rights for men and women'[89] while for Penney Kome its '167 recommendations . . . became the blueprint for mainstream feminist activism during the 1970s'.[90] In other words, the public attention which 'women's issues' received as a result of the RCSW's work and the agenda for change which it set down in its resolutions provided a focused definition of 'feminism' and 'women's issues'.[91]

The terms of reference of the RCSW were confined to equal opportunity issues, albeit broadly conceived. The discourse of the RCSW was based on 'the human rights concept [which] provided an ideological framework in which individuals and organizations who did not all share the same feminist perspective could comfortably situate women's rights'.[92] The way to ensure women full human rights, according to the RCSW, was through an improvement in their economic conditions, particularly their participation in the paid labour force. In addition, reforms of the political process, to give women more influence in electoral and governmental politics, were important because with political power women could begin to make the changes they required.

The RCSW utilized the ideas of 1960s' human rights liberalism. It displayed a belief in the importance of state support for the disadvantaged until they could become equal competitors, a great deal of optimism about the possibilities of reform, especially through actions within the institutions of liberal democracy, and the belief that historic disadvantages could be overcome via proper state action and voluntary effort. From within its human rights liberalism the RCSW transmitted to the Canadian population the feminist message that women were individuals equal to any other in society, although some women needed help to overcome the effects of discrimination and achieve equality.

Within the collective identity of genderless personhood thus celebrated, there were no words for talking about 'difference', about the fact that only women bear children and that reproduction places women in a different situation than it does men. Nor, then, was there any space for feminists to promote a vision of society in which women as a group, as an identifiable and politically viable entity, had rights differing from those of other citizens. When the goal was to deny the existence of legitimate defences of 'difference', as liberal feminism did in the name of a common humanity, politics stressing the specificity of women and their situation appeared contradictory and unsustainable. Silence could only surround the unspeakable, and liberal feminism focused primarily on strategies for achieving access to the labour force and equality in civil and political rights for women.

This was not simply a problem of discourse; there was also an important strategic issue. The RCSW did recommend liberalization of the abortion law. It advocated in Recommendations #126 and #127, that 'the Criminal Code be amended to permit abortion by a qualified medical practioner on the sole request of any woman who has been pregnant for 12 weeks or less' and after 12 weeks if a qualified practitioner determined the woman's physical or mental health was threatened. However, for the Commissioners themselves, these resolutions were the most controversial of any made. Three of the five dissenting statements distanced Commissioners from the recommendations about reform of the Criminal Code; no other topic generated so much dissent.[93] The message clearly imbedded within this important document was that linking improvements in women's condition to greater reproductive freedom would lead to controversy and loss of support.

The lesson was not lost on the women's movement. For liberal feminists, concerned with equalizing opportunity and moving women into the mainstream of economic, social, and political life, the abortion issue created a dilemma. Therefore, while continuing to demand improvements in the law and agitating against the worst abuses and conditions of the current situation—the harassment of Dr Morgentaler, for example—the issue was never allowed to dominate the agenda or become a defining one for feminism.[94] Instead, public activity was left either to Morgentaler defence committees or to single-issue organizations, like CARAL. The extent of this downplaying of abortion was seen during the debates about the *Charter of Rights and Freedoms* in 1980-81. The 1981 Ad Hoc Conference quickly abandoned its original resolution that the Charter 'be amended to include the right to reproductive freedom'. This demand was never pressed in the struggles which women waged around the Charter.[95]

For these and other reasons, the women's movement did not concentrate on, albeit always supporting, further liberalization of the abortion law in the 1970s and 1980s. The RCSW had encased feminism in a language of human rights, which made it difficult to find words for speaking of women's real 'difference', their reproductive lives. Moreover, the largest part of the women's movement, which itself located women's historic difficulties in discriminatory practices and traditional attitudes rather than in control over reproduction *per se*, accepted this discourse. Finally, instead of the campaign for abortion reform creating solidarity around a common sense of identity, the questions of whether and how to pursue reform fragmented the movement from the start. Abortion politics remained constrained by the discourses and institutions of liberalization and medicalization. No wing of the women's movement was strong enough to force other visions and arrangements into the centre of the universe of political discourse.

Response to Assault

The women's movement was not simply asleep at the switch or unappreciative of the importance of abortion rights. There was an important factor limiting the attention the issue garnered: time. The 1969 reform had preceded the institutionalization and consolidation of the new women's movement. Then, it took time for the full impact of the ineffective law to be felt. Through the 1970s legal abortions *were* available to women with the knowledge, energy, and money to seek them out. The urban areas and central Canada, where feminists were concentrated, did have hospitals that performed abortions. Therefore, the moral compulsion that might have followed from a complete ban on abortions did not exist. The 1969 reform, as McDonnell says:

> knocked the wind out of the sails of the reform movement at a critical time, saddling it with a half-measure that made abortion just accessible enough to neutralize pressure for outright repeal of the law.[96]

It took a decade and a half of attrition of access before it became glaringly obvious that the possibility of 'legal' abortions had no meaning if no doctor agreed to perform them or if no TAC existed. It also took the increasing success of the pro-life movement to demonstrate that an immense threat to women's right to choose abortion came from the New Right. Once this was clear, feminists began to mobilize to protect and guarantee legalized abortion.

The Quebec women's movement was the first to begin to use the abortion issue as a major focus for mobilization. After the victory of the Parti Québécois (PQ) in the 1976 provincial election, charges against Dr Morgentaler were dropped by the Quebec Minister of Justice. Nevertheless, this 'victory' for abortion reformers remained a hollow one because hospitals were still not performing abortions in sufficient number. By 1978 a co-ordinating organization linking women's groups, female unionists, and neighbourhood and other popular groups, had become a large-scale feminist movement for free and accessible contraception and abortion. These actions marked the first real extension of the Québécois women's movement beyond Montreal and the solidification of its support beyond the intellectual milieu. Concrete consequences of the mass-based actions were that the provincial government acknowledged that its own locally based health clinics or private clinics could perform abortions, with costs reimbursed by the provincial health care system. By the 1980s, abortion was a widely accepted medical practice in Quebec, according to principles long demanded by the pro-choice movement.[97] The nationalism of the PQ legitimated breaking federal law, under pressure from the newly regrouped women's movement.

In English Canada large-scale mobilization came later and under much more difficult circumstances. By the mid-1980s the women's movement was again beginning to take up the issue of abortion in a serious way, but by then the high ground had been seized by the pro-life activists. Moreover, within the women's movement, the representation of abortion in the straightforward terms of pro-choice had begun to trouble some feminists. In Toronto, for example, single-issue campaigns and the broad-based International Women's Day Coalition, a major linking organization for feminist action, came to be deeply divided along racial lines. Particularly singled out was white women's uncritical support for abortion, while women of colour often faced a different situtation. Poverty, immigration laws, and racism acted as barriers to their right to bear and raise children. Women of colour, moreover, feared both contraception and abortion as potential weapons in the state and men's hands to limit some women's child-bearing.[98]

In response to the pro-life movement's successes in reducing access and the criticism that pro-choice rhetoric was racist, too narrow, and too liberal, in 1982 a new organization appeared in Toronto. The Ontario Coalition for Abortion Clinics (OCAC) redefined the issue as one of reproductive rights, by which it meant not only the right to choose abortion but also the right to bear healthy children, for women's health and sexuality to be within their own control. Constructing a wide-ranging socialist feminist analysis which linked reproductive rights and health to child care, pay equity, and new power relations between women and men, the Coalition took inspiration from the successes in Quebec as well as from the long-standing demand of the abortion reform movement for equitable and meaningful access. This group invited Dr Morgentaler to establish a free-standing clinic in Toronto, and then undertook to provide the necessary financial and other support for his legal defence. Defence of the clinic was to be used to mobilize expanding attention to reproductive rights.

It was to be a long and hard battle fought not only in the courts but through daily confrontations in the street outside the clinic.

Pro-life groups fire-bombed the clinic, picketed it constantly, and harassed its users. Such confrontational tactics on the part of pro-life groups reflected both their growth in the 1970s and their increasing frustration in the face of new feminist mobilization.

Pro-life groups had appeared immediately after the 1969 reform of the Criminal Code, organizing for its repeal. Birthright, providing social services for pregnant women so they would carry their pregnancy to term, was founded in 1968, even before the Criminal Code was reformed. The pro-life movement then gained a great resource as the Catholic Church became more active in opposing abortion. A further source of support came from conservative women reacting to what they perceived as the threat of feminism. The first of such groups was the Alberta Federation of Women United for the Family, established in 1981. This initative was quickly followed by the group REAL (Real, Equal, Active, for Life) Women in 1984.

All of these New Right groups represented abortion as a murder, as the first line of attack on family values, and as the source of much social instability. These anti-feminist groups joined with existing single-issue pro-life groups to produce a movement with enough strength to close down TACs in many hospitals and to eliminate abortion services in some provinces altogether. Indeed, non-targeted hospitals, in fear of being singled out, often reduced their abortion services in anticipation.

The movement then began to diversify its activities, moving directly to the electoral and partisan process. The Liberals and Conservatives had never really been allied with the feminists advocating reproductive control. Politicians in both parties considered that the 1969 reform had been quite sufficient. This enthusiasm for the status quo became even greater as the Roman Catholic Church left the more liberal phase that had kept it out of the fray in the late 1960s and became active in the movement to rescind the 1969 reform. This renewed activity affected the Liberal party in particular, given its long-standing reliance on Catholics for electoral support and because of the number of Catholics among its MPs. For the Tories, the growing link between economic conservatism and pro-family activists under the banner of the New Right meant that they could not risk alienating a potential source of new support by pushing any change in the law. Both parties felt most comfortable operating within the familiar terms of medicalization. 'Letting the doctors decide' meant that the political parties did not have to disturb a delicate balance which had grown up between the massive support in public opinion for legal abortion, and the small but vocal group of anti-choice militants.[99] Therefore, in the 1984 election campaign, in which so much was made in the media of so-called 'women's issues', both Brian Mulroney and John Turner held the same position. They supported the law as it had stood since 1969.[100]

Only the NDP adopted a strong pro-choice position and often participated in the alliances of organizations which helped to solidify, at least in the Ontario NDP, support for women's right to choose.[101] There is some evidence that this stance helped the New Democrats in the 1984 election, while the Liberals and Conservatives may have suffered from their reliance on the old, familiar terminology and politics. Beginning in the late 1970s, pro-life forces had begun targeting candidates for office who were publicly committed to a pro-choice position.[102] By 1984 this strategy meant that many of the women in Parliament, of whichever party, were targeted. The so-called 'Campaign Life' ran a candidate against Flora MacDonald, but she managed to defeat the challenger. Iona Campagnola on the other hand was defeated after being selected as a target by anti-choice groups. Because, in part, of the wishy-washy position taken by her party, she gained no support from feminists, despite the fact that her personal position was pro-choice. NDP MPs Lynn McDonald and Pauline Jewett, in contrast, retained their seats, at least in part because they gained new support based not only on their own pro-choice position but also because of their party's greater commitment to moving beyond the analysis of abortion as a health issue.[103]

Targeting in the 1984 election campaign was only another indication that the pro-life forces were on the offensive. They gained a foothold in the Conservative Party when some Tory candidates accepted funding and help from 'Campaign Life' in 1984. Anti-choice militants lobbied Parliament.[104] They pressured MPs to support a private member's bill which would give foetuses the rights of living persons.[105]

Such militancy succeeded over the decade of the 1980s in recasting the discourse of abortion. Abortion as health care was swamped by a language of 'rights'. For pro-life activists a foetus' rights override those of the woman who carried it. Feminists responded that women's rights should prevail, with every woman having the right to make a choice about abortion. Despite the best efforts of groups like the Ontario Coalition for Abortion Clinics to broaden the meaning of reproductive rights and health, this shift to a pro-choice discourse had the effect of jettisoning many of the social arguments for abortion which had been present both in the language of medicalization and in the left's discussion of abortion in the 1960s.

By the mid-1980s two groups faced off. One represented the issue as being about life, babies, and rights. The other represented it as about women, freedom of choice, and rights. When on 28 January 1988 the Supreme Court used the discourse of medicalization again, to strike down a law which no longer had the support of anyone, the way was open for these two diametrically opposed discourses to shape the parliamentary and public debates. With the Court's decision women had finally emerged from the shadow of the doctors. But the victory had its terrifying side. Now, instead of facing the doctor and the state in hospital consulting rooms, women faced in the streets and Parliament those who would charge them with bloody babies and destruction of society. This would be a battle very hard to win.

Chapter

3

Choice and No Choice in the House

Janine Brodie

The scene outside the Morgentaler free-standing abortion clinic in Toronto the day of the Supreme Court decision was highly symbolic of the previous nineteen years of struggle around Canada's besieged therapeutic abortion law. It was the existence of the Morgentaler clinics which had forced the abortion issue into the courts after both pro-life and pro-choice forces had failed to persuade successive federal governments to consider changes to the existing legislation. It was only fitting, therefore, that the two emotionally charged coalitions awaited the Supreme Court's ruling outside this rather unassuming red-brick on Harbord Street.

As it had religiously since its establishment, one group, representing Canada's determined anti-abortion minority, began to picket the clinic early on the especially cold winter morning of 28 January 1988. Its numbers mushroomed when the media announced that the Supreme Court had ignored the pro-life lobby's non-negotiable claim that abortion was tantamount to murder and should be banned. At one point, the pro-life ranks outweighed those of their declared enemies, pro-choice advocates, by a ratio of twenty to one. As the day drew to a close, however, this group was dwarfed by jubilant supporters of the clinic and other feminist organizations who compared the decision to the granting of female suffrage and celebrated the court's apparent recognition of women's constitutional right to reproductive control.

The two sides, separated by a police barricade, closed the street for most of the evening while the police and the media waited for a confrontation between these long-time adversaries. But this was a characteristically Canadian demonstration: it was polite and orderly. The pro-life group, decidedly older and more male, kept its vigil waving its familiar placards of mutilated foetuses and chanting 'Give Life a Chance.' Across the way, pro-choice supporters, almost all women, relished their apparent victory with embraces and cheers.[1] But amidst this fragile truce and celebration there were two troubling elements: first, no one was really sure what the Supreme Court decision actually meant for Canadian women and second, politicians, who were invited by the Court to formulate a new abortion law, were conspicuously absent.

Much to the federal government's consternation, the landmark decision of the Supreme Court of Canada in *R. v Morgentaler* catapulted the abortion issue onto the centre stage of Canadian politics.

In deciding that Section 251 of the Criminal Code was unconstitutional, the Court indicated that the formulation of abortion policy was a political rather than a legal matter. It was up to federal politicians, if they so desired, to devise a new law which reflected a balance between the state's 'legitimate' interest in the foetus and the constitutional protection guaranteed to Canadian women under the *Charter of Rights and Freedoms*.

The decision was immediately interpreted as a feminist victory because it represented a significant shift in legal discourse concerning women's rights and reproductive control.[2] The Supreme Court appeared to have at least partially accepted strains of the pro-choice movement's 'rights' rhetoric asserting women's right to bodily integrity and reproductive control. The pro-choice movement understandably took the decision as a victory because it transplanted the rhetoric of choice into the domain of law. It appeared to place the coercive power of the state behind the pro-choice movement's vocabulary and interests.[3]

This apparent victory, however, proved to be both partial and short-lived. The majority of the judges (5 of 7) had decided that Section 251 violated Canadian women's constitutional rights to the security of the person. Only one, however, Madam Justice Bertha Wilson, declared that women had a *right* to an abortion in the early stages of pregnancy. Moreover, all of the majority decisions conceded the state's interest in protecting the foetus.[4] The Court avoided suggesting the content of any future abortion legislation, explicitly designating the political sphere as the most appropriate forum for that decision. From a strictly legal perspective, then, the decision simply struck from the Criminal Code the conditions established in 1969 under which legal abortions could be performed in Canada. Importantly, however, the decision reopened political space for pro-life and pro-choice forces to strip the abortion issue of its previous medical and technical guises and recast the issue as a social and moral debate about the respective rights of a woman and foetus.

The Supreme Court decision initiated three years of political manoeuvring and struggle culminating in the legislative stalemate of 1991. The state continued to employ a medicalized discourse, in a sense talking in a different language than the pro-life and pro-choice movements, but it could not depoliticize the abortion debate. In the end, the pro-choice movement could claim victory because abortion remained out of the Criminal Code. In another sense, however, it had failed because the state did not embrace its discourse on women's right to reproductive choice. The struggle over meaning continues but, after 1991, the site for this struggle has been shifted to the provinces.

This chapter traces the tortured and complicated journey from the Morgentaler decision to the defeat of the federal government's abortion legislation in the Senate in 1991. It examines the numerous attempts by the federal government to establish a political balance between pro-choice and pro-life forces through legislation; the parliamentary rhetoric surrounding the abortion issue and the rights of women; and the defeat of the abortion law.

The Political Prelude to Morgentaler

In retrospect, the primary importance of the 1988 Supreme Court decision was to break the political stalemate that had come to characterize the politics of abortion in Canada, and to demand response from all the federal parties and the federal government. While the New Democratic Party (NDP) had long condemned Section 251 of the Criminal Code, the Liberal and Progressive Conservative Parties, in and out of power, had consistently tried to avoid the issue. Both major parties officially supported the 1969 legislation, which essentially delegated the question of access to abortion to the medical profession, as a necessary compromise between two irreconcilable positions. As brokerage parties, neither the Liberals nor the Conservatives were willing to take a position on what they saw as a 'no-win' issue which could only fracture their volatile electoral coalitions. Indeed, as late as 1984, while under pressure from the medical profession and women's groups to change the legislation, then Justice Minister John Crosbie refused to reconsider Canada's increasingly unenforceable abortion law because it was 'an issue on which there is no social consensus'.[5]

But almost twenty years of debate in the 'court of public opinion' had forged a tentative social consensus on abortion. In fact, a number of public opinion polls suggested that there was wider agreement in the electorate about abortion than other issues—such as free trade and privatization—on which the government had already acted. For example, a 1985 poll indicated that 53% of

Canadians favoured easier access to abortion.[6] By April 1988 another poll showed that 69% of Canadians agreed that 'the decision to have an abortion should rest with the woman in consultation with her doctor', while only 26% disagreed.[7]

Public opinion on the abortion issue is fragile, however, sometimes appearing contradictory depending on the specific wording of the question asked. Nevertheless, when responses to the same questions are measured over a period of months and years, Canadian public opinion on abortion appears quite stable. Approximately one-quarter of Canadians agree that abortion should be legal under any circumstances, another 13% believe that it should be illegal under all circumstances, and the vast majority think abortion should be allowed in certain circumstances. Among this latter group, Canadians are more likely to support abortion for the so-called 'hard cases' of rape, incest, the woman's health, and fetal deformity and less likely to support 'soft cases' relating to socio-economic and life-style factors. In other words, the public is more likely to favour free access to abortion when a woman is cast in terms of victim than when abortion is associated with decisions relating to women's self-determination.[8] These proportions and tendencies also characterize the American public.[9]

Although public opinion has favoured changes to Canada's abortion regime for some time, it is also clear that the federal government would not have touched this issue if it had not been for the Supreme Court's ruling. Unlike the late 1960s, when the federal government last legislated abortion policy, the political terrain upon which the abortion issue now rests has been deeply politicized by both the pro-life and pro-choice coalitions. Both groups, as we know them, grew out of and were galvanized by the 1969 amendments to the Criminal Code.

As Jane Jenson argues in Chapter Two, women were marginalized in the 1969 parliamentary debate, but the passage of the legislation brought almost immediate condemnation from Canada's nascent second-wave feminist movement and the organization of a pro-choice lobby. Over the past two decades, the pro-choice coalition has concentrated its organizational energies in three fields—public education, financial support for the Morgentaler court challenges, and lobbying politicians. While its goal always has been the decriminalization of abortion, by the mid-seventies its political agenda also turned to the issue of access. The Badgley Committee, which reported in 1977, confirmed what the pro-choice movement had long suspected: the operation of the 1969 abortion law was working extremely inequitably across Canada. The criteria of Therapeutic Abortion Committees (TACs) differed from one hospital to another and many Canadian women effectively had no access to a therapeutic abortion in their communities.[10]

The problem of diminishing access, as the previous chapter explains, partially reflected the political impact of the pro-life movement in Canada. Like the pro-choice movement, it organized quickly after the passage of the 1969 legislation. While representing a minority of Canadians, pro-life groups could boast of a number of important victories before 1988. At the local level, they were instrumental in restricting access to abortion by electing their supporters to a hospital board and then putting its TAC out of business. This tactic effectively halted abortions in Prince Edward Island and severely limited access in New Brunswick, Newfoundland, and many rural communities throughout Canada. In addition, their constant political pressure intimidated federal politicians, making them reluctant to pursue abortion reform even though the need for reform had been painfully obvious for some years. The activities of pro-life groups also put the pro-choice coalition on the defensive by forcing it to defend the limited gains it had achieved in 1969 as well as its broader feminist-inspired political agenda.[11] Nevertheless, the pro-life coalition had failed in its primary objective—a total ban on legal abortions in Canada. Almost twenty years of reproductive politics, then, had resulted in a political stalemate.

The Politics of the Morgentaler Decision

Given this legacy of conflict and inertia the reactions of the pro-life and pro-choice coalitions and federal parties to the Morgentaler decision were predictable. True to form, a leading activist of the pro-life coalition condemned the decision as 'a licence to any doctor in the country to set up a corner butcher shop'.[12] Laura McArthur, president of the Toronto Right-to-Life (RTL), announced that the pro-life forces would immediately pursue a two-fold strategy in response to the decision: they would fight against the establishment of free-standing abortion clinics which had 'sprung up like hamburger stands' in the United States and they would intervene in the next federal election to elect a 'pro-life Parliament'.[13] In response, the Canadian Abortion Rights Action League (CARAL) indicated that, having achieved the decriminalization of abortion through the courts, it would 'fight to keep it out'.[14] The battle lines for a renewed struggle over Canada's abortion policy had been drawn.

The reactions of the federal parties were also predictable. The NDP welcomed the decision because it was consistent with the party's official platform, while John Turner, leader of the Liberal Party, waffled, suggesting that his party would read the decision carefully, review its implications, and decide how to proceed. Meanwhile, Barbara McDougall, the Minister Responsible for the Status of Women in the Conservative cabinet and a public supporter of decriminalization, gave the official party line: 'there's not a consensus among women on the role of the state on this issue, so that's why I must look at the issue and consult with my colleagues.'[15]

The Supreme Court decision put the Conservative government, which was sitting in the basement in public opinion polls in an election year, in an extremely difficult position. Unlike economic issues, compromise on abortion policy is difficult, if not impossible, to achieve because organized proponents on both sides of the issue see it as an 'all or nothing' proposition. The federal government essentially had five options:[16]

First, it could accept the Supreme Court decision and do nothing. This strategy would have won the support of pro-choice groups but certainly would not have put the issue to rest. Inaction would have provoked pro-life groups and their many supporters on the Conservative backbench as well as open political space for pro-life organizations to demand a legal definition of the rights of the foetus. It also promised to create an environment in which access to abortion would vary widely from one province to another.

Second, the government could reintroduce Section 251 and invoke Section 33 of the *Charter of Rights and Freedoms*—the so-called 'notwithstanding clause'. This response, however, would have mobilized a broad coalition of lawyers, civil libertarians, and women's organizations against the government and only offered a five-year reprieve on the issue.

Third, the government could delay taking any action by appointing a Royal Commission or Task Force on abortion policy. But, again, this strategy would only postpone the decision and give further opportunity for the mobilization of pro-life and pro-choice groups.

Fourth, as is so often the case in Canadian politics, the federal government could attempt to defuse the issue by passing it to the provinces. Prior to the Morgentaler decision, the federal Criminal Code (Section 251) established national conditions for entitlement to abortion while the provision of abortion services was a provincial responsibility. This constitutional division of powers promised, if only temporarily, to obscure the controversy in an endless web of federal-provincial negotiations.

Finally, the government could accept the invitation of the Supreme Court and draft a new law which would attempt to strike a balance between the rights of women and the state's interest in the foetus as well as between the competing claims of the pro-life and pro-choice lobbies.

The government's first response was to reject options one through three and pursue the fourth. Although Prime Minister Mulroney announced on the day of the decision that the federal government would not leave this dimension of Canadian life unregulated, one day later Ray Hnatyshyn, the Minister of Justice, suggested that the federal government would not move immediately because 'these matters are shared responsibilities with the provincial governments'.[17] The Minister of Health, Jake Epp, then began to consult with his provincial counterparts.

The obvious tactical advantages of this strategy proved short-lived. In the absence of federal legislation, the provincial balkanization of abortion services was almost immediate. Ontario and Quebec announced the immediate dissolution of their hospital TACs and agreed that abortions would be funded through their respective medicare schemes, regardless of whether they were performed in hospitals or clinics. In addition, the Ontario government announced that it intended to establish a number of regional women's health clinics which would provide the procedure. The NDP government in Manitoba indicated that it would pay for abortions performed in hospitals or clinics and would encourage the establishment of non-profit community health clinics. This brought charges from the provincial Conservative party that the government was establishing a regime of 'abortion on demand, paid by the people of Manitoba'.[18]

A decidedly different scenario was developing in British Columbia—a province with both the highest ratio of abortions to live births in Canada and a committed pro-life, neo-Conservative premier.[19] Premier Bill Vander Zalm announced that the province would no longer provide public funding for abortions except in 'life-threatening' situations—a term which, much to the dismay of doctors in the province, the Social Credit cabinet left undefined. The Premier, however, indicated that, in his opinion, 'rape and incest' were not 'life-threatening' and that the province would not fund abortions for these reasons.[20] Instead, the province planned to unveil a multi-million dollar scheme designed to assist women in carrying their pregnancies to term. The plan would be implemented on a user pay basis.

British Columbia's haste broke the temporary calm offered to the federal government by the strategy of passing the buck to the provinces. Provincial women's organizations, civil liberties associations, and the NDP attacked the BC government for placing its biases above the law, but the Social Credit government held firm, responding that it was actually the opposition that was biased. The provincial debate was heated and sometimes comical. Health Minister Peter Duek, for example, charged that the provincial NDP leader was 'obviously very biased that everyone should have an abortion whether they were pregnant or not'.[21]

British Columbia's actions were roundly condemned in Ottawa. The federal NDP, CARAL, and the Ontario Coalition of Abortion Clinics (OCAC) demanded that the federal government withhold health care funding from any province that refused to abide by the Supreme Court decision or failed to meet the principle of universality provided under the Canada Health Act. Similarly, the federal Liberal Party attacked the Conservative government for allowing a situation to evolve where all Canadians were not entitled to equal access to medical services. The integrity of universal medicare rather than women's reproductive freedom, however, was the Liberals' chief concern.

The fiasco was temporarily resolved on 23 February 1988 when the British Columbia Supreme Court, acting on a challenge from the BC Civil Liberties Association, ruled that the Social Credit cabinet did not have the authority to enforce its new regulations on abortion. The court did not argue that the provincial government could not end the funding of abortions. Instead, it concluded that the provincial government did not have the authority to determine what constituted a medically required service. The BC case, therefore, left open the distinct possibility that other provinces might declare abortion an uninsured procedure under their respective medicare schemes. Indeed, there was already some precedent for this. In 1987, for example, the Alberta government 'de-insured' sterilization, birth control counselling, and the provision of birth control devices. Faced with the looming spectre of a provincial checker-board of abortion regimes and new court challenges, the federal government had little option but to devise new legislation.

The Illusive Compromise

The Conservative government approached the difficult task of formulating a new abortion policy only reluctantly and within the context of sustained pressure from pro-choice and pro-life advocates outside and within party ranks. Outside Parliament, the pro-choice groups, co-ordinated by CARAL, were quick to make their position known, sending an open letter to all Members of Parliament that explained both the rationale and depth of public support for keeping abortion out of the Criminal Code. Meanwhile, national women's organizations such as the Canadian Advisory Council on the Status of Women (CACSW) and the National Action Committee on the Status of Women (NAC) as well as the Canadian Medical Association (CMA) passed resolutions that abortion should be a private matter, decided by a woman and her doctor.

The pro-life lobby mobilized a massive public letter-writing campaign which urged MPs to vote for a restrictive abortion law, legalizing the procedure only when the life of the woman was at risk. As important were the intense lobbying activities conducted by pro-life MPs within their respective caucuses. The largest group of pro-life MPs were housed within the Conservative Party, especially on the backbenches. All of them were men and all were very committed to the pro-life cause. Only a year before, one of their most vocal leaders, Gus Mitges, had succeeded in bringing to a vote in the House of Commons a private members bill which ascribed constitutional rights to the foetus. The vote was 62 in favour of creating such rights in law and 89 opposed. Support for the bill came overwhelmingly from the

Conservative backbench, none of the eleven Conservative cabinet ministers attending voted for it. After the Supreme Court decision this group of pro-life Conservative MPs mobilized once again, pressuring fellow MPs to join their ranks. Assisted by pro-life organizations, they called an information meeting for Members of Parliament, with some sixty attending, to hear Dr Bernard Nathanson, an American physician best know for his narration of the graphic pro-life film, *The Silent Scream*.

Partly because of the strength of the pro-life forces within the Conservative Party, the Prime Minister found it impossible to find a compromise policy in his parliamentary caucus. Even after five meetings of the Conservative caucus, agreement on a new policy proved illusive. Thus, on Friday, 13 May 1988 Prime Minister Mulroney announced that a new abortion law, like the capital punishment issue before it, would be put to a free vote in the House of Commons. Members of Parliament would be allowed to vote according to their conscience on this contentious issue. The call for a free vote was a tacit admission on the part of the government that abortion was a moral issue to be decided by individual conscience.[22]

The government's first attempt to establish a new abortion law was fraught with procedural difficulties. In fact, it was unprecedented in the annals of Canadian parliamentary democracy. The Conservative government proposed to have the House of Commons vote on a complicated motion. The main motion would 'prohibit the performance of an abortion, subject to the following exceptions':

> When, during the earlier stages of pregnancy: a qualified medical practitioner is of the opinion that the continuation of the pregnancy of a woman would, or would be likely to, threaten her physical or mental well-being; when the woman in consultation with a qualified medical practitioner decides to terminate her pregnancy; and when the termination is performed by a qualified medical practitioner; and
>
> When, during subsequent stages of pregnancy: the termination of the pregnancy satisfies further conditions, including a condition that after a certain point in time, the termination would only be permitted where, in the opinion of two qualified medical practitioners, the continuation of the pregnancy

would, or would be likely to, endanger the woman's life or seriously endanger her health.

The proposed legislation, in other words, favoured a gestational approach in which access to abortion would be relatively free during early pregnancy and more restrictive later. What was unique about the Conservative motion was that it appended two quite distinct and contradictory amendments to the main motion. One gave 'pre-eminence to the protection of the foetus', prohibiting the performance of an abortion except when 'two independent qualified medical practitioners have, in good faith and on reasonable grounds, stated that in their opinion the continuation of the pregnancy would . . . endanger the life of the pregnant woman or seriously and substantially endanger her health'. The other amendment would give primacy to women's freedom to choose to terminate a pregnancy 'in consultation with a qualified medical practitioner'.[23]

Appending two contradictory amendments to the main motion represented a significant departure from Canadian parliamentary tradition and practice. Normally the government presents a resolution to the House and all MPs have the right both to present amendments to the proposed legislation and to speak to every amendment proposed. In this case, however, the government indicated that no amendments, other than the two contained in the government's resolution, would be allowed and that Members could speak only once during the debate and for no longer than twenty minutes.[24]

The government's strategy brought immediate condemnation from the opposition party leaders who regarded the manoeuvre as a threat to Canadian parliamentary democracy. Accordingly, the House refused to grant the government the unanimous consent it required to introduce its motion and follow the unconventional procedure. The government returned to its strategy rooms but the issue would not rest. In the Senate, Senator Stanley Haidasz, a former Liberal cabinet minister and ardent pro-lifer, introduced a private bill calling for life imprisonment of 'abortionists', a two-year sentence for women having abortions and five years for anyone who 'shows wanton or reckless disregard for the life or safety of an unborn human being'.[25]

In mid-July, 1988 the Tory government renewed its efforts to legislate on abortion. This time the government decided not to introduce new legislation, simply seeking instead 'a sense of the House' which would guide it in formulating any future legislation. It reintroduced its main motion of two months earlier without the two contradictory amendments. And this time MPs would be allowed to air their views and to introduce their own amendments to the government's resolution. Again, however, the Opposition parties as well as both pro-life and pro-choice forces were unsatisfied. The opposition argued that the government had opted for the path of least resistance, allowing MPs to air their views about abortion without presenting specific legislation to structure the debate or reveal the government's future intentions. The pro-life movement interpreted the resolution as the government's commitment to establish a permissive abortion law, while pro-choice saw it as offensive to women and potentially unconstitutional. Nevertheless, both extra-parliamentary groups were heartened by the fact that sympathetic Members of Parliament could introduce amendments reflecting their respective positions.

The House of Commons debated the abortion issue from Tuesday, 26 July, into the early morning hours of Thursday, 28 July. In all, seventy-five Members (27% of the House) gave speeches. Of these, 57% were clearly pro-life, 21% were clearly pro-choice and 21% pressed for a middle position or focused on procedure. Fully 79% of the pro-life speakers came from the ranks of the Conservative Party while the remaining were provided by Liberal members. Moreover, all of the pro-life speeches were given by men. Some 30% of the women sitting in the House gave speeches and all but one were uncompromisingly pro-choice. While the other women in the House supported a pro-choice option, many were reluctant to speak for fear the pro-life groups would use their speeches as ammunition against them in the next federal election.[26]

These speeches measure the successful representation of pro-life and pro-choice discourse in an official political forum. This representation has important implications in the policy process. The content of any law reflects a particular representation of a social problem and, thereby, advances the claims and interests of specific groups over others. Abortion politics, as we have seen, has been waged on a number of fronts—in the streets, the hospitals, the courts etc.—but ultimately the substance of abortion legislation reflects the law-makers' understanding of the issue. It is important, therefore, that we examine the content of the 1988 debate.

Constructing the Meaning of Abortion in the House

Parliament is only one among many forums for the representation of competing discursive constructions of abortion. Parliamentary debates are an exercise in public rhetoric, part of the process through which the underlying interests of differently empowered social groups struggle with each other for particular outcomes through the negotiation of persuasive meanings.[27] Although the House of Commons has long since lost its mythical image as 'the hub of parliamentary democracy', parliamentary debates are extremely relevant in our examination of the politics of abortion because they provide a measure of the success of competing social forces in having their particular meanings and understandings represented and legitimized by an institutional forum. In turn, the 'official' representation of one discourse to the exclusion of others increases the likelihood that this particular set of social meanings will be reflected in public policy.[28] Nevertheless, as discussed in Chapter One, the dominance of one interpretation over others cannot be separated from the unequal social relations structuring power in any society. The substance of the parliamentary debate reflects the power of competing social forces as well as the fact that the composition of the legislature makes it more receptive to particular interpretations. The abortion debate occurred within a broader social and political context which largely excludes women from economic and political power and marginalizes feminist discourse in Canada's legislatures.

As the previous chapter demonstrates, the meaning and social construction of abortion has been subject to ongoing political struggle. In the 1960s, it was successfully defined as a medical procedure, enabling politicians to provide limited access to abortion by means of the therapeutic exception. With the rise of second-wave feminism and the pro-life movement, however, this medicalized definition was challenged by competing views framed within liberal rights discourse. Pro-choice discourse advocates women's right to chose while pro-life advocates the primacy of the right to life of the foetus. The meaning of abortion, however, is 'only the tip of the iceberg' within each discourse.[29] Many students of abortion policy readily observe that the respective discourses of the pro-choice and pro-life movements about abortion *per se* represent a much broader debate about the social construction of women.[30] The manner in which women are represented in the discourse surrounding abortion is not a trivial matter. Shared understandings of what abortion is and who women are go a long way toward informing the content of abortion legislation as well as defining women's interests in the matter. For example, a medicalized definition takes control from women and places it in the hands of medical practitioners. Further, it discourages the growth of a collective consciousness and mobilization because abortion is defined as a individual matter necessitated by unpredictable and uncommon medical indications. In contrast, the representation of abortion as a collective right based on women's difference both mobilizes women as political actors against state regulation of reproduction and gives primacy to individual women as the relevant decision-maker and moral agent.

Pro-Choice Discourse

Over the course of the past three decades, four types of arguments have been used to advance the cause of liberalized abortion laws. The medical rationale suggests that considerations of a woman's health sometimes make an abortion a medical necessity. Accordingly, the state should relax legal restrictions on abortion both to preserve the health of women and to protect them from unqualified 'backstreet' abortionists whose practices flourish in a restrictive legislative environment. Related to this are the legal and pragmatic rationales. Both readily accept that women obtain abortions, regardless of the specific legislative regime regulating the procedure. The legal posture, therefore, argues for liberal abortion legislation in order to protect the integrity of law. A law that is consistently broken is obviously a bad law and bad laws only serve to discredit the rule of law. The pragmatic rationale also accepts the reality of abortion and argues that the regulation of abortion should be tempered with sociological considerations. In particular, the pragmatic position sees abortion as part of a broader spectrum of policies relating to reproduction. Accordingly, abortion should be integrated into a comprehensive system of reproductive education and control which would, in the long run, reduce its incidence. Last, the principled rationale frames the issue of abortion as a women's right.[31]

All of these rationales for a liberalized abortion regime were voiced during the 1969 debate although the medicalized version clearly predominated. The argument that women had a right to reproductive control, including abortion, was decidedly muffled, but it was quickly embraced by the emerging second wave of Canadian feminism and the pro-choice movement. The pro-choice argument for women's reproductive control rests on two different sets of ideas, one pragmatic and sociological and the other rights-based. The sociological argument, which was echoed at the margins of the 1969 debate, recognizes that it is women who are ultimately responsible for the birth and care of children and that they, therefore, should have the choice to bear a child.[32] The extension of this position is that every child should be a 'wanted' child and that the onus on women is less to provide a child with 'life' than to provide it with a 'good life'. In other words, motherhood should be a matter of a rational and instrumental choice factoring in quality of life criteria for the woman, the potential child, and the family.[33]

The notion that women have a right to abortion, independent of any sociological considerations, was popularized by second-wave feminism. This rationale is firmly lodged within classical liberal rights discourse.[34] The feminist and pro-choice movement's call for reproductive rights rests on the fundamental liberal principles of 'bodily integrity' (i.e., citizens have a right to make decisions about their own bodies free from state interference) and 'individual conscience' (i.e., women are autonomous, rational, and moral agents capable of exercising choice).[35] This new public construction of abortion, therefore, challenges the medical definition and associated rationales for abortion. Abortion is no longer a matter of medical intervention allowed by state-defined 'health' indications but, instead, a fundamental right of all women.

Both the sociological and rights-based constructions of abortion are largely silent on the moral or scientific status of the foetus. The former assigns primacy to the quality of life of children, while the latter depicts abortion as a woman's right and accords no *a priori* moral standing to the foetus.[36] In fact, the most extreme forms of the liberal-rights variant depicts the foetus simply as women's 'property' with a moral status no greater or different than other forms of property. Following from this, it is only women who have the right to decide.[37] The pro-choice movement's appeal to rights gave it a powerful tool for creating a collective identity among women and for representing women as autonomous social agents. But pro-choice's silence on the moral dimensions of the issue, and its construction of abortion in terms of rights, opened discursive space for the pro-life movement to advance competing claims about the rights of the foetus.[38]

All of these themes in pro-choice discourse were expressed, with varying degrees of intensity, in the House of Commons during the July 1988 debates. As noted above, only 21% of the speeches were clearly pro-choice—a statistic which, in itself, is a partial indicator of the success of the pro-choice movement in having its particular constuction of abortion represented in an official political forum. Put simply, the majority of the legislators did not express a pro-choice position in the House. The NDP caucus, however, formed a united front against the proposed reintroduction of abortion into the Criminal Code. Their primary strategic manoeuvre was to largely ignore the moral and philosophical questions about abortion that the pro-life forces were to raise during the debate and focus instead on the growing issue of access. Marion Dewar, the first NDP member to speak in the House, was quick to assure the Canadian public that her party was not 'pro-abortion'. Instead, she asserted that her party was firmly committed to the proposition that 'women should have some right to choose' and that, therefore, the 'same type of services [should be] available to all Canadian women so that they can have equal access'.*(3)* (Speakers are identified by number. See Appendix B, page 151.) The NDP introduced an amendment to the effect that the Canada Health Act be amended to ensure equality of access to abortion. This call was reiterated by the NDP speakers but it was later ruled out of order by the Speaker of the House and, thus, not called to a vote. The pro-choice position of decriminalization and easier access to abortion was faithfully represented in the House by the NDP but that party's minority status precluded this position from becoming the 'sense of the House'.

The Rhetoric of Pragmatism

All of the pro-choice speeches reflected the familiar themes developed over the past twenty years. Without exception, they offered pragmatic and rights-based rationales for maintaining a liberalized abortion regime. The first thread of pragmatism was, in fact, reminiscent of the 1969 debate. Put simply, the speakers argued that abortion was a fact of life and that legislative restrictions only promised a return of the 'bad old days'. The House was reminded that:

> We cannot go back to making abortions illegal because it will not stop abortions from taking place. It will simply force women to seek illegal abortions in unsafe, completely unhealthy ways, that will cause damage to the women in our community.*(49)*

These speeches often made reference to the backstreet abortionist, to make the point that new restrictions on abortion would be both ineffective and harmful to women.[39] Terms such as 'unhealthy', 'unsanitary', 'used coathangers', and 'vacuum cleaners' reinforced the picture. As an ultimate statement of pragmatism, it was argued that the backstreet abortion was 'not a very attractive picture, but it was real life'.*(25)* Moreover, the proposed legislative restrictions would be useless because 'if women can't get an abortion here, they will go across the border'.*(10)* This would only disadvantage young, poor women, especially those living in remote areas.

The pragmatic theme downgrades issues of morality by arguing that whether we like it or not, women will seek out abortions and that it is up to the state to protect them. It is, therefore, a woman-centred discourse but the women are largely passive and in need of protective legislation. A woman-centred protective theme also underlies the second strain of pragmatism contained within the pro-choice discourse—the need to focus on the living. According to this line of argument, the government's pro-life posturing was hypocritical because it made little effort to support women and families. In fact, Conservative cutbacks in welfare funding disadvantaged women and children and indirectly encouraged women to terminate their pregnancies. The House was reminded of the feminization of poverty and how growing numbers of Canadian children were undernourished and deprived of adequate housing and support. 'After all this neglect of born children and mothers . . . our society cannot really expect to stop abortions just by punishing pregnant women.'*(29)* The key to limiting the incidence of abortion in

Canada did not rest with regulations on the procedure but, instead, with an adequate family policy, 'enabling women to make proper choices . . . a choice not dictated by economic necessities'.*(46)* In other words, these speakers argued that abortion should not be debated on the high moral terrain occupied by the pro-life movement. It had to be contextualized sociologically in order to be understood. As summarized by one pro-choice MP:

> No child is born into a vacuum, rather, every child from conception is readied for life in a complex network of family and community relationships. But many Canadian women today feel that they must resort to abortion as the only way of coping with a society which has no place for pregnant women or their children. Women feel that they must restructure themselves by emptying their wombs, whereas it is really society that must be restructured . . . . [We must] deal with such crucial matters as birth control, counselling, social services, violence, battering, child care, housing or conditions of remorseless poverty.*(44)*

This sociological argument, like the backstreet narrative, is woman-centred and protective. In the former, the woman is a victim of a sinister charlatan and, in the latter, a victim of the gender division of labour and the neo-conservative state. However, the sociological argument also shares commonalities with some threads of pro-life discourse. In particular, it tends to see women as mothers or potential mothers who, when forced by pragmatic considerations of economic necessity, act unnaturally when they terminate a pregnancy. In both cases, the point of convergence is a 'family policy'.

The Rhetoric of Rights

Other pro-choice speeches were more clearly reflective of the pro-choice movement's discourse on rights and the representation of women as something other than mothers or potential mothers. The first step in this argument relates to the liberal notion of bodily integrity: i.e., women's bodies, women's choice. Many of the male pro-choice speakers took as their point of departure women's difference and argued that 'only [women] can make [the choice] about the product of their womb'.*(46)* Moreover, 'women are the only ones who bear children in our society. Therefore, they must make the decisions.'*(53)* On the rare occasion when the foetus was recognized, the House was reminded that 'it was nevertheless inside another person'.*(29)*

The second step in this argument, again consistent with classical liberal theory, is to represent women as responsible moral agents who are fully capable of making rational decisions. 'What men are challenged for', one male MP told the House, 'is to believe that women may be just as responsible as men. It shakes our egos a little bit but the facts seem to bear it out.'*(29)* Others pointed to the obvious contradiction in the fact that women have the right, and indeed are held accountable, to make responsible decisions in every aspect of their lives with the exception of control of their reproductive capacity. The representation of women as full moral agents, however, was most forcefully argued by women MPs, regardless of party affiliation. An older and otherwise conservative government MP told the House that while she was personally opposed to abortion, 'Every woman has her own conscience [and] the government cannot and should not tell women what they can think and do.'*(24)* The Minister Responsible for the Status of Women, Barbara McDougall, put the argument to the House most eloquently.

> A woman is a whole being. She has a body, an intellect, and a soul and spirit, whatever the magic is that makes us a unique species. I remind you that frequently the body makes its own choice. The miscarriage of an unborn child is a natural abortion. It is the body saying 'no'. Why, if the woman is a whole being, cannot her mind, her intellect, her spirit make that same decision? . . . And make no mistake, women make the right choice, a far better choice than you or I or all the pageantry of institutions that have been invented . . . from the beginning of time.

The final step in the pro-choice argument, following from the liberal themes of bodily integrity and moral agency, is that Parliament, an overwhelmingly male legislature, did not have the right to proclaim a new abortion law because women were not adequately represented in that forum. A number of male MPs indicated that they felt uncomfortable with the debate both because of the underrepresentation of women in the House and the obvious pro-choice position of the women MPs. By what right, one male MP asked, did he as a man have to say, 'You women can't have an abortion unless your health is really in danger . . . That I don't mind allowing you.'*(71)* Another charged that it was 'sheer nonsense' for the House to attempt to legislate 'women's morality'.*(10)* Yet another argued that it was preferable to leave the decision to 'the female half of the race rather than telling them that father knows best'.*(29)*

To summarize, the pro-choice speeches reflected two very different rationales for maintaining a liberalized abortion regime in Canada, and two very different representations of women. One stream, pragmatic and sociological, argued that abortions were a reality and that women, represented as vulnerable mothers or potential mothers, needed protection either from unsafe abortions or from a hostile economic environment. The other stream represented the issue of abortion and women within the abstract discourse of liberal individualism. Women were represented as rational moral agents who had the right to make decisions about their bodies free from state interference. As already noted, fewer than one-quarter of the speeches in the House conveyed either variant of the pro-choice case and most were silent on the moral dimensions of abortion and the status of the foetus. These issues as well as a much more threatening representation of women would be taken up by the majority of speakers, who were firmly situated in the pro-life camp.

Pro-Life Discourse

The pro-life campaign is about twenty years old and, by now, most of us are familiar with its depiction of abortion as murder. Since the liberalization of abortion policy, pro-life groups have shifted the centre of their rhetorical campaign from the condemnation of the immorality of irresponsible sex and abortion to a positive campaign to protect 'life'. We are also familiar with pro-life narratives which vividly describe the murder of the foetus. The stories depict the knowing foetus being torn limb by limb in a suction procedure or the viable foetus being left to die in a surgical dish after a saline-induced abortion. This rhetorical strategy has been effectively reinforced, as Petchesky's analysis so convincingly demonstrates, with photographic images of the foetus which arouse public identification with it and obscure the pregnant woman's body.[40]

Public opinion polls show that committed pro-lifers constitute a small proportion of the Canadian public, but their influence in the abortion debate far outweighs their relatively small numbers. This is partly because of their militant devotion to a single issue, effective organizational tactics, and lobbying and electoral activities. More important, however, is their construction of a powerful new discourse around abortion which is consistently advanced in public forums. This certainly was the case during the 1988 parliamentary debates. In reading the pro-life speeches one is struck by their similarity and the interlocking steps in their argument. The success of the pro-life movement reflects the power of its discourse and, therefore, the underlying assumptions and linkages in its argument deserve in-depth examination.

Science as Foe and Friend

The fundamental premise of pro-life discourse is that life begins at conception. This proposition was also often voiced in the 1969 debate but it was then frequently grounded in moral and religious rationales. This grounding was successfully countered with the argument that it was inappropriate for the state to legislate morality, thereby opening space for medicalized definitions of the foetus and the practice of therapeutic abortions, at least in the early stages of pregnancy. The first task in the rhetorical revival of pro-life, therefore, has been to shift the abortion issue back onto a moral terrain. To do so, it had to discredit the prevailing medical definition of abortion and reconstitute its claim that life begins at conception. Its strategy has been to deny that abortion is a medical matter to be decided by doctors and, at the same time, to draw on medical science to legitimize its claim that life begins at conception. We can clearly discern this rhetorical strategy in the 1988 parliamentary debates.

The first claim advanced by pro-life speakers was that abortion is not about medicine because 'pregnancy is not a disease and abortion is not therapeutic'.*(12)* Moreover, when abortion was liberalized to allow therapeutic exceptions, it was misused by the medical profession to provide abortions for non-medical reasons. The 1969 reforms, argued one pro-life MP, 'resulted in doctors authorizing thousands of abortions which had nothing whatsoever to do with the health of the mother . . . . These reasons . . . were given as excuses to destroy an innocent baby's life.'*(54)* The final link is that, since abortion is not about medicine, doctors are ill-equipped to make the decision about who should be allowed to terminate a pregnancy.

> Why her doctor? Surely the question to kill unborn human beings is a philosophical and moral issue . . . . By training, by experience, by education, [doctors] are probably the least qualified group to decide philosophical questions . . . most medical people could not tell the difference between a philosophical precept and a wet paint sign.*(37)*

As critical theorists have long recognized, attaching scientific status to a claim both depoliticizes it (i.e., it is not contestable because it is a proven 'fact') and gives it power (i.e., because modernity attaches greatest legitimacy to scientific 'truth'). A scientific guarantee of truth, in turn, helps create public acceptance of the implications of particular discourses.[41] In the evolution of pro-life discourse, medical science is both a foe and a friend. This discourse discredits the medical profession as arbitrators in moral disputes and, at the same time, embraces medical science as the irrefutable guarantor of the claim that life begins at conception. This rhetorical twist, although internally contradictory, sets the foundation for the social construction of the foetus as a full-fledged human being in possession of natural rights. Pro-life's strategic embrace of science reads as follows: '. . . the biological and physiological facts speak for themselves . . .'*(26)*; '. . . medical evidence is concrete. It is objective. It is compelling. Life is an uninterrupted continuum which begins at conception and ends at death'*(6)*; '. . . to hold otherwise is bad science'.*(38)*

Armed with the 'truth' of science, pro-life discourse then challenges the pro-choice movement to lend similar scientific legitimacy to its claims. One pro-life MP after another argued to the effect that 'the burden of proof [is] on those who would snuff out the lives of the unborn by abortion'.*(12)* What is implied here is that without scientific grounding, the pro-choice position is both invalid and untrue.

In fact, the most liberal variants of pro-choice discourse have been silent about the scientific status of the foetus and are, therefore, particularly vulnerable both to pro-life's capture of science and its claim of foetal personhood. Instead, the pro-choice position has tended to link the concept of foetal personhood to viability.

Over the past twenty years, however, medical and technological developments have made 'viability' an increasingly elastic concept. Indeed, new medical technologies, foetal imaging, and pro-life discourse increasingly give the illusion that the foetus can somehow survive outside of a woman's body, or, at least, much earlier than could have been imagined twenty years ago.[42] The pro-life movement has used these technological advances as reasons, if not to achieve a total ban on abortion, at least to compress the time period when women are allowed to choose.[43] Nevertheless, pro-life's most serious challenge to existing abortion legislation does not relate to the viability factor. Rather, it is the rhetorical construction of the foetus as the new and maligned 'character' in the abortion saga. The social construction of the foetus is the next central block in pro-life discourse.

The Social Construction of the Foetus

The major rhetorical device of the modern pro-life movement, following from its 'scientific proof' about when life begins, is to 'create' the foetus as a full member of the human family with all the attributes and rights ascribed to human beings. The first step in this argument is to provide proof, again often 'scientific', that there is no difference between the foetus and you and me. But there is a difference. The foetus lives inside and is wholly dependent on the woman's body. The pro-life's rhetorical challenge, therefore, is to make the foetus complete and autonomous by rendering the woman's body invisible and irrelevant to foetal personhood.[44] This is asserted in the following manner:

> Science tells us that when the sperm and ovum unite, they become a complete genetic package programmed for development into a mature adult. Nothing will be added except time and nutrition . . . . the fertilized egg is like a computer chip.*(9)*

> [at conception] The colour of our eyes, the size of our feet, and the capacity of our brains have all been established. Nothing needs to be added other than food, shelter and care . . . The unborn can cry, hiccup, develop individual tastes, be startled, and feel pain.*(6)*

The pregnant woman, according to this discursive construction, represents shelter, nourishment, and time. She is a mechanical incubator who, so long as she is functional, is irrelevant to the outcome of the pregnancy. The foetus, from conception, is autonomous and self-propelling. It is like us all biologically, but pro-life discourse tells us that it is different socially and politically. We are told that 'the unborn is innocent';*(9)* that it is 'the weakest stage of all of us';*(38)* that it 'has done no wrong';*(54)* and that it is 'without defences'.*(61)* Why then should 'he or she be punished, let alone murdered?'*(54)* Thus, it follows that each and every one of us must protect the foetus through law as we would wish ourselves to be protected. The pro-life speakers thus called for constitutional rights for the foetus as well as representation by 'legal counsel'*(31)* and in the cabinet.*(12)*

The power of current pro-life discourse is the representation of the foetus as a person with biological and political sovereignty. This construction promotes a model of pregnancy as a condition which, by definition, pits the rights of one autonomous citizen (the foetus) against the rights of an invisible and passive body (the woman).[45] Nevertheless, the creation of the foetus as an autonomous citizen does not solve the problem of whose rights should prevail in the case of abortion. In order to ensure the primacy of foetal rights over women's rights, pro-life discourse must counter the pro-choice claim of women's right to bodily self-determination by both expropriating the female body and disenfranchising the female subject.

The Discursive Campaign Against Women

Clearly, one of the central threads of pro-choice discourse over the past twenty years is the representation of women as autonomous moral agents who have the right to make unfettered decisions about both their bodies and their reproductive capacity. The demand for reproductive control has been particularly challenging to patriarchal discourse and social relations because it displaces the definition of women as simple child-bearers and disenfranchises men in the politics of reproduction. Thus, while it is necessary for the pro-life movement to represent the foetus as a person, it is equally necessary to counter and diffuse feminist discourse about women.

Pro-life's campaign against women occurs on a number of interrelated terrains. The first relates to the meaning and purpose of women's sexuality. A number of pro-life speakers indicated that women do have 'choice' in the abortion decision. This choice, however, is limited to whether or not to engage in heterosexual relations. Once pregnant, the woman loses her choice to society. Pro-life spokesmen reject the central tenet in pro-choice discourse that abortion is a woman's choice or a 'feminist issue'.*(6)* Instead, the speeches frequently assert that abortion is a 'family issue',*(43)* a concern of the entire 'human family'*(6)* and 'above all, . . . a societal issue'.*(27)* As such, 'society must have the right to limit [women's] choices'.*(33)*

In other words, pro-life discourse asserts that the choice to terminate a pregnancy is not a woman's but society's. This rhetorical construction thus conflates patriarchy with society and denies women's autonomy and self-determination. These cannot be granted to women because they are inconsistent with the broader universal (read patriarchal) values of family and society. To say that it is not a woman's but society's choice to terminate a pregnancy is to cast the woman outside society and make her a object of social control. When the interests of 'society' and women collide, society takes precedence and the woman becomes a disenfranchised social actor. Importantly, this disenfranchisement only applies to *pregnant* women.

The representation of the foetus in pro-life discourse further alienates and disenfranchises women in issues of reproductive control. The idea of foetal personhood requires that it be detached from the pregnant body so that it can be perceived as independent and autonomous. Nevertheless, pro-choice discourse relating to women's bodily integrity draws the foetus back into the pregnant body as a contingent entity subject to women's choice. To counter this claim, pro-life must argue that it is not a woman's choice because it is not her body: it belongs to the foetus. In a rather incredible biology lesson, for example, one pro-life MP told the house that 'the umbilical cord and the placenta belong to the baby. They are not part of the mother's body.'*(12)* Another argued that the feminist call for bodily control was 'distressing' because 'we are not talking about their own body'.*(28)*

Pro-life discourse, therefore, dictates that upon the act of conception women lose their choice to society and their body to the foetus. Control of the womb is of primary importance here and in these pro-life speeches it is ascribed great symbolic importance. The womb is a contradictory site which acts as a metaphor for patriarchy as well as revealing deep currents of sexism and gyno-phobia. It is both a sanctuary—'the first family home'*(33)*—and a site of terrible violence against the foetus. The pro-life representation of the womb reflects its conflicting visions of women and pregnancy. Although pregnancy is promoted as the natural course for women to follow, when women are allowed to control their womb, they act in anti-social and unnatural ways. One MP argued 'abortion is an extreme form of child abuse inside the womb'*(4)*, while another lamented that 'it is chilling for me to realize that the most violent place in Canada today is not some dark side street in a decayed section of an inner city; it is, rather, the human womb.'*(5)*

Because women are the major threat to foetal life, there is an obvious political imperative to protect the foetus against the destructive impulses of the pregnant woman.[46] Choosing whether or not to terminate a pregnancy should not be left to the woman because, as we have seen, it is neither her choice nor her body. Even more fundamentally, however, women are incapable of making the choice because they are not full moral agents. They are either too selfish to act for the social good, or they have been tricked and need legislation to protect themselves against themselves.

The Immorality of Women

The demand for reproductive choice erodes the long-standing patriarchal definition of women and its complementary web of social organization. Patriarchal discourse defines women as different because of their reproductive capacity. Childbearing and motherhood are seen as 'natural' and inevitable for women. This biological destiny, in turn, informs other socially constructed gender differences. According to this discourse, women are selfless, nurturing, and passive, both worthy of and in need of protection from men. They are also closer to nature and thus less rational and less morally responsible for their behaviour than men.[47] Men are capable of objectivity: women are governed by their irrational subjectivity.

Abortion breaks the patriarchal link between reproductive destiny and the gendered division of labour. By asserting their right to reproductive control, women are asserting that childbearing is not the most important thing in their lives and that their definition of self is not limited to motherhood.[48] From a patriarchal perspective, abortion represents an act of mutiny against motherhood as well as a rejection of 'natural' feminine qualities. To reject motherhood is to defy all those qualities ascribed to mothers—absolute dedication, marital chastity, selflessness, total sacrifice.[49] In other words, it is to be selfish. More seriously, the social construction of the foetus means that women seeking abortion are pursuing their own selfish ends at the cost of another's life.

The representation of women who seek abortions as selfish was repeatedly offered by the pro-life MPs. Abortion, according to one, allowed a woman 'the absolute legal right to have another killed in order to solve her own personal, social or economic problem'.*(4)* Another, recounting a letter from a constituent, asked the House '[how would you like it] if your mother at the present moment would come with a knife and stab you in the back because you were a nuisance to her social life'.*(45)* According to this construction, then, women are morally bankrupt and society must use the law to tame their self-centred and hedonistic nature. As one MP put it: 'For those who have no moorings, no ethical guidance mechanisms, no moral guidance mechanisms left, the only thing left is the law.'*(14)*

While pro-life discourse constructs women as incomplete moral agents, it stops short of assigning this deficiency to biology. The essential gender difference is that women are more easily lead astray. According to this argument, women are passive and have been 'manipulated by society to do the most unnatural thing in the world, to kill their own tiny child'.*(4)* Moreover, 'the radical feminist lobbyists, supported by taxpayers' money,' want to destroy the family 'which history has already revealed as the strength of the nation'.*(20)* Women have been duped by feminists and the prochoice movement which is without a 'value system'.*(52)*

Abortion threatens the foetus and the family but it has also done 'a terrible disservice to the well-being of the mother herself'.*(6)* According to the pro-life MPs, 'more and more people are beginning to recognize that women themselves are victims of abortion . . . more and more women are realizing that they are being terribly exploited by our selfish abortion oriented society. This is discrimination against women and against the very nature of womanhood.'*(4)* Although there is little medical evidence to support any widespread incidence of post-abortion syndrome, the pro-life MPs maintain that abortion leaves 'physical and psychological scars . . . etched on the souls of many of our women, our wives and mothers'*(27)* Added to the long list of why women should be denied choice, therefore, is the idea that women must be protected from themselves because they have been diverted, at great personal costs, from their true and natural identities by the immoral pro-choice movement.

The thrust of pro-life discourse is directed against the pro-choice movement's rights-based rhetoric. There are a number of inconsistencies and contradictions in its argument. For example, medicine is both discounted in abortion and the guarantor of foetal life. Similarly, this discourse privileges social values over individual choices in the decision to carry a pregnancy to term. At the same time, it asserts the foetus' absolute right to life irrespective of the values of the collectivity.[50] Finally, pregnancy is constued as a natural and desirable condition for women but, once pregnant, women seem to act in decidedly unnatural and undesirable ways.

Recruiting the Pregnant Body

Pro-choice discourse also stresses pragmatic and sociological considerations. How then does pro-life discourse counter the pragmatic rationale for a liberal abortion regime? Put simply, its alternative is adoption. The pro-life MPs completely rejected pro-choice's assertion that every child should be a wanted child by arguing that 'there is no such thing as an unwanted child'.*(35)* They contended that 'children certainly can be unplanned but someone always wants them, though that someone may not be a biological parent'.*(58)* Who is that someone? It is 'childless couples, desperate to adopt'*(58)*, who 'hunger for parenthood'*(14)*, and who are 'willing and anxious to enjoy the beauty and richness of parenthood through adoption'.*(27)* In so arguing, pro-life discourse juxtaposes the image of the careless and morally bankrupt woman against that of the infertile heterosexual couple, arousing sympathy for childless women who are trying to follow the 'natural' and selfless course of motherhood.[51] The demand for children for adoption, therefore, provides an alternative to abortion, if only the selfish pregnant women can be encouraged to bring their pregnancies to term.

Pro-life MPs suggest that the state can recruit the pregnant body to serve the infertile couple by severely restricting access to abortion, devising an encompassing family policy, and assisting the unwed mother. The House was told that 'we, as individuals, and our society need to walk alongside [teenage pregnant girls] . . . care for them, provide support mechanisms for the life they are creating'.*(14)* The challenge facing Canadians is 'to nurture a mother facing an unwanted pregnancy . . . so that women can give their children a future . . . and respond to a childless couple'.*(27)* None of the pro-life speeches asserting the adoption link, however, discuss the trauma teenage girls or women might experience by carrying the pregnancy to term and then giving up the baby. The representation of women seeking abortions as selfish both trivializes the abortion decision and desensitizes us to the possibility that these women might have emotions or other priorities. The pro-life representation of women, then, is ultimately reducible to a pregnant body.

No Sense in the House

By the end of the debate, twenty-one amendments to the government's resolution had been tabled. The Speaker of the House ruled that all but five were either identical in intent or introduced a new element in the debate, and were therefore out of order. The thrust of the five amendments, to be voted on in order, were as follows:

1) The Collins amendment, which would have made an early abortion a matter of choice between a woman and her doctor while requiring that later abortions (for reasons of the woman's health or physical health) be approved by another doctor.

2) The James amendment, which would allow abortions in the first twelve weeks of pregnancy and impose restrictions thereafter.

3) The Mitges amendment, which would have prohibited abortions except when two doctors agreed that continuing the pregnancy would endanger the life of the mother.

4) The Sparrow amendment, which defined the early stage of pregnancy as the first eighteen weeks.

5) The Bosley amendment, which would have simply

> required that abortions be conducted by qualified medical practitioners. The decision to have an abortion would be determined by a woman and her doctor.[52]

The pro-life lobby had made an impressive showing in the House during the first two and one-half days of debate and they were clearly heartened by the prospect that the parliamentary exercise might result in the adoption of the blatantly pro-life Mitges amendment. As one pro-life MP after another rose to speak, pro-choice MPs became convinced that, if the Mitges amendment came to a vote, it would represent the 'sense of the House'. This outcome could only be avoided if a majority coalition could be constructed around the Collins amendment, which would be the first to come to a vote. Thus, strong supporters of the choice option within the government's ranks approached the NDP, seeking support for the Collins amendment even though it restricted choice and kept abortion policy within the Criminal Code. Such a strategy would block the Mitges amendment while leaving the NDP members free to vote against the government's main motion. In the end, however, key strategists within the NDP argued that the party's strong commitment both to choice and decriminalization prevented it from entering into such a coalition. The vote would have to proceed without any backroom agreement to block the pro-life amendment.

The vote was called in the early morning of July 28. Neither the Prime Minister nor Liberal leader John Turner was present. The Collins amendment was the first put to a vote: it lost, 191 to 29. The James amendment was called next and was defeated, 202 to 17. Next was the decidedly pro-life Mitges amendment which when called to a voice vote, appeared to have won a majority. A formal vote count, however, revealed 105 Members in favour and 118 opposed. Following this, the Sparrow amendment was defeated on a voice vote and the Bosley amendment was rejected 198 to 20. In the end, the government's main motion was also defeated 147 to 76. The result of the whole exercise was that, while the pro-life amendment came perilously close to winning, the government had still gained no 'sense of the House' to devise new legislation.

None of the coalitions had won, but then again, none had lost. For the pro-life forces, the chance of winning a ban on abortion in the next round of debate remained an inspiring possibility. In contrast, the stalemate in Parliament meant that the pro-choice movement had achieved, if only by indecision, its preferred policy outcome—choice and decriminalization. Meanwhile, the government could be seen to be acting on the abortion issue without doing anything concrete. Lost in most accounts of this confusing episode in Canadian parliamentary democracy was one disturbing fact. If the women in the House of Commons had not voted unanimously in a cross-party coalition against the Mitges amendment, it would have been adopted as the sense of the House. Of the 118 Members voting against the pro-life amendment, 96 were men and 22 were women—all of the women MPs voting. The 105 Members supporting the amendment were men. With regard to the politics of abortion, then, the nominal representation of women in the House of Commons did make a difference.

Soon after the vote, Prime Minister Mulroney dissolved Parliament and called a federal election for 21 November 1988. During the campaign the abortion issue was, of course, largely muffled by the Free Trade debate. Nevertheless, pressure to reform Canada's abortion policy continued to flow from a variety of sources. In August 1988, both the Canadian Medical Association (CMA) and the Law Reform Commission of Canada urged the government to establish a regime of abortion on demand during the early weeks of pregnancy. In the meantime, pro-life groups were engaging in their campaign to elect a 'pro-life Parliament' but they found the electorate to be far less concerned about the abortion issue than was the pro-life membership. Public opinion polls, conducted during and after the 1988 campaign, indicated that voters were preoccupied with free trade and not abortion. Only 1.5% of a national sample identified abortion as the most important issue of the campaign but this apparent public disinterest did not deter the pro-life coalition. As promised, it published the position of all candidates on the abortion issue, targeted ridings where pro-choice MPs were contesting re-election, lent its organizational resources to pro-life candidates, and spend some $400,000 on the election campaign.[53]

Pollsters are still uncertain about the impact of these efforts but many pro-choice MPs did not return to the House. Included among these were Ray Hnatyshyn, Lynn McDonald, Flora MacDonald, Lucie Pépin and Marion Dewar. In addition, approximately 74 strong anti-abortion candidates were elected. Twenty were newcomers and all but two of these were Liberals. At least one, Thomas Wappel, gained his nomination because pro-life groups packed the nomination meeting.[54]

Back to the Courts

The Conservatives returned to power with a majority but they gave little indication that they would act quickly on the abortion controversy. The absence of a federal abortion law, however, was having impact both in the courts and in the street. A year without federal regulation had resulted in extreme provincial variations in entitlement and access. Abortion remained a decision between a woman and her doctor in Nova Scotia, Quebec, Ontario, British Columbia and the Northwest Territories. In contrast, Newfoundland replaced its TACs with the requirement that women seeking an abortion must do so within the first twelve weeks of pregnancy and only after seeking counsel from a psychiatrist, gynaecologist, social worker, and registered nurse. New Brunswick and Alberta required referrals from two doctors while Saskatchewan required the referral of one doctor and counselling. Finally, the Prince Edward Island government passed a motion condemning abortion in the province but indicated that it would fund out-of-province abortions if a woman obtained the approval of five doctors.[55]

These inequities in provincial regulation brought Dr Morgentaler once again to the courts. The first case involved the government of New Brunswick. Shortly after the Supreme Court decision, the province indicated that it would pay for an abortion only when two doctors certified that it was a medical necessity and when it was performed in a provincially accredited hospital by an obstetrician or gynaecologist. Court action arose when the province refused payment to Dr Morgentaler after three New Brunswick women obtained an abortion at his Montreal clinic. Morgentaler challenged the government's actions and requested that the court order the province to pay. The New Brunswick Court of Queen's Bench sided with Morgentaler in April 1989, freeing women in the province to obtain an abortion elsewhere and have it covered by the provincial medical insurance scheme.[56]

A month later Dr Morgentaler announced his attention to open a free-standing abortion clinic in Halifax in defiance of a new provincial regulation. Nova Scotia had effectively outlawed free-standing abortion clinics in the province by disallowing certain medical procedures including abortion from being performed other than in hospitals. Morgentaler proceeded in defiance of the regulation and began performing abortions in his Halifax clinic in the fall. He invited the police to arrest him and they obliged, initially laying seven charges against him under the act.[57] The case came to trial in the spring of 1990.

These legal and legislative manoeuvres were coupled with a sustained attack by pro-life groups on free-standing abortions clinics, primarily in Vancouver and Toronto. Frustrated by their defeat in the Courts and the inaction of the federal government, pro-life groups began a crusade of civil disobedience designed, depending on one's interpretation, either to 'save the unborn' or engender guilt and fear among women seeking abortions. 'Operation Rescue' which began in late 1989 was primarily directed against Everywoman's Health Clinic, British Columbia's first free-standing abortion clinic, and the Scott and Morgentaler clinics in Toronto.

This new pro-life strategy consisted of blocking the entrance to the free-standing clinics so that women seeking abortions could not enter. The tactic inevitably brought in the police to break up the blockade, court injunctions ordering the protesters desist these practices, and defiance of the court orders by the pro-life activists. In Vancouver this predictable succession of events brought protesters the threat of a five-month jail sentence for defying the court's injunctions and a thousand dollar court fine for first offenders.[58] In Toronto, protesters were eventually prohibited from demonstrating within 500 feet of the Morgentaler Clinic.

Successive court action against Operation Rescue only seemed to convince the pro-life militants of the correctness of their defiance. They likened their civil disobedience to the American Civil Rights movement of the 1960s and themselves to the great martyrs of history. Spokesmen for the militants announced that they were willing to go to jail to 'save one baby' and to 'serve the Lord'. Moreover, when brought to trial for disobeying court injunctions, they stood in silent protest 'because when Jesus Christ was on trial, he said nothing'.[59] Pro-life leaders indicated that, without help from the government, these acts of civil disobedience and intimidation were the only tools left to them to save the unborn. They predicted that in the absence of a federal ban on abortions, 'people will realize that this is what they're going to have to do'.[60] By the summer of 1989, however, Operation Rescue was winding down; other options were presenting themselves.

July of 1989 brought a series of events which both heartened pro-life groups and drew many Canadians who had not previously been engaged in abortion politics under the pro-choice banner. The first event took place in the United States, but it alerted pro-choice activists to the fragility of legal victories in the domain of reproductive choice. On Monday, 3 July, the Supreme Court ruled on *Webster v Reproductive Health Services*, a case which involved a challenge to a Missouri statute. The state law declared that life begins at conception and prohibited public employees from aiding in, or public monies and facilities being used for, non-emergency abortions. The legislation further required that doctors test for foetal viability before terminating pregnancies which were more than twenty weeks advanced. While the lower courts had ruled that the legislation breached *Roe v Wade*, the American Supreme Court declared the law constitutional. The immediate effect was to severely limit access to abortion in Missouri since Reproductive Health Services provided almost three-quarters of the state's abortions and would no longer be eligible for public funding. More important, it opened the door for other pro-life state legislatures to pass similar laws restricting entitlement and limiting access to safe and legal abortions.[61]

On the same day as the American Supreme Court decision, an Ontario judge opened a much more disturbing legal minefield concerning the rights of fathers in abortion. The Dodd case involved a boyfriend, with uncertain claims to paternity, obtaining a court injunction to prevent his former girlfriend from obtaining an abortion. Similar cases had been repeatedly spurned by Canadian courts. Only a year earlier an Alberta court rejected such a request and in 1984 the Ontario Supreme Court ruled in the *Medhurst* case that a man did not have the right to stop a woman from obtaining an abortion.[62] In these cases, the prevailing medicalized definition of abortion protected women from third party vetoes because medical treatment was seen to be the choice of women alone.

The Dodd case was heard by the Ontario Supreme Court with neither Barbara Dodd nor representatives of Women's College Hospital, where the abortion was to be performed, present. Gregory

Murphy, the boyfriend seeking the injunction, told the court that the child was wanted and that he was capable and willing 'to provide for all his needs'. In response, Judge O'Driscoll declared the 15-week-old foetus to be under the Court's protection restraining the woman, the hospital, 'John Doe, Jane Doe and other persons unknown' from 'taking the life of the infant . . . . either by performing an abortion or a cesarean operation or otherwise'.[63]

While Women's College Hospital decided to remain neutral, judging it to be a private dispute, the decision brought immediate and strong reactions from various players in the abortion saga. Pro-choice forces condemned the decision as treating women as little more than 'an unconscious womb' and held public rallies to protest against the decision. Groups such as OCAC saw a dramatic rise in contributions and membership.[64] Meanwhile, pro-life forces saw it as a legal breakthrough 'because it recognized the right of the father and made a dent in the argument that abortion is a decision between a woman and her doctor'.[65]

An appeal was heard on 11 July 1989 and Dodd's private life was again paraded before the public. This time the Supreme Court of Ontario ruled in Dodd's favour and she went immediately to the Morgentaler clinic for the procedure. Importantly, the Court came to its decision on procedural grounds, ruling that Dodd was not given sufficient notice of the original hearing. The Court remained silent on the crucial question of whether such injunctions were legal.[66]

Although Dodd had obtained an abortion, a bizarre turn of events continued to excite media attention. Immediately after the injunction was lifted, Dodd informed the press that the experience had convinced her to work for the pro-choice cause. Meanwhile, pro-life supporters, including Murphy, held a mock funeral for Dodd's foetus in front of the Morgentaler clinic. Only a week later, and much to the dismay of pro-choice activists, Dodd denounced her decision of the previous week. Granting a press interview from the Toronto office of the Campaign Life Coalition, she suggested that she had been manipulated by pro-choice representatives and that, even though this had been her third abortion, she no longer believed either that women should have them or that they should make the decision without the father. Spokeswomen for the OCAC steadfastly denied that they had pressured Dodd but the damage to the coalition had already been done.

The Dodd case appeared to open the floodgates for third party interventions in abortion cases. By mid-July, the Manitoba courts heard a case demanding an injunction but the request was denied. In Quebec, however, a much more disturbing scenario was unfolding. On July 7 Jean-Guy Tremblay successfully obtained a temporary injunction preventing his former girlfriend, Chantal Daigle, from terminating her 18-week pregnancy. On July 17 the Quebec Superior Court upheld the injunction. Daigle, who had left Tremblay some weeks earlier because he had been physically and mentally abusive to her, appealed to the Quebec Court of Appeal on July 26. Daigle, as well as her distinguished legal counsel, were convinced that the Court would put an end to the fiasco and rule in her favour, but it did not.

In a stunning 3-2 decision, which shocked both the legal community and pro-choice forces everywhere, the Quebec Court of Appeal issued an unprecedented ruling which prevented Daigle from having an abortion. It declared that, in accordance with the Quebec Charter, the foetus was a 'distinct human entity' which 'has a right to life and protection by those who conceive it'. Even though Daigle had told the Court that Tremblay had been abusive and persuaded her to discontinue birth control, it ruled that she had become pregnant voluntarily. Moreover, the court suggested that an abortion was not therapeutic because 'pregnancy is not in itself an attack on a woman's physical well-being'. Instead, it pronounced a biologically determinant rationale that 'rule of nature is that pregnancy must lead to birth'.[67] The rationale provided by the Court clearly echoed the central themes of pro-life discourse.

Tremblay, with the financial backing of pro-life groups in Quebec, had been victorious although he was no longer sure that he wanted to raise the child as he had indicated earlier. He told the press that he wanted 'to be a father but he didn't have the time right now'. Later, he reasoned, 'I don't give milk. Women give milk. I guess the baby needs his mother.' Most of all, Tremblay told the press that he just wanted the much-publicized episode to end, especially the accusations relating to his abuse because he never hit her hard enough 'to leave any marks'.[68] Daigle, however, indicated that she was still determined to have an abortion even though she was rapidly approaching the point in her pregnancy when Quebec hospitals would no longer accept her for the procedure. Daigle was clearly overwhelmed by what had transpired and told the press that she simply could not believe that 'in 1989, people are still toying with the idea that a woman is not the master of her own body'.[69] She would, nonetheless, abide by the Court ruling and appeal to the Supreme Court of Canada.

The Daigle decision sent shock waves throughout the country. Thousands of pro-choice activists demonstrated in the streets in Montreal, Toronto, Vancouver, Halifax and elsewhere in protest against the decision which gave ex-boyfriends control over 'the most basic decision' in a woman's life and reduced them to 'walking wombs'.[70] Pro-life spokesmen were obviously delighted with the ruling because it represented a 'light at the end of the tunnel' and provided the opportunity for more men in Quebec 'to save their babies'.[71] Doctors, lawyers, and politicians reeled at the implications of the decision. The Quebec Medical Association urged its membership to consult with lawyers before performing any more abortions while lawyers and politicians deplored a situation in which the foetus was legally recognized as a human being in only one province, thereby suggesting that all abortions were illegal in Quebec and legal elsewhere. The Prime Minister is said to have been taken aback by this series of events; both he and Barbara McDougall hinted that new legislation would be introduced in the fall to prevent further chaos.[72]

The Daigle case, like the American Supreme Court decision, demonstrated how vulnerable women's reproductive control was to the biases of individual judges, the embrace of pro-life discourse concerning foetal rights by some, and the fragility of the Morgentaler decision. The case would obviously have to go to the Supreme Court both because Chantal Daigle insisted on her right to terminate her pregnancy and because the Quebec court had opened grounds for granting constitutional protection to the foetus. The Justices of the Supreme Court would have to be called back from their summer vacations to deal with the issue in an emergency session.

The Daigle case could have been circumvented earlier in the year if the court had chosen to rule on the Borowski case. Joseph Borowski, a committed anti-abortion crusader, had resigned his cabinet post in Manitoba's NDP government in 1971 to fight for the rights of the foetus. Angered over Morgentaler's successive court victories, Borowski decided to launch a court case in 1977 to have the rights of the foetus recognized in law. His efforts were immediately frustrated by the intricacies of the Canadian judicial system. Federal lawyers intervened in the case arguing that Borowski as an interested third party did not have the standing to bring such a case to trial. There also was legal wrangling over the question of whether a federal or provincial court should hear the case. These procedural issues occupied the courts for nearly four years. Finally the Supreme Court ruled that Borowski had standing and that the case could be heard in a provincial court. In the interim, the *Charter of Rights and Freedoms* had come into effect. Armed with this new legal ammunition, Borowski appeared before the Saskatchewan Court of Queen's Bench in 1983 to argue that the foetus should be protected under Section 7 of the Charter which guaranteed the security of the person.[73] The Court, however, ruled that the foetus was not a legal person and, therefore, was not protected under the Charter. This judgement was upheld by the Saskatchewan Court of Appeal in 1987.[74] Borowski would take the case to the Supreme Court for final determination.

The Mulroney government had, in fact, used the indeterminate legal status of the foetus as a stalling tactic in the long road to creating a new federal abortion law. After failing to gain a 'sense of the House' in the summer of 1988, Mulroney indicated that he would wait until the Supreme Court ruled on the Borowski case before introducing new legislation. The Court ruled on 9 March 1989 but, much to everyone's disappointment, it dodged completely the issue before it—the question of whether the foetus had a right-to-life under the constitution. It argued that, since Section 251 of the Criminal Code had already been struck down in the Morgentaler decision, Borowski's case was moot.

For Borowski, news of the unanimous ruling was devastating. He argued that Supreme Court had used 'a gimmick' and had played 'a trick' on the pro-life movement. He ruled out any further challenges to the court, reasoning that 'it would be a waste of my time to ever go back before those gutless . . . judges who wasted ten years of our time'. The Supreme Court decision simply added fuel to the resolve of Operation Rescue whose spokeswoman declared that 'if the court will not act to save babies then . . . people . . . will have to do it themselves'.[75]

The Daigle case landed the issue of foetal rights squarely back on the doorstep of the Supreme Court. Moreover, the advancing stages of Chantal Daigle's pregnancy meant that the Court had to act quickly. Thus, on August 8, the Supreme Court sat in emergency session to deal with the issue. A number of key players in the politics of abortion were granted intervenor status including the Attorney Generals of Canada and Quebec, CARAL, the Women's Legal Education and Action Fund (LEAF), the Canadian Civil Liberties Association (CCLA), the Campaign Life Coalition, Canadian Physicians for Life, and REAL Women of Canada. But, before the judges could hear all the submissions, Daigle's lawyer dropped a bombshell into the proceedings. The court was informed that the young woman, then twenty-four weeks pregnant, had disguised herself, crossed the border, and obtained an abortion.

The Daigle case was now effectively moot, but this time the Supreme Court decided not to skirt the issue and struck down the injunction against Daigle. It issued its reasons for doing so in November 1989. The Court indicated that it would not enter into 'the philosophical or theological debates about whether or not a foetus is a person'. Moreover, it argued that this issue 'cannot be settled by linguistic fiat'. Instead, as in the case of the Morgentaler decision, the court held fast to its contention that the issue of foetal personhood had to be resolved in the political arena. It would base its decision on existing Canadian law which, according to the judges, did not recognize the foetus as a person. Precedents indicated consistently that 'legal personality is acquired at birth'. Moreover, the judges indicated that 'no court in Quebec or elsewhere has ever accepted the argument that a father's interest in a foetus . . . could support a right to veto a woman's decision'.[76] The legal status of the foetus and the rights of the father in the abortion debate appeared to have been settled, at least with respect to the constitution and existing law. Once again the Supreme Court had frustrated the pro-life coalition.

The Making of Bill C-43

The events of the summer of 1989 convinced the Mulroney government that it could no longer postpone introducing a new abortion law. Shortly after Parliament reconvened from the summer recess, a Conservative caucus committee was struck to recommend a new course of action. The committee, constructed to represent the party's pro-choice, moderate, and pro-life factions, was given the difficult, if not impossible, task of recommending new legislation which would both pass in the House of Commons and meet the constitutional supervision of the Supreme Court. By the end of September, it had settled on three options to form the basis for new legislation. The first would allow abortion on demand up to the first fourteen weeks of pregnancy, add restrictions during weeks 14 through 20, and ban abortions after 20 weeks. The second would allow abortions during the first five months of pregnancy, and the third would apply some regulation to abortion but without reference to the stage of the pregnancy.[77]

Some sort of gestational approach in which free access to abortion applied during the early stages of pregnancy and restrictions were imposed later had been advocated for some time by many key players in the abortion debate, among them the CMA, the Canadian Bar Association (CBA) and, most recently, the Canadian Law Reform Commission on Crimes Against the Foetus. The Supreme Court implied, in the Morgentaler decision that a gestational approach might be the proper course of future action. Moreover, most other countries applied a gestational formula in their abortion legislation. Nevertheless, this approach provided a moral and tactical dilemma for the ardent pro-life MPs in the Conservative caucus. It promised state restrictions on access to abortion, at the cost of allowing relatively free access during the early stages of pregnancy. This distinction was an affront to those who maintained that life began at conception and, therefore, after considerable debate, the caucus committee rejected a gestational approach to any new federal legislation.

The government finally presented its new abortion law to the House of Commons on 3 November 1989. Bill C-43 attempted to respond to Canada's unique constitutional constraints and, at the same time, strike a compromise between the competing demands of the pro-choice and pro-life coalitions both within and outside Parliament. Yet, like many attempts to find a compromise on an issue which defies compromise, the government's proposed solution satisfied no one. As in other countries which have attempted to balance the demands of opposing forces in the politics of abortion, a general prohibition of abortion was maintained within the Criminal Code, subject to special exceptions. In other words, the pro-life position provided for the 'morality of the law' while a medicalized discourse supplied 'the practical regulations'. The Canadian version of 'no abortions, unless . . .' read as follows:[78]

> 1) Every person who induces an abortion on a female person is guilty of an indictable offence and liable to imprisonment for a term not exceeding two years, unless the abortion is induced by or under the direction of a medical practitioner who is of the opinion that, if the abortion were not induced, the health or life of the female person would be likely to be threatened.

The proposed new law reintroduced a ban on abortions in the Criminal Code while, at the same time, created a gaping loophole whereby a doctor could decide, without the constraints of seeking a second opinion or the certification of any hospital committee, that a woman's health indicated that the procedure was necessary. Bill C-43 went on to define a women's health liberally, if not ambiguously, as 'physical, mental and psychological health'. 'Opinion' was defined as the 'generally accepted standards of the medical profession'.

The Opposition parties were quick to criticize the government's new legislation. Members of Parliament decried the recriminalization of abortion and Bill C-43's failure to ensure equitable access to the procedure for women across the country. The Minister of Justice, however, maintained—as he would throughout the debate on Bill C-43—that the intent of the legislation was to define a national standard for 'entitlement to abortion' based on 'health grounds'. The question of access and the delivery of health services was a matter of provincial jurisdiction and responsibility.[79]

The government indicated that, after long hours of deliberation and careful drafting of Bill C-43, it believed that it had achieved a workable compromise. But none of the key actors in the politics of abortion agreed. A Campaign Life lobbyist immediately denounced the proposed legislation as 'a piece of junk'. Similarly, Canadian Physicians For Life expressed their 'profound disappointment' because the bill offered 'no real protection for the human foetus at any point in the pregnancy'.[80] From the opposite side, C-43 was criticized for, once again, marking women seeking abortions for reasons unrelated to their health (and doctors providing them) as criminals, and for failing to ensure equitable access for all Canadian women. In fact, as discussed below, the provisions of the bill promised to restrict or deny access to legal abortions to women in many regions of the country.

Justice Minister Doug Lewis remained confident that a workable compromise had been struck and predicted that Bill C-43 would become law before the end of the year. Its first crucial test was gaining the approval of the House on Second Reading so that it could go to the committee stage for public hearings and refinement. But its passage at this preliminary stage was by no means certain. Both the pro-life and pro-choice coalitions within the House were opposed to the bill, although for very different reasons. Only two days before the vote was scheduled the *Toronto Star* published a poll of MPs which indicated that the government did not have the votes to see the proposed legislation to the committee stage.[81]

Bill C-43 was reintroduced to the House for Second Reading on 28 November 1989. Prime Minister Mulroney, who had been conveniently absent during the government's previous attempt to gain a 'sense of the House', made a long and impassioned speech demanding compromise from all sides so that the controversy could be finally laid to rest. He also indicated that this time he would only allow the Conservative backbench a free vote on the bill while the cabinet was expected to toe the party line. Cabinet Ministers and those aspiring to Cabinet were sent a clear message to hold their noses and pass the bill.

Surprisingly, Bill C-43 received approval-in-principle by a rather wide margin—164 to 114. Among those voting against it were 12 Conservatives (the hard pro-life faction), 60 Liberals and 42 NDP members. Unlike the previous exercise, the women in the House did not vote in unison: all of the Conservative women voted for the bill while all the women in opposition voted against it.[82] What surprised political pundits was the strength of support for the bill on the Tory backbench. The ardent pro-lifers were expected to reject it but it soon became apparent that some of this group was willing to see the bill go to committee so that more restrictive conditions could be introduced at the committee stage. C-43 moved to its legislative committee comprised of eight men and six women MPs selected to reflect a 'balanced representation' on the issue.

From late January until late March of 1990 the committee engaged in an intensive series of public hearings. In all, it heard testimony from three federal cabinet ministers, forty-six groups, thirty of which represented the pro-choice position, and five individuals. It received briefs from another one hundred and seventy-five groups and one hundred and forty-one individuals. With the exception of the Conservative cabinet ministers, none of the witnesses appearing before the committee supported the legislation in an unamended form. Unlike the 1988 debate which focused on the broader issues evoked by abortion, most of the submissions to the parliamentary committee focused on the specifics of C-43. Granted, the terms of the new legislation were related to broader issues such as the medical and moral status of the foetus, the rights of women, paternal rights, the medical status of abortion, eugenics, and family policy. Nevertheless, both the pro-life and pro-choice coalitions as well as other participants focused on the substance of the legislation. Our review of the committee hearings, therefore, will focus on these groups' specific and numerous objections to the bill.[83] In particular, we will concentrate on the ambiguities contained in the language of the bill, the likelihood of private or third party prosecutions, and the issue of access.

The Assault on C-43

Bill C-43 provides entitlement to abortion according to medical rather than eugenic, socio-economic, or personal criteria. In a strict reading of the legislation, women and doctors in Canada are not allowed to terminate a pregnancy unless a doctor determines that the health—physical, mental, or psychological—or life of the woman is likely to be threatened. Medical technology has advanced to the state where few pregnancies actually threaten the life of the woman. Thus, the interpretation of the word 'health' has considerable importance in determining the restrictiveness of the legislation. Both the pro-choice and pro-life movements were quick to suggest amendments to the committee which would make the definition either more inclusive or more exclusive.

Pro-life groups predictably argued that the definition of health in C-43 should be more restrictive by amending the legislation to include phrases like 'seriously threatened' (Salvation Army) or 'likely to lead to the loss of her life or permanent and serious disability of her person' (Focus on the Family) or 'substantial' and 'serious'. Others such as the Canadian Congress of Catholic Bishops (CCCB) and REAL Women suggested that the threat to the woman's health should be serious and 'not treatable by any other commonly accepted medical procedure' (CCCB) or 'that no other medical treatment is available' (REAL Women). This position was also advanced by Canadian Physicians for Life which brought an angry response from one of the women MPs sitting on the Committee. After a spokesman for the group indicated that abortion was not an appropriate treatment for an adolescent victim of incest, Lise Bourgault responded in the following manner, to cheers of 'bravo' from the other women MPs sitting on the committee.

> Who are you? Who are you to impose such a concept to a poor 13-year-old, and to a woman? In the case of a woman who has been violated by six men, one after the other, what do you do if she wants an abortion? Because she cannot, for many reasons, have that child! You are going too far. It does not make sense. You are physicians!

Of particular concern to the pro-life groups was the meaning of the term 'psychological' health, because they argued it opened the door to abortion on demand. The Canadian Congress of Catholic Bishops argued that the term was 'nebulous' and 'capable of abuse' while REAL Women indicated that the term was 'simply absurd' and should be dropped. Others suggested that the admission of psychological criteria would allow abortions for 'any form of distress' including stress arising from socio-economic factors. In other words, 'psychological' was an extremely elastic concept that would permit legal abortions independent of so-called 'health' criteria.

This interpretation was, in fact, not far off the mark. When Justice Minister Doug Lewis appeared before the parliamentary committee he conceded the worst fears of the pro-life movement. Asked what the term would include he responded that:

> To me, the definition of psychological health goes beyond mental. It includes our environment: just exactly how is the problem an individual is dealing with within the environment they have, sociological or physical, going to affect their health? . . . . In my opinion, 'psychological' is broad enough to utilize the word 'socio-economic'.

This position was also reinforced by the Law Reform Commission. Pro-choice groups, however, argued that if it was the government's intent was to allow abortions for environmental and socio-economic factors, it should have clearly specified this in the proposed legislation. These groups correctly pointed out that 'many women are forced to seek abortion for social and economic reasons' (Canadian Labour Congress [CLC]). All the pro-choice groups deplored the fact that the government was reintroducing abortion in the Criminal Code but they also argued that if it were determined to do so, its criteria for eligibility should reflect the realities of abortion in Canada. They, therefore, recommended that the criteria should be expanded to include socio-economic and family planning considerations or, at the very least, reflect the World Health Organization's definition of 'health' which is more expansive.[84]

Although the psychological category potentially provided a loophole in the legislation for women seeking abortion for non-health related reasons, many groups saw it as threatening equality of access. Psychological health is an extremely subjective diagnosis; the same woman might well get a very different assessment from two different doctors. Moreover, if psychological health was meant to include socio-economic factors, doctors would be 'required to weigh non-medical factors in their decision-making' (National Association of Women and the Law [NAWL]). LEAF argued persuasively that this requirement also contradicted the Morgentaler decision. The bill labelled 'women as criminals who seek abortions on the basis of their own priorities and aspirations if those priorities do not coincide with those of a doctor and the state'.

Clearly, the new legislation, framed within a medicalized discourse, placed inordinate power in the hands of the individual doctor deciding whether a woman qualified for an abortion. It also put doctors in a precarious situation because they too would be subject to criminal prosecution if they performed an abortion under conditions which did not meet the letter of the law. The government indicated time and again that doctors need not fear prosecution because they were allowed, under the new law, to make their decision according to generally accepted medical standards. The criminal penalties against those procuring abortions, the Minister of Justice insisted, were only 'aimed at persons who are not medical practitioners but [those who] carry out abortions in unsanitary and unsafe conditions, commonly referred to in the past as backstreet butchers'.

The Canadian Medical Association was not so convinced. In a stinging indictment of Bill C-43, the CMA argued before the Committee that it could not live with the new legislation. Its objections were five-fold. First, while the association commended the government for defining abortion as a medical procedure, it questioned why the bill 'singles out abortion as the only specified medical act' subject to Criminal Code sanctions. Second, the CMA argued that the bill jeopardized the physician-patient relationship. The bill would force many women seeking an abortion to discount their own priorities and aspirations and feign the criteria specified by law. Moreover, the possibility of third party interventions would break the bond of trust between a woman and her doctor. Third, the CMA took issue with the government's contention that Bill C-43 enhanced either access or entitlement to abortion in Canada. It predicted that the threat of criminal prosecution and harassment would reduce the already small pool of doctors willing to perform abortions and, at the very least, force doctors into practising 'defensive medicine'. Fourth, the CMA indicated that it was not sure 'exactly what [was] meant by psychological' and that doctors would likely insist upon some sort of psychiatric consultation before providing an abortion. This would only lead to delays for women, thereby risking their health as well as adding financial burdens to an already stressed health care system. Finally, the CMA questioned why, if the government had faith in the professional standards of the medical profession, it felt it necessary to police doctors through the Criminal Code.

From the time that the new legislation was introduced in the House, pro-choice activists and doctors alike had expressed concerns that pro-life groups would use it to charge and harass doctors providing abortions. Although the Supreme Court had ruled in the Daigle case that male partners did not have the right to veto a woman's decision to have an abortion, there was nothing in the new legislation to prevent third parties such as pro-life groups or male partners from charging that a doctor was not acting in good faith and according to the letter of the law when providing the procedure. In fact, on the unveiling of the legislation, Judy Rebick, speaking on behalf of NAC, immediately recognized this flaw in the legislation. It potentially provided 'an additional tool' in the hands of the anti-abortion coalition.[85] Considering that pro-life militants were already harassing abortion clinics, this was not an extreme assessment. Some legal experts appearing before the committee suggested that it would be difficult for pro-life groups to prove in court that doctors had made an illegal decision, especially given the ambiguity surrounding the term 'psychological'. Nevertheless, other legal experts, such as the spokeswomen for LEAF, indicated that the mere threat of prosecution and harassment would be sufficient to deter most doctors from providing the service in the future. The legislation might provide relatively easy access to abortion and, at the same time, discourage doctors from performing the procedure.

The invisible but threatening link between private prosecutions and access was repeatedly drawn to the attention of the parliamentary committee during the hearings. Groups as diverse as NAC, the YMCA, the Humanist Association of Canada, the CLC and LEAF argued that there was nothing in the legislation to prevent the initiation of prosecutions by third parties against doctors or women. Moreover, the question of whether such prosecutions were likely to succeed in the courts was irrelevant. As NAC (and others) argued 'even one prosecution will stop 90% . . . of the doctors who perform abortions from performing them, because they are not willing to take the risk of prosecution'. The overwhelming consensus of pro-choice, medical, and legal groups was that the simple threat of third party prosecutions of medical practitioners would severely restrict access to abortion in Canada, especially for women in rural areas and in some provinces.

Not wanting to lend credence to these claims, pro-life groups remained silent on the subject or denied that they would engage in the harassment or prosecution of doctors performing abortions. But the threat of doctors withdrawing their services was by no means a trivial one. Testimony before the parliamentary committee revealed that, although approximately 800 physicians in Canada occasionally provide abortions, the majority are performed by approximately 325 doctors. In some areas of the country, women's access to abortion services depended on only one or a few doctors. And, many, according to the CMA, were already contemplating withdrawing their services if the legislation passed in an unamended form. Attempting to still the doctors' fears, the Minister of Justice and the Law Reform Commission suggested that frivolous prosecutions could be prevented if the legislation were amended, as is the procedure with hate literature, to allow private prosecutions only when approved by a provincial Attorney General. Although the CMA had numerous other objections to the bill, it also recommended an amendment be inserted into the legislation stating that 'no prosecution under this section will be instituted without the consent of the Attorney General'.

The proposed amendment may have provided a margin of security for the CMA's membership, but pro-choice groups were less convinced. The decision to prosecute would simply revolve around the personal biases of provincial politicians, many of whom were on the record as pro-life activists and actively hostile to pro-choice organizations. For example, the Attorney General of British Columbia had been responsible for the surveillance of pro-choice groups in his province. Such a make-shift solution promised only to exaggerate the problem of unequal access and uncertainty. Doctors might feel relatively free to perform the procedure in some provinces but face the likelihood of harassment and prosecution in others or when governments changed. Within the present context, CARAL argued that 'requiring the agreement of the Crown to proceed with prosecution will not help in provinces like BC, Nova Scotia, PEI, and Newfoundland and Saskatchewan where governments have clearly indicated their opposition to abortion'.

The role of the provinces raises the third major complaint about Bill C-43—the provision of abortion services. Predictably, the pro-life witnesses appearing before the committee argued vehemently that the proposed legislation opened the door to abortion on demand, i.e., unrestricted access. Their objections revolved around the inclusive and ambiguous definition of health, the lack of gestational limits on abortion and the requirement that only one doctor need approve the procedure. Groups like Campaign Life saw the latter provision as an incentive for doctors to increase access to abortion services. Why would a doctor who makes his or her living providing abortion services turn away a potential customer? Moreover, the legislation did not prohibit abortion clinics or require that only doctors could perform the procedure. Pro-life groups objected to the phrase in Bill C-43 suggesting that abortions could be performed by others, 'under the direction of a medical practitioner'. For them, the legislation raised the spectre of greedy abortionists pressuring women into obtaining abortions, the proliferation of abortion clinics, and the creation of a new occupation—abortion technician.

Pro-choice groups had a much more negative assessment of the access issue. As discussed above, these and other groups argued before the committee that the definition of 'health' in the proposed legislation was too narrow and did not reflect Canadian women's real needs or motivations for seeking abortions. In addition, the threat of third party prosecution was likely to severely reduce rather than expand the pool of doctors willing to perform the procedure. The Minister of Justice, Doug Lewis, however, responded that the intent of the legislation was not to restrict access. In fact, Lewis argued that the bill corrected the procedural roadblocks which had restricted access under Section 251 of the Criminal Code. He defended the proposed legislation, indicating that it required the consent of only one doctor rather than a committee, that eliminating the hospital requirement had thereby facilitated the establishment of abortion clinics, that health had been given a definition which permitted stress as a relevant criteria, and so on. Moreover, both Lewis and the new Justice Minister, Kim Campbell, repeatedly assured their critics that the new legislative regime was preferable to no federal legislation because it set national standards for entitlement within the Criminal Code. This position was supported by the Law Reform Commission which suggested that a national framework would make it 'very difficult for the provinces to restrict access'.

The pro-choice forces took issue with the government's case that it had established a right to entitlement for all Canadian women in the legislation. For one thing, the vagueness of the term 'health' promised that doctors would not assess patients similarly (CARAL). Under the 'psychological' criteria women might be allowed an abortion motivated by socio-economic concerns by some doctors in certain areas but not in others. Moreover, legal groups such as LEAF and the National Association of Women and the Law argued strenuously that the Criminal Code was an entirely inappropriate place to specify national entitlement. Bill C-43 simply asserted the conditions under which women could legally obtain an abortion. It did nothing to ensure that the government of any province (Prince Edward Island, for example) was responsible for providing abortion services.

Pro-choice groups suggested that if the federal government was sincere about ensuring women across the country equal access to abortion facilities, it should have amended the Canada Health Act rather than the Criminal Code. Under the former act, the federal government could withhold medicare funding from provinces that failed to provide 'reasonable access to abortions and other reproductive health care services on a regional basis' (Saskatchewan Reproductive Rights Coalition [SRRC]). The Minister of Justice, however, responded that the government had no intention of using the Canada Health Act in a manner which would infringe upon the constitutional prerogatives of the provinces. 'The lack of or extent of medical facilities in any region of the country', according to Lewis, was 'the responsibility of the province in question'. The federal government had not in the past used the Canada Health Act to legislate the provision of any medical procedure and would not do so in the future.

The Minister failed to acknowledge the obvious contradiction in his logic. With Bill C-43, the federal government was specifying, under the threat of criminal sanction, the conditions under which women could obtain a medical procedure although no other medical condition was subject to similar federal legislation (CMA). Moreover, he suggested that if any province failed to provide reasonable access to abortion services then pro-choice groups would have to litigate the province in question. The federal government would not take any responsibility for the nature or the extent of the provision of abortion services in any province. Later, the new Minister of Justice, Kim Campbell, indicated that if the provinces chose to exercise their jurisdiction and restrict abortion services it would be 'out of the federal government's hands'.[86] In other words, the federal government fully intended, with the passage of the proposed legislation, to relieve itself of the issue and shift the politics of abortion to the provincial sphere of Canadian politics.

Throughout the parliamentary committee hearings group after group introduced amendments which would either relax or tighten state restrictions on women's reproductive control. But from the beginning the Minister of Justice urged the committee 'not to make amendments to the bill which affect the delicate constitutional balance' which, he argued, the bill embodied. He warned the committee that Bill C-43 had been constructed to meet both the requirements of the Morgentaler decision and the state's interest in protecting the foetus and that unnecessary tampering would make it vulnerable to judicial veto. Pressed by the Committee members, Justice Minister Lewis allowed that the legislation might be amended to the effect that there could be no private prosecutions without the consent of the provincial Attorney General. Anything more, he believed, would upset the balance purportedly achieved in the new legislation.

At the end of the hearings, representatives of all three parties proposed twenty-four amendments to Bill C-43, only one of which was pro-choice in intent. Proposed by NDP member Dawn Black, the amendment would have repealed any section of the Criminal Code which restricted women's access to abortion services. The remaining twenty-three amendments either dealt with the issue of private prosecutions or attempted to restrict access. None were adopted by the committee, signalling a significant loss for both pro-life forces and the medical profession. The former had passed the bill on its Second Reading in order to make it more restrictive but they had failed, while the latter remained vulnerable to the threat of prosecutions. Moreover, the rules of the House provide that once an amendment has been rejected at the committee stage, the same amendment cannot be reintroduced in the House on Third Reading.[87] Only the government, which had insisted on passing the legislation in an unamended form, could claim victory. The goverment's failure to protect the medical profession from legal liability, however, would make its victory a short-lived one.

The Vote is Over, Girls

The bill was now set to return to the House for final reading and passage. Again the government appealed for co-operation from all key players in the politics of abortion. The Minister of Justice, Kim Campbell, attempted to assure her pro-choice opponents that the bill was the best possible compromise that could be achieved. Identifying herself as 'a pro-choice woman of child-bearing years', she indicated that she was 'very comfortable with the bill'. To the pro-life coalition, she issued a warning. If the bill was defeated, 'this government, in this mandate, would probably not attempt to draft another'.[88] To defeat the bill, in other words, would simply maintain the status quo of decriminalization.

On 22 May 1990, Bill C-43 was reintroduced in the House of Commons for its final three days of debate. Both pro-choice and pro-life advocates remained guardedly optimistic that the bill would be defeated, if opponents from both sides of the debate voted against it. The politics of Bill C-43, therefore, encouraged an alliance between militant pro-choice and pro-life forces which a spokeswomen for CARAL admitted was an unusual coalition involving 'two very strange bedfellows'.[89] In the House, however, the passage of the bill seemed to be a foregone conclusion. The government had exerted strong pressure on its caucus to toe the party line and the debate itself was not well attended. One amendment after another was defeated in the House and, on the final night of the debate, there were insufficient government members in the House to comprise a quorum. This prompted the NDP to stage a strategic manoeuvre to kill the bill, but the government was able to pull enough MPs back into the House to defeat the NDP motion.

The debate concluded and the vote was scheduled for Tuesday, 29 May at 3 p.m. With only a few days remaining, pro-choice groups rallied in a last-ditch campaign to keep abortion out of the Criminal Code. Pro-choice activists gathered outside the Conservative Party headquarters in Toronto while demonstrations against Bill C-43 were held in fifteen other Canadian cities. Over the weekend, pro-choice groups also conducted a telephone blitz of Members of Parliament urging them not to vote for the bill on its final reading.[90] In the meantime, the National Association of Women and the Law announced that it would immediately mount a constitutional challenge to the law in the Supreme Court arguing that it violated three sections of the Charter.[91] Others such as OCAC in Ontario and the Regroupement des Centres de Santé des Femmes in Quebec warned that, if the bill passed, they would openly defy the law and encourage doctors to ignore the new legislation.

The pro-life groups remained inactive in the face of this eleventh-hour campaign, indicating with an air of resignation that they had done all that they could to influence the outcome of the vote.[92] Their confidence had been visibly shaken both because their committed proponents proved unable to change the legislation in committee and because many self-proclaimed pro-life MPs now appeared willing to support the bill. Some were prepared to vote 'yes', reasoning that this legislation was better than none. This rationale was constantly fuelled by the Justice Minister who warned that if C-43 failed its final test the House would not have the opportunity to address the issue for many years to come. Other committed prolifers appeared to be persuaded by the threat of the party whip which the government had recently used to discipline two caucus members who broke rank with the party on the proposed Goods and Services Tax. One cabinet minister and strident pro-life advocate, obviously fearful of losing his cabinet post, cast his desertion from the cause in terms of a difficult but strategic virtue. 'I have to face in my heart', he said, 'as to whether it's going to further my own pro-life commitments to have one less voice in cabinet in support of the pro-life position.'[93] His 'heart' persuaded him to support the legislation and, in the process, maintain the prestige and paycheque of a cabinet minister.

The floor of the House of Commons took on the air of a circus as MPs reluctantly filed in to determine the fate of Bill C-43. Pro-choice militants who had filled the public gallery threw women's clothing to the floor and chided the MPs in chorus: 'No new law.' 'MPs can choose. Why can't women?' 'You're supposed to represent us.' But the desperate campaign was brought to an abrupt halt. Uniformed and plainclothes security guards dragged one after another from their seats, even those who sat quietly awaiting the vote. And, in a few minutes it was over. The bill passed but with a surprisingly small majority—140 for and 131 against. Only 13 Conservatives voted against the legislation, none of them women. A House of Commons security guard approached the women remaining in the gallery saying, 'All right, girls. The vote's over. You can leave.'[94]

The Doctors Play Hardball

Bill C-43 would now move on to the Senate. Considering that the Liberal-dominated Senate had grown very adept at frustrating the Conservative government's legislative initiatives, and that the body was itself divided on the abortion issue, an easy passage through the Second Chamber seemed highly unlikely. At the very least, C-43 would not pass into law until after the summer recess. By the fall, however, the Senate was deeply embroiled with the federal government over the passage of the proposed Goods and Services Tax (GST). Weeks of procedural wrangling and filibuster over the new tax delayed the Senate hearings on the abortion bill until late October, 1990.

Even though the bill still had not become law, the impact of the passage of C-43 through the House of Commons was felt almost immediately. Across the country, doctors who had performed the procedure began to withdraw their services, forcing hospitals to turn away women seeking abortions. During the summer, four of the five doctors performing abortions at the Winnipeg Health Sciences Centre, Manitoba's biggest hospital, stopped performing the procedure; the fifth served notice that he would stop as soon as the bill became law. Throughout the country hospitals announced variations of the same story. Victoria General Hospital in Halifax, which provides 85% of abortions in Nova Scotia and the majority in the entire Atlantic region, announced that one of its eight doctors was no longer performing abortions; two others were consulting lawyers, and the rest would likely follow their lead. At the Peter Lougheed Hospital in Calgary, all seven doctors who performed abortions withdrew their services, forcing as many as thirty-five women a week to travel to the United States to obtain the procedure. In Toronto, doctors performing abortions in hospitals began to refer their clients to the Women's Health Centre in order to obtain more documentation before deciding to terminate a pregnancy. Meanwhile, provincial medical associations urged their members to exercise caution in selecting patients and, in Alberta, advised their membership to obtain a second opinion. Even Dr Morgentaler announced his intention to have women sign a statement attesting to their physical and mental health before providing the service.[95]

The critics of Bill C-43 could not have been more accurate in their prediction that the mere threat of criminal prosecution would deter many doctors from performing abortions and thereby cause needless delays as well as denying access to women in many regions of the country. The doctors readily admitted that their silent protest would cause hardships for women. Asked who loses, one prominent Manitoba obstetrician angrily assessed the emerging status quo as follows: 'I'll tell you who loses—a 16-year-old girl in Flin Flon, Manitoba loses.' Another doctor described the new legislation as 'so anti-women' and MPs as 'a group of post-menopausal men in Ottawa . . . harming the lives of desperate women'.[96] While recognizing and condemning the conditions created by Parliament, the doctors maintained that they would have to practise this kind of defensive medicine until it was 'crystal clear' what the implications of the bill were 'for patients, for doctors and for hospitals'.[97]

By the time the Senate hearings on Bill C-43 began in the late fall of 1990 the doctors' campaign against the new law was making itself felt among Canadian women as well as federal politicians. Over the summer, an estimated sixty doctors stopped performing the procedure, causing a logjam in urban centres, such as Toronto, where abortion services remained available. Metro women were forced to wait as much as a month for the procedure because women from many other Ontario cities, including Sault Ste Marie, Brampton, and Waterloo, to name a few, could no longer obtain abortions locally. Pro-choice groups voiced their growing concern that the problem of access was 'getting worse than it was in 1969'.[98] Over the summer and fall, the doctors turned up the heat. The Society of Obstetricians and Gynaecologists conducted a series of surveys of its membership indicating that only 158 doctors would continue to perform abortions in Canada if Bill C-43 became law.[99] It warned the government that the law would bring back the 'back-street' abortionist and effectively deny the procedure to Canadian women living in the Atlantic and Prairie provinces.

The doctors, who feared criminal liability under the new law, were voting with their feet. Justice Minister Kim Campbell steadfastly maintained that they misunderstood the law and that it would not affect them. However, rumblings in the pro-life camp suggested otherwise. Although pro-life groups had remained silent on the question of prosecutions before the passage of the bill, they now readily admitted that they would try to persuade women, like-minded doctors, and ordinary citizens to lay charges against doctors performing abortions. The national president of the Campaign Life Coalition admitted that 'we've told our people to become watch-dogs'. They also planned to convince women who had abortions to sue their doctors for medical malpractice. By July, pro-life militants announced that they had already begun to prepare a case against one Toronto doctor whom they refused to identify. By the fall, the Canadian Rights Coalition, modelled on the American Rights Coalition, made available to Canadian women a toll-free number in Tennessee which provided information on how to sue a doctor for malpractice.[100] In response, pro-choice groups began to mount legal defence funds for doctors who might fall victim to these tactics.[101]

The federal government had pushed C-43 through Parliament by the narrowest of majorities, but it clearly had not anticipated the extent to which the doctors would rebel. Justice Minister Campbell continued to maintain that the doctors simply did not understand the legislation, and sent them an information package in the fall designed both to explain the legislation and to quell their fears.[102] During the Senate hearings, however, she turned on the offensive. She accused the doctors of 'ignorance', of 'exploiting pregnant women by refusing their requests for abortion', and for 'using the interests of women as a tactic in a political battle'.[103] Campbell finally conceded that, if proclaimed, the law would not be implemented until the doctors' concerns were addressed. But the doctors as well as the Ontario Criminal Lawyers Association were keenly aware that 'under the provisions of the Criminal Code, [she would have] no power to do anything'.[104] The doctors, as Campbell recognized, were playing 'hardball politics' and, judging by the Senate committee's reactions to these exchanges, they were winning.[105]

The federal government had rested its case for a new abortion law framed within the Criminal Code on the contention that there had to be national standards for entitlement. Without it, the Minister of Justice suggested that the provinces would step into this legislative void, create their own regulations, and limit access. The Nova Scotia courts, however, took the wind out of this argument in October 1990. Once again, the case involved Henry Morgentaler. As discussed earlier in this chapter, Morgentaler opened a free-standing abortion clinic in Halifax in defiance of the province's Medical Services Act. The Act dictated that abortion and eight other medical procedures could only be performed in provincial hospitals, thereby making free-standing abortion clinics illegal in the province. The Court, however, ruled that the law was invalid both because it was designed to 'control and restrict abortions within the province' and, more importantly, because the legislation was 'in the pith and substance criminal law', an exclusive preserve of the federal government.[106]

The Nova Scotia decision effectively signalled to the provinces that they could not use their constitutional powers in the health field to prevent the establishment of free-standing abortion clinics. Morgentaler, vindicated once again by the courts, announced that he now planned to open clinics in all the provinces beginning with Newfoundland and Alberta.[107] But the decision did not stop certain municipal and provincial governments from setting obstacles in his way. In St John's, for example, the city council attempted to rescind the zoning permit it granted to its new Morgentaler clinic. Only two months after losing the battle, the Nova Scotia government refused to pay for abortions performed at the Halifax clinic, forcing Morgentaler back into the courts for payment.

Sober Second Thought

For any number of reasons, then, prognosis for Bill C-43 appeared bleak. Over the two months of Senate hearings, the Committee heard from 38 individuals and groups and, with the exception of two Tory cabinet ministers, the Law Reform Commission of Canada, and the Plymouth Brothers, none favoured it. A national poll conducted in December also indicated that 66% of Canadians did not favour recriminalizing abortion.[108] And nothing that the cabinet members told the Senate seemed to justify its passage. Justice Minister Kim Campbell told the Senate that, even though the bill satisfied almost no one in its present form, the government would accept no amendments resulting from the hearings.[109] Meanwhile, Health Minister Perrin Beatty admitted that the bill did nothing to ensure access.[110] The Senators seemed quite justified in asking why they should pass a law that appeared to be fatally flawed and that few Canadians felt was needed.

Apart from the issue of whether the Senate should pass C-43 was the practical question of whether it could. The Senate, like the House of Commons, was deeply divided on the abortion issue and, even though the Senate was now dominated by Conservative appointments, the vote would be a free one.[111] Clearly, the chamber of 'sober second thought' did not house sufficient numbers of prochoice advocates to defeat the bill, although some Senators did identify with the choice position. Opposition to the bill came from a variety of quarters. Some Senators were attuned to the objections of the public and the doctors while others objected to the bill because it did not give protection to the foetus. Even before the committee hearings were completed, a poll found the Senate equally divided on the bill (34 for, 35 against).[112]

The pro-life forces in the upper chamber, however, used the hearings as another opportunity to thwart the bill. Most active among these was Stanley Haidasz who appeared before the Committee with the Reverend Alphonse de Valk, the editor of a pro-life publication, and later attempted to amend the bill to restrict legal abortions only to cases where the woman's life was threatened. The pro-life forces also recruited Dr Bernard Nathanson to testify before the Senate. He told the hearings that medical technology, with sufficient funds, could within two years develop techniques whereby the foetus could be withdrawn from one womb and inserted into another woman who wanted to carry the pregnancy to term. He appealed to the Senate to recommend a total moratorium on abortions until such techniques were perfected.[113]

On the eve of the vote in the Senate, parliamentary insiders began to suspect that the federal government was ambivalent about the bill's passage. There had been very little pressure exerted on Conservative Senators to toe the party line and the Justice Minister had indicated that, even if passed, the bill might not be implemented, at least initially.[114] Thus, when the vote was called late in the afternoon of 31 January 1991, no one was betting on the outcome. And, as it turned out, no one could have. In a rather extrodinary page in the annals of Canadian parliamentary democracy, the Senate vote was tied—43-43. Such a tie vote had never happened before. The Senate first reacted with confusion, but it soon became clear that under Senate rules a tie meant defeat. Bill C-43 became the first government bill that the Senate had defeated in thirty years. And, since C-43 had few supporters, there were few tears when it met its demise. With an air of resignation, Kim Campbell told the press that, while she still saw the need for federal legislation, parliament had spoken and the government would not try again within its present mandate.

After three full years of political manoeuvring, the unusual status quo dictated by the Supreme Court's Morgentaler decision remained intact; Canada still had no abortion law. This round in the politics of abortion had been a struggle over meanings and, in the end, no single discourse prevailed. The government had relied on the tried-and-true discourse of medicalization, but this time the discourse was followed to its logical conclusion. If abortion were indeed a matter of medicine, what business did the government have in regulating it or establishing criminal sanctions for doctors exercising the tools of their trade? Others, both inside and outside of Parliament, had long since adopted alternative discourses which interpreted abortion in terms of the rights of women or the foetus. C-43 spoke to neither camp. And, like the Tower of Babel, the weight of competing languages led to its collapse.

Of course, both the pro-choice and pro-life forces have interpreted the defeat of Bill C-43 as a victory. Reminiscent of the Morgentaler decision, the pro-choice forces saw the continuing decriminalization of abortion as an affirmation of women's rights. Said one, 'we have won a right today, the right to reproductive freedom, that is as important as our right to vote'. But no rights were granted to Canadian women amidst the clash of meanings in the Senate. In fact, pro-life spokespersons seemed to have a better understanding of what had transpired. 'We have a clear slate now to bring forth good legislation that will protect the pre-born child.'[115] What will eventually be transcribed on that slate—the rights of women, the rights of the foetus or some other representation of abortion—remains the crucial arena of struggle in the on-going politics of abortion.

Chapter

4

Morgentaler and Beyond: Abortion, Reproduction, and the Courts

Shelley A.M. Gavigan

Feminism, Law, and the State

Throughout the 1970s and 1980s, the Canadian feminist pro-choice movement identified the state and especially the law as its principal adversaries, calling for decriminalization of abortion and demanding that the state 'keep its laws off women's bodies'. Parliament never acceded, and ultimately it was left to litigation in the courts, in particular criminal prosecution and a Charter challenge, to determine the status of the Canadian abortion law. The celebrated *Morgentaler*[1] victory in the Supreme Court of Canada led to a partial realignment of feminist posture *vis-à-vis* the law, however. The critique of the legal system became more selective: juries were applauded, the Supreme Court became preferred over certain provincial Courts of Appeal (notably those of Ontario and Quebec), and the call for 'No New Law' was amended to 'No New Criminal Law'. As astute students of Canadian politics, Canadian feminists and pro-choice activists alike realized that decriminalization alone did not guarantee women's access to abortion. While the Criminal Code continued to be resisted, the Canada Health Act, the bedrock of Canada's medicare system, came to be seen as having a different legal complexion. Thus, feminists in Canada developed a more refined appreciation of the distinction and relationship between coercive and other forms of law.

This chapter examines the legal legacy of the *Morgentaler* decision, and the challenges it poses for feminist analysis of and engagement with law. The Supreme Court's decision, profound as it was, did not create a right to abortion for Canadian women, nor did it offer any resolution of the abortion issue. While feminists were galvanized to resist any new law, the problem of how to *ensure* women's access to medically insured abortions loomed larger than ever before. Several provincial governments were equally moved to restrict both doctors and women, while the medical profession likewise resisted any new criminal law which might put its members at risk of either criminal prosecution or harassment.

Several of these protagonists found themselves in curious positions in their relationship to the law. While Henry Morgentaler continued to be prosecuted by the Crown in Nova Scotia, he himself applied to the Court when the New Brunswick government refused to pay his fees for abortion services rendered to New Brunswick women at his Montreal clinic. While the Right to Life movement continued to press for new foetal rights and men's rights, several of its supporters, participants in Operation Rescue (characterized by one author as 'Operation Oppress You')[2] found themselves on the other side of the law, prosecuted and convicted for their defiance of court orders to stay away from abortion clinics.[3] It is my argument that no groups found themselves in a more contradictory position *vis-à-vis* Canadian law and the Canadian state than did feminists and their allies who found themselves enjoying an unprecedented series of legal victories.

The implications of a feminist turn to law to challenge power and to create new rights claims have been carefully and critically interrogated by left and feminist scholars alike.[4] British feminist Carol Smart, noting that 'it is almost as hard to be against rights as it is to be against virtue',[5] urges feminists to be wary of the appeal of the rhetoric and legal practice of 'rights'. Smart argues that feminists have ceded too much to law at the expense of more important alternative extra-legal strategies, and they now find themselves in a difficult contradiction: 'the appeal to law on the basis of basic rights was no less than an appeal to the state to re-order power relations.'[6] Whether in the areas of sexual assault, child custody or reproductive freedoms, Smart argues that law transforms feminism's claims and issues, and imposes new and superior redefinitions; and it is 'this power to define [that] is part of the power of law . . .'.[7] She urges feminists to 'discourage a resort to law as if it holds the key to unlock women's oppression', to 'de-centre law wherever this is feasible' and thereby to resist 'the move towards more law and the creeping hegemony of the legal order'.[8]

Yet, Smart draws back from analysing the state as a site of women's subordination and feminist struggle. While she illuminates the uneven and refracted relation of law to women and argues against imprecise and simplistic conceptual frameworks such as 'power as commodity', 'law as tool', it is clear that she also regards 'the state' as analytically vacuous and anachronistic: 'a concept like the state is so imprecise and misleadingly implies a monolithic unity of interests and regimes. . . '.[9]

The cogency as well as the limits of Carol Smart's argument have begun to be illustrated in the Canadian context as feminists grapple with the weaknesses, perhaps even false promise, of the Charter of Rights and Freedoms.[10] Judy Fudge argues that by advancing women's equality claims through Charter litigation, feminists have neglected both the nature of the state's contribution to the maintenance of women's subordination and the significance of the particular form of the public/private split entrenched in the Charter. She illustrates that the inequalities and despotism of the private sphere remain beyond the scrutiny of the Charter, irrespective of whether one's concept of the private realm includes the family as well as the market. She cites, for example, the state's legislatively expressed commitment to the primacy of 'private' responsibility for spousal or child support, which is nothing less than a commitment to state-enforced patriarchal relations. In the same way some feminists do, the state wants men to be responsible for children, to be accountable, and most importantly, to pay. But, in her view, '[i]t is impossible to regard a [judicial] decision that reinforces women's economic dependency upon men by privatizing the obligation for support as a progressive victory.'[11]

This chapter illustrates that a concern with the law-state relation is still appropriate, indeed imperative. Smart reminds us that the state is often asserted to be, and less often illustrated as, a leviathan-like source of power, for men or capital or both. Rather than ignoring it because of these analytic problems, however, it is still better to insist upon an analysis of the law-state relation. This is particularly so in the Canadian context because the abortion issue cannot be understood as separate from the state, its form, its division of powers,[12] its social policies and coercive practices, and the law, both legislative and adjudicative.

To detach the law from the state is effectively to participate in efforts to depoliticize the former. Indeed, as this book argues, the medicalization of abortion, the use of criminal prosecution and the courts, the 'free vote' in Parliament, have all been aspects of the state's strategy to depoliticize both abortion struggles and abortion law. Feminists must both recognize this strategy and work with conceptual tools that allow it to be exposed and thereby analyzed. The specificity of both state and law need to be acknowledged. Thus, without collapsing law into the state, or the state into law, it is necessary to examine each in relation to the other.

Even ostensibly private disputes, such as those involving the women and men in the abortion injunction cases,[13] illustrate the importance of the posture and action of the state *vis-à-vis* abortion. Such cases demonstrate how recriminalization explicitly defines the interest of the Canadian state in abortion and, implicitly, defines an interest of men who, regarding themselves sufficiently affected, attempt to intervene to ensure compliance with the law.[14] Beyond the issue of criminalization are state decisions about whether or not to provide medicare funds for 'non-therapeutic' abortions,[15] to permit the establishment of free-standing abortion clinics,[16] and otherwise to create conditions of meaningful access.[17] The resolution of the abortion issue is more likely to be determined by political struggle than by legal right. In this the role played by the state is of central importance.

An analysis of this role and the nature of the law-state relation is aided by the concept of ideology, which illuminates the contradictory nature of law. Understanding the significance of law as a site of ideological struggle permits a reconcilation of the contradictory experiences and assessments of pro-life and pro-choice legal challenges. Therefore, this chapter proceeds from the proposition that law within Western capitalism is principally, but not exclusively, an ideological form.[18] It sets normative standards and informs, shapes, and constrains the content of collective and conventional thinking about social structure and the possibilities and necessity for change, and it is simultaneously informed by these conventional ideas and beliefs about social relations.[19] Not simply nor even accurately characterized as a 'reflection' of society, or its 'hammer', the law (including its agents—lawyers, legislators, and judges) is both a product of and reproducer of the existing social order.[20]

Conceptualizing law and ideology assists us in analysing the current abortion debates, as well as demonstrating the extent to which the law is a site of struggle. The sections which follow describe the ways in which the pro-life movement has made claims with increasing authority that 'abortion is murder' when this is not, and has never been, the definition provided in Canadian criminal law. They also describe how the startlingly novel claim that the foetus is a person has gained popular currency, notwithstanding the consistent position in law that a live birth is a prerequisite for personhood. Ideologies become dominant not necessarily through law, and indeed occasionally in opposition to law, but emergent as well as dominant ideologies may nonetheless be imported or incorporated into law. Interestingly, the strongest weapon in the anti-choice rights arsenal in Canada has not yet proven to be a legal one.

After reviewing the *Morgentaler* decision in detail, we will examine related litigation, including the pro-choice and pro-life cases, the fathers' rights cases, and cases involving the provincial clawbacks of *Morgentaler* and medicare. Notwithstanding the many legal defeats experienced by anti-choice advocates, and the recent spate of legal victories achieved by pro-choice advocates, the *extra-legal* cultural struggle that is currently being waged may prove to be the decisive one.[21] To argue that both the law and the state are sites of struggle ought not to lead to the position that they are inevitable, necessary, or exclusive sites; the legal victories are never conclusive. In other words, while the law cannot be ignored, it should not mesmerize those endeavouring to achieve social change.

From Victory to Defeat to Victory: Morgentaler in the Courts

Although there was unevenness in levels of feminist activity in the years following the 1969 amendments to the Criminal Code, Canadian feminist and pro-choice activists consistently identified the inequality created by the abortion law and called for decriminalization.[22] They voted with their feet in the streets, in hundreds of demonstrations and several blustery March 8 International Women's Day marches. The cold feet really belonged, however, to male elected representatives in Parliament. For all their lobbying efforts, political activity, careful analyses and documented inequality, Canadian women met the stony intransigence of a federal government ostensibly committed to equality in its legislation, yet lacking the political will to move on this important issue.

In the early 1980s, the women's movement paid increasing attention to the abortion issue. Feminists were frustrated by their failed efforts to have abortion decriminalized, and were foiled in their attempts to work within the existing law.[23] Activists in English Canada looked to the successful free-standing clinic experience in Quebec and decided to extend the Quebec experiment to other communities, specifically Winnipeg and Toronto. In Toronto, the Committee for the Establishment of Abortion Clinics was formed by feminist and pro-choice activists. The Committee sought and received the support of Henry Morgentaler and two other doctors, and the Morgentaler Clinic on Harbord Street in Toronto was opened. A public campaign was launched, and the challenge to the federal law was explicit and direct.

As in the 1970s in Quebec, a raid on a Morgentaler clinic resulted in criminal charges. And, once again, following a prolonged but unsuccessful pretrial motion to quash the indictments against them,[24] Dr Morgentaler and his two colleagues, Drs Leslie Smoling and Robert Scott, were acquitted by yet another jury. Once again, at the hands of a Court of Appeal, the verdict was set aside; a new trial was ordered.[25] The Ontario Court of Appeal was not moved by defence arguments that the *Charter of Rights* had altered in a significant way the fabric of the law. In fact, the Court of Appeal comforted itself with the knowledge that abortion had long been a criminal offence and offered this analysis of the right to life, liberty, and security of the person under section 7 of the *Charter*:

> Some rights have their basis in common law or statute law. Some are so deeply rooted in our traditions and way of life as to be fundamental and could be classified as part of life, liberty and security of the person. The right to choose one's partner in marriage, and the decision whether or not to have children, would fall in this category . . .
>
> We agree with Parker A.C.J.H.C. in the court below that, bearing in mind the statutory prohibition against abortion in Canada which has existed for 100 years, it could not be said that there is a right to procure an abortion so deeply rooted in our traditions and way of life as to be fundamental.[26]

The Ontario Court of Appeal also held that Dr Morgentaler's understanding of the law relating to the defence of necessity was 'misconceived'. The Court, clearly offended by the doctors' scrupulous advance preparation to rely upon this defence, held:

> Taking the most favourable view of the evidence for the defence, the respondents were dissatisfied with the present law relating to abortions in Canada.[27]

It was left to Morgentaler to proceed with an appeal to the Supreme Court of Canada and to argue in that court that the abortion provisions of the Criminal Code violated the Canadian Charter of Rights and Freedoms, in particular section 7, which provides:

> Everyone has the right to life, liberty and security of the person and the right not to be deprived thereof except in accordance with the principles of fundamental justice.

Although the named appellants before the Supreme Court were Drs Morgentaler, Smoling and Scott, the case was argued in the name of women whose access to abortion, including therapeutic abortion, was inhibited by the operation of the provisions of section 251. Clearly, the voluminous evidence led at trial by the doctors convinced the majority of the Court that the procedure enunciated in section 251 was, in the words of the Chief Justice, 'manifestly unfair'.[28] While Justice McIntyre in dissent insisted that any problems identified with the abortion law were caused by 'external' forces, specifically 'a general demand for abortion irrespective of the provisions of section 251',[29] Dickson held that 'many of the most serious problems with . . . section 251 are created by the procedural and administrative requirements established in the law'.[30] Although the heart of Dickson's judgment centred upon the 'manifest unfairness' of the procedures, the lack of any definition of health, and the inherent delays in the 1969 amendments, his judgement had some unequivocal resonances for women:

> Forcing a woman, by threat of criminal sanction, to carry a foetus to term unless she meets certain criteria unrelated to her own priorities and aspirations, is a profound interference with a woman's body and thus a violation of her security of the person.[31]

Despite this apparently strong criticism of compulsory pregnancy, it is important to remember that Dickson would have upheld the legislation had its procedures complied with the principles of fundamental justice; the fact of criminalization *per se* was not rejected. Beyond this, Dickson, as all members of the Court, contemplated that state protection of 'foetal interests' 'might well be deserving of court protection'[32] under section 1 of the Charter which: '. . . guarantees the rights and freedoms set out in it subject only to such reasonable limits prescribed by law as can be demonstrably justified in a free and democratic society'.

In other words, provided that restrictive abortion legislation contained a standard or procedure that was fair and not arbitrary, Dickson might well uphold it in the name of state protection of the foetus.

Madam Justice Wilson's judgement focused less on procedural unfairness which might be remedied. Unlike her brothers on the bench, Wilson rested her decision on the right to liberty within section 7, and insisted that the right to individual liberty is 'inextricably tied to the concept of human dignity',[33] which for Wilson included the right to make fundamental personal decisions within a sphere of personal autonomy:

> The right to reproduce or not to reproduce which is in issue in this case is one such right and is properly perceived as an integral part of modern woman's struggle to assert *her* dignity and worth as a human being (emphasis in original).[34]

Wilson also held that a woman's security of the person was violated by section 251. In particular, the requirement of a therapeutic abortion committee meant that:

> She is the passive recipient of a decision made by others as to whether her body is to be used to nurture a new life. Can there be anything that comports less with human dignity and self-respect?[35]

Wilson's 'sphere of personal autonomy' did not involve an atomized libertarianism. She situated her individual 'woman' within her context[36] while insisting that within this social or collective context, the individual (pregnant woman) had to be able to make decisions which might well defy the imaginative capacities of (non-pregnant) men. Nonetheless, Wilson too contemplated that, as in *Roe v Wade*, a woman's right of access to abortion was not to be absolute:

> At some point the legitimate state interests in the protection of health, proper medical standards, and pre-natal life would justify its qualification.[37]

For Wilson, section 1 of the Charter would authorize 'reasonable limits to be put upon the woman's right':[38]

> In the early stages the woman's autonomy would be absolute;

> her decision, reached in consultation with her physician not to carry the foetus to term would be conclusive. The state would have no business inquiring into her reasons. The precise point in the development of the foetus at which the state's interest in its protection becomes 'compelling' I leave to the informed judgement of the legislature which is in a position to receive guidance on the subject from all the relevant disciplines. It seems to me, however, that it might fall somewhere in the second trimester.[39]

As for the rest of the bench, both Beetz J. (writing with the majority) and McIntyre J.(in dissent) held that protection of the foetus was the primary purpose of the abortion legislation; Beetz found the procedural problems in section 251 fatal. McIntyre, the only judge to use the language of the pro-life movement, would have upheld the legislation designed to protect the interests of the unborn child:

> There has always been a clear recognition of a public interest in the protection of the unborn and there has been no indication of any general acceptance of the concept of abortion at will in our society.[40]

In the end, section 251 was struck down.

Although few people anticipated complete success with the Charter challenge, it is clear in retrospect that it was an all-or-nothing proposition. In an oddly dialectical way, the seed for this successful assault on the abortion section had been sown in Justice Dickson's own analysis of it as 'a comprehensive code . . ., unitary and complete within itself' in his 1976 judgement which upheld Dr Morgentaler's conviction in the first round.[41]

The result was, of course, an historic decision in which the Supreme Court of Canada struck down in its entirety section 251. It marked the culmination of two decades of hard-fought feminist struggle in which the legal victories had been few and the political victories even fewer.[42] However, it quickly became clear that this, like many victories, particularly legal victories, was fragile, incomplete and contradictory. The victory was fragile because the federal government, though bruised, attempted for two years to recriminalize abortion. Threats, and in some cases action, by provincial governments responsible for hospitals, to refuse or limit funding for abortions in the absence of a therapeutic exception in the Criminal Code further attested to the fragility.[43] It was an incomplete victory because the unequivocal commitment of all the Supreme Court judges to 'foetal interests' or the 'state's interest in the foetus' invited Parliament to limit women's access to abortion (and indeed other medical procedures) in the later stages of pregnancy and opened the door to other legislative proposals, which purported to carve out a 'specific' foetal interest, if not full legal personality.[44]

Finally, the victory was also contradictory in that the Court reinforced the notion that abortion is a medical matter. Contradictions abound in this maintenance of a medicalized conception of abortion. On the one hand, Canadian feminists and pro-choice activists have articulated a long-standing critique of the implications of denoting of abortion as a medical or therapeutic matter.[45] Yet, on the other hand, in very important and paradoxical ways the continued denotation of abortion as a *health* matter has been significant in the Canadian context. Health care in Canada has come to be regarded as a social right, enshrined in a comprehensive and fully funded health care system based upon principles of accessibility and universality.[46] In the years following the Supreme Court's decision, the issue of women's right of access to health care has fuelled the pro-choice movement. Indeed, the fragility of women's access to abortion has helped to illustrate the more general fragility of medicare in Canada.

By focusing on these contradictions we can better understand the situation Canadian women face. Obviously, the language of the Morgentaler judgements of the majority was a ringing restatement of an *individual* right to life, liberty, and security of the person and is thus consistent with the emphasis on abortion as a private and individual matter.[47] While this reflects the language of lawyers and judges, it has *not* been the characterization of Canadian pro-choice and feminist activists, who have consistently framed abortion as an issue of equality and access.[48] Access to abortion by Canadian women should not be as vulnerable to the kind of legislative and judicial erosion as in the United States, where the US Supreme Court began to undermine *Roe v Wade*[49] in a series of decisions which upheld federal provisions restricting the expenditure of

Medicaid funds for all but medically necessary abortions, thereby and thereafter depriving poor American women access to medically insured abortions.[50] In 1989, the US Supreme Court upheld Missouri legislation which prohibited publicly funded health-care centres and public employees from providing abortion services.[51] The Canadian political and social context is different in an important respect by virtue of the comprehensive public health-care system. And so in Canada we are in the rather paradoxical position of now having to insist that abortion is a health-care matter, in order to ensure equal access and availability of publicly funded abortions.

Right to Life versus the Law

The 1969 abortion law was also assailed by the right to life movement who insisted that even the limited therapeutic provisions of the Criminal Code went too far. The thrust of their campaign, legal and otherwise, has been to limit women's access to legal abortion, to advocate striking down the therapeutic abortion provisions, to construct and advance new rights for men (*qua* husbands and fathers) and for the foetus, and to threaten and harass everyone involved in the delivery of abortion services. These challenges to Canadian abortion law are as important as the pro-choice challenges have been.

One important early extra-legal tactic of the right to life movement was to exert constant, concerted pressure on hospitals to dismantle their Therapeutic Abortion Committees. Paradoxically, a hospital's decision to dismantle its committee (often after a struggle for control of the composition of the hospital board) sometimes became a source of tension between hospital boards and doctors. Doctors were able to force the reinstatement of abortion committees by refusing to sit on other hospital committees. The outcome in at least one such case, however, was the appointment by a hospital board of a new committee with 'conservative' views on abortion.[52] Moreover, during a doctors' strike in Ontario in the fall of 1986 (provoked by the prohibition of extra-billing in the medicare system) one of the first services affected was the Therapeutic Abortion Committee.[53] This experience again demonstrated the political nature of the therapeutic abortion process and the tenuous status of women's access to legal abortion.

The most tenacious legal challenge undertaken by the anti-choice movement was to be found in the *Borowski* case. In 1981, the Supreme Court of Canada granted standing to long-time pro-life activist Joseph Borowski to bring an action challenging the validity of the therapeutic abortion amendments to the Criminal Code. Speaking for the majority of the Supreme Court, Martland J. held that Borowski did not have to establish that he was directly affected by the abortion legislation in order to bring his legal challenge because he met a second test: 'he has a genuine interest as a citizen in the validity of the legislation and . . . there is no other reasonable manner in which the issue may be brought before the court.'[54] With the entrenchment of the *Charter of Rights*, Borowski amended his action to argue that the therapeutic abortion amendments were unconstitutional under sections 7 and 15, violating a foetus' right to life and equality.

He was unsuccessful at trial.[55] Moreover, in the spring of 1987, the Saskatchewan Court of Appeal dismissed his appeal, holding that a foetus is not an 'everyone' entitled to the protection of section 7 or section 15 of the Charter.[56] Because the *Morgentaler* appeal was heard by the Supreme Court before the *Borowski* appeal, the decision in the former sealed the fate of the latter. Once the legislation he undertook to challenge had been struck down by the Supreme Court in *Morgentaler*, Mr Borowski's own appeal to the Supreme Court was dismissed as moot.[57]

The legal argument advanced by Borowski and others for foetal personhood goes thus: Protective mechanisms available to the unborn which crystallize at birth are already recognized by law. There is no logical reason why legal personality and the rights which flow therefrom should not be concomitant in time.[58] The medical and health needs of a foetus are analogous to and continuous of those of a child; thus, the child and the foetus should be considered juridical persons in the same sense and for the same reasons.[59] While any 'right to property' thus far afforded to the foetus is and has been a contingent right[60]—contingent on live birth—this requirement is regarded as anachronistic.[61] Indeed, Joe Borowski's counsel insisted he was arguing the new 'Persons Case'—a reference to the *Persons* case of 1930 which extended women's political rights.[62]

Foetal Personhood: The Ideology of Foetal Rights

Feminists across a range of disciplines[63] have noted the many and contradictory ways that the new visibility of the foetus has rendered pregnant women invisible, likened them to 'ambulatory chalices'[64] or flower pots[65] and, less benignly, seen them as the principal adversaries of the foetus. Advocates of legal recognition of foetal personhood such as the American legal academic John Robertson[66] and Canadian law reform consultant Edward Keyserlingk[67] have turned their minds to a whole panoply of forms and degrees of maternal misconduct. In his assertion that 'mothers are arguably those with the most serious and extensive duties and obligations toward the unborn, and therefore the likeliest class of defendant',[68] Keyserlingk clearly regards pregnant women as the likeliest adversaries and perpetrators of 'foetal neglect'.

The current characterization of hostility and antagonism between pregnant women and foetuses is one which has been carefully constructed. In right-to-life legal arguments and factums, in literature (legal and otherwise) and films, the pregnant woman is increasingly put in the position of adversary to her own pregnancy either by presenting a 'hostile environment' for foetal development or by actively refusing medically proposed intervention.[69] Clearly, upon closer analysis, the conflict is not one between maternal and foetal rights,[70] but rather between women and self-appointed curators of the foetus or guardians of 'foetal interests'.

The ubiquitous presence of the foetus in the abortion debate is of rather recent provenance, the earlier medical and legal literature and case law having focused on the sexual immorality which gave rise to abortion rather than the value of embryonic life.[71] Now it seems, the foetus itself has become the apparent target of the engagement, our culture having 'discovered' what women have long known: babies do not come from hospitals; they are 'with us' throughout 'their' pregnancy. Moreover, prior to its birth the foetus is already the new kid on the block. Foetal personhood advocates emphasize the 'biological' unity of the 'pre-born' and 'born'[72] and de-emphasize the biological unity of woman and foetus.

Feminists both acknowledge the fundamental unity of woman and foetus and insist that the relationship is not 'symmetrical'.[73] Indeed, feminist insistence upon pregnancy as a 'relationship'[74] between a pregnant woman and a foetus is as significant as the insight that this relationship is neither symmetrical nor inherently antagonistic. Feminists are thus currently engaged in a concerted struggle to resist the emerging if not yet prevailing image of pregnant women as menacing vessels, an image offensive to the integrity and moral agency of pregnant women. But feminists have also had to contend with the new invisibility of pregnant women in this campaign; witness Edward Keyserlingk:

> *In most respects but one*, the transfer from the protections of the womb to the protection of the crib and nursery, there is unbroken continuity between the unborn and the child. (emphasis added)[75]

Has the law similarly been rendered invisible, an empty vessel or an enemy alien, by the various contestants? Certainly, advocates for the recognition of legal personhood for the foetus have reason to feel that they have received a chilly reception in Canadian courts. In the *Sullivan and LeMay* case,[76] involving two lay midwives who had been charged with criminal negligence in the death of the foetus during delivery, the Court restated the axiomatic position that prior to live birth, the foetus is not a human being for the purpose of the Criminal Code. In the 'father's rights' cases of *Daigle v Tremblay*[77] and *Murphy v Dodd*[78] both 'potential fathers' and foetuses ultimately had to yield to the rights of the women.

While acknowledging the Canadian legal victories which have given rise to pro-life chagrin, feminist advocates and scholars need to be attentive to the various ways in which the foetal personhood campaign has been waged extra-legally, that is, culturally and politically. Here the ideological dimensions of the matter are particularly striking. Despite the claim that the foetus is the named object of their attention, it is clear that the real objects of the foetal personhood campaign are *women*.[79] Foetal personhood has implications for all women; all pregnant women experience some form of surveillance, but it is the poor who are most vulnerable to the 'pregnancy police'.[80]

The new foetal imagery is not one-dimensional, however. Indeed, two powerful if contradictory images of the foetus have emerged as part of what Rosalind Petchesky has characterized as a strategy to make foetal personhood a self-fulfilling prophecy by making the foetus a public presence in a visually oriented culture:[81] the tiny, helpless, and innocent unborn child and the active, virtually autonomous foetus trapped in its mother's womb, begrudgingly serving a nine-month sentence of confinement. Petchesky argues that our collective understanding of the foetus has been in large measure constructed by the visual images presented and insisted upon by pro-life advocates.

The potential cultural and political successes of the foetal rights movement, then, lie in its ability to both capture the imagination and tap the anxiety of people who are receptive to the notion that pregnant women are capable of extreme acts of selfishness and irresponsibility. The foetus is presented as helpless and vulnerable, the most innocent of innocent victims. Again, what is striking is that this campaign has been so successful *without* significant support in Canadian law for its fundamental underlying premise: that the foetus is a person with legal rights.

A window on this issue presents itself in part in the child welfare cases in Canada and the forced obstetrical treatment cases[82] in the United States. A small but significant body of case law to date reveals[83] some judicial sympathy for the proposition that for the purposes of child-welfare legislation, a child is deemed to include the unborn.[84] In both Canada and the United States it is clear that the women who are feeling the coercive edge of foetal attraction are poor women, women on welfare who have a 'history' with either welfare or child welfare authorities or both. Poor women, homeless women, and mentally ill women have supplanted the 'lewd' women who vexed previous generations of lawmakers and law enforcers. And the net will widen if Edward Keyserlingk's view—that those who pose the greatest threat to foetuses are their pregnant mothers—prevails.

Thus, although abortion is never far from its agenda, it is fair to observe that the foetal rights movement tackles more than abortion. In the United States, in the aftermath of the significant yet modest pro-choice victory in *Roe v Wade*, the strategy has been to work within and against the letter of *Roe*. While for some, the insistence that life begins at conception obviously means that there can be no compromise with *Roe*, for others the short-term concession of the first trimester to pregnant women has enabled them to declare 'open season' on the second and the third. The argument is that once a pregnant woman has foregone her option for an early, legal abortion, her rights as a citizen diminish increasingly in favour of her obligations (and, they argue, her legally enforceable duty) to her foetus. In John Robertson's words, although a woman is under 'no obligation to invite the fetus in or to allow it to remain, once she has done these things, she assumes obligations to the fetus that limit her freedom over her body'.[85] Secondly, they are supremely confident that medical science will soon render the foetus viable at increasingly earlier points in pregnancy and, that as a result, the parameters for women to exercise their right to early abortion will be increasingly narrowed.[86] Thus, in the US, right to life advocates have worked both within and against the letter of the *Roe* judgement. As Janet Gallagher has argued:

> This attempt to use Roe as a legal weapon against pregnant women—to claim it as justification for detention, criminal charges of 'abuse', drastic restraints on liberty, and even unconsented-to surgical invasion—stands the decision on its head, and not merely in terms of the right to abortion. Roe v Wade may have its flaws, but granting open season on pregnant women after viability is not one of them.[87]

Paternal Legal Claims: The Abortion Injunction Cases

In this section, I revisit some ground recently well travelled by activists, courts and academics:[88] the fathers' rights claims in the area of abortion. Reviewing the various judicial victories achieved by women against the seeming odds of law and patriarchy illustrates that the right of women to abortion unencumbered by the interference of men is one which principally and paradoxically has been acknowledged by the law alone. In other words, a woman's right to autonomy and self-determination in her fertility control is still a contentious claim within a society committed to the idealized (patriarchal) nuclear family.

Given the great importance placed on the issue of fathers' rights by groups opposing the liberalization of abortion law, it is not surprising that the issue of husbands' and fathers' rights in the matter of abortion has been raised in Canada. Indeed, after Marc Lepine murdered fourteen women at the Ecole Polytechnique in Montreal in December 1989 and injured a dozen more in his antifeminist rampage, a spokeswoman for REAL Women of Canada opined that he 'just might have been a man whose child had been aborted by a feminist'.[89]

There is of course some irony in the concern that anti-choice groups express on behalf of men who have 'lost their rights' in the context of legal abortion. Although there has never been an express requirement for a husband's consent in abortion law or medical procedure, they have not ever really been left out in the cold.[90] Notwithstanding the absence of any legislative requirement for either spousal or parental consent in the old abortion provisions, the Badgley Report found that in practice Therapeutic Abortion Committees across Canada operated with diverse consent requirements relating both to the age of the woman and to the father. More than two-thirds (68%) of the hospitals surveyed by the Committee required the consent of the husband. A few hospitals required the consent of a husband from whom the woman was separated or divorced and the consent of the father where the woman had never been married.[91]

Despite these practices, under the previous therapeutic provisions of the Criminal Code, Canadian courts had held that a husband had neither a right to be consulted nor a right of veto in the matter of his wife's application for a therapeutic abortion.[92] They have been, however, more loath than courts in other jurisdictions[93] to rule these men completely out of court. In two early reported cases, Canadian courts adopted the reasoning of an English court in *Paton v Trustees of B.P.A.S.*,[94] in which a husband applied unsuccessfully for an injunction to prevent his wife from proceeding with an abortion approved in accordance with the English abortion legislation. In 1981, the British Columbia Supreme Court dealt with an application by a husband for an injunction to restrain his wife and the Campbell River and District Hospital from proceeding with her therapeutic abortion.[95] The BC court held that the facts were virtually identical to those in the *Paton* case and similarly held that the therapeutic abortion provisions of the Criminal Code could not accommodate a husband's 'veto'.

Three years later, an Ontario Court was faced with a similar, highly publicized application.[96] Alexander Medhurst commenced the action on his behalf and that of his unborn child for an injunction to restrain his wife, her doctor, and the hospital from proceeding with an abortion. Although he was initially successful, the court ultimately held that as an unborn child is not a person, there was no legal entity for whom the husband could be appointed guardian. Although both husbands were unsuccessful in their legal challenges, a close reading of these two early cases reveals judicial angst about abortion, along with considerable sympathy for the position of the applicant husbands.

The insistence by the women's movement that men take children and child care seriously has contributed to the now prevalent assumption that men as fathers actually do much more than they once did. As Carol Smart has illustrated in her work, the *image* of new fathers, especially with babies (as opposed to children) now informs popular culture.[97] Thus it seems inevitable that we should have witnessed an apparent surge in men's interest in 'their pregnancies' and 'their' unborn children and, for some, their struggles for custody before birth. Another twist to the law's relation to and regulation of women resurfaced in the aftermath of the Supreme Court's decision in *Morgentaler*. Men (supported by the pro-life movement) once again began to litigate to prevent women from terminating pregnancy. To the women's movement's clarion call that 'This uterus is not government property', these 'post-Morgentaler' men responded: 'No, it's mine.' To them, abortion was not a women's issue; it was their issue about their 'issue'.

The apparent legal vacuum created by the Supreme Court's decision in 1988 spurred some men to litigious direct action. Consistent with the pre-Morgentaler cases,[98] in all but one of these cases the men were successful initially. Judges who were confronted with the application, usually ex parte, were persuaded to issue the interim order.[99] The respondent woman had to apply to a different judge of the same court to set aside the initial ex parte restraining order.[100] When she lost again, as Chantal Daigle did in the Quebec Court of Appeal, she had then to appeal to the Supreme Court of Canada.[101]

Only Justice Hirschfield of the Manitoba Court of Queen's Bench of his own initiative (as the woman was not represented by counsel before him) was unequivocal in recognizing the woman's right to choose, although the importance of his caveat should not be lost:

> It is apparent to me that when the Respondent decided she was going to terminate the pregnancy she was exercising a freedom of choice which she has the right to exercise. And,

> that she was exercising the control over her body which she has the right to exercise. . . . [the] overwhelming consideration from my point of view is the fact that a human being, that is the Respondent has an absolute right, subject to criminal sanctions, to the control of her body. There is no criminal sanction against her exercising that right, in my opinion, *as the law stands today, and until changed, she is entitled to do so*. (emphasis added)[102]

In the end, in the post-Morgentaler cases, none of the injunctions stood. The women won in court; the men lost.

To refuse to characterize these legal victories in the abortion struggle as defeats does not absolve one from the requisite analysis of the nature of the victories and their manifest fragility and weakness. Nor is it to deny the fact that they often do not feel like victories, even where the ex parte restraining orders are lifted, enabling the woman to proceed unencumbered by legal sanction. It is also important to acknowledge the lack of legal determinacy in these cases; for instance, in a number of the injunction cases in both Canada and the United States, the woman proceeded to have an abortion, notwithstanding the fact that the case was still before the court.[103] In one case where a British woman survived the judicial ordeal with her legal rights intact, she elected not to have the abortion and gave the baby to the man, who in turn gave the child to his mother to raise.[104] And of course, in Canada in the summer of 1989, the spectacular conversion by Barbara Dodd to the Right to Life Movement made news for weeks. Ms Dodd's attempt to obtain an abortion was initially thwarted by her boyfriend, who may or may not have been the 'father', and his lawyer, Angela Costigan. The pro-choice movement championed Dodd's cause, and she was eventually able to proceed with the abortion. Almost immediately following her successful struggle to resist her boyfriend and proceed with her abortion, she recanted, and made the cover of *Maclean's*.[105] Legal victories clearly are not to be taken for real victories.

One reason these legal victories often *feel* like defeats is the clear empathy expressed in many of the cases for the men, especially the husbands, especially by the male judiciary.[106] In the early Ontario case, *Medhurst*, Mr Justice Reid was clearly moved by the husband's plight:

> The husband has a direct interest in the issue of the compliance with the [criminal] law which, in my view, entitles him to bring this application on his own behalf, and his lack of any right to withhold his consent or to be consulted does not deprive him of the right to resort to this court to assert or protect that interest. *I cannot think of anyone more entitled to the court's protection of that interest than a husband. . . . [I]t is difficult to think of anyone who could have an interest equal to that of a husband in the pregnancy of his wife.*[107] (emphasis added)

Reid J.'s holding permitted the husband to apply immediately to review the Therapeutic Abortion Committee's decision in the matter of his wife's application for a therapeutic abortion, and although he 'lost' in that round as well,[108] he had been empowered by the judicial assertion of a husband's inherent interest and virtual 'natural right' in respect of his wife's pregnancy. This was so notwithstanding the fact of their marital separation, and the husband's clear attempt to force his wife back into the marriage. The legal form of the substantive law as it then was inhibited the husband's power. But the generosity of Canadian courts toward the granting of standing to men in the matter of abortion,[109] including in the injunction cases under the Criminal Code, makes it clear that any recriminalization of abortion will invite and facilitate procedural harassment of women seeking abortions and doctors prepared to perform them.

Not only have men *qua* men been somewhat inhibited by law; so too have some American judges who find they 'must, with reluctance' accept that '[t]he [US] Supreme Court has made it crystal clear that a pregnant woman, without the permission or consent or advice from anyone else' has a right to an abortion in the first trimester, while noting that '[m]any individuals who specialize in religion or ethical concerns are appalled by the Supreme Court decisions'.[110] In the course of his reported judgement in *Medhurst*, Reid J. also insisted:

> It is not possible to approach this matter without personal convictions—I am personally appalled at the prospect of abortion—or to be left unmoved by the emotion and anxiety that suffuse this issue.[111]

In light of his views 'at the prospect of abortion', one imagines that Mrs Medhurst was relieved that the criminal law inhibited not only her husband but also the Bench. One doubts that it was *her* 'emotion and anxiety' that moved the judge in his remarks.

Not every man who lost in court received condolences from the bench. The fact of allegations of violence contributing to the separation (Mr Paton) and/or abortion (Mr Tremblay) was noted (without comment) by the tribunals/bench. The men who were trying to hold marriages together (Medhurst, Anderson, Whalley) were regarded as sincere men in tragic circumstances. Significantly, the failure to conform to the ideal of the sincere family man was fatal to at least one American man's claim.[112] John Doe commenced an action in Indiana to prevent Jane Smith from proceeding to terminate her 10-12 week pregnancy. He managed to get himself before a justice of the US Supreme Court within two weeks. Jane Smith had become pregnant toward the end of their two-month relationship during which time he had been separated from his wife of six months, by whom he also had a child. He had since reconciled with his wife. Significantly also for Justice Stevens, John Doe had been 'sporadically employed at low paying jobs for the last eighteen months'.[113]

Following an earlier decision of the US Supreme Court in *Planned Parenthood v Danforth*,[114] Stevens J. noted that in order to 'require a mother to carry a child to term against her wishes, the father must demonstrate clear and compelling reasons justifying such actions.'[115] Here, *inter alia*, the plaintiff 'has showed substantial instability in his mental and romantic life. Based upon the plaintiff's romantic patterns over the last eight months, it would be impossible for the Court to predict the stability of his family unit at the time of birth.'[116] Therefore, John Doe's claim was held to provide a 'particularly weak basis for invoking the extraordinary judicial relief sought'.[117] Had John Doe been a stable family man with a good and steady income, Justice Stevens, it seems, might have been persuaded to rule differently.

The risk of relying on the characterization of the 'facts' of men presumably 'suffused by emotion and anxiety' (and indeed their equally suffused lawyers) in their quests to prevent their estranged wives or girlfriends from obtaining legal abortions has been illustrated in the 1989 Ontario case *Murphy v Dodd*.[118] Angela Costigan, counsel for the applicant boyfriend, had served the court documents herself upon Barbara Dodd on Friday afternoon before the July long weekend; the return date was the Tuesday morning immediately following the holiday Monday. On Tuesday, the presiding Judge noted in the endorsement of his order:

> The time is 10:40 a.m.; counsel for the Applicant advises me that she has had indirect communication with the Respondent Dodd; neither Respondent appears nor does Dodd intend to appear by counsel. No one is here to represent the hospital.[119]

In his affidavit in support of the application, Gregory Murphy deposed that he was the father of the Respondent's unborn child, that her doctor had said that an abortion would endanger her health, and that he was from an 'intellectually superior' family.[120] In the subsequent application by Ms Dodd to set aside the initial order, Gregory Murphy's conduct (and by implication his counsel) was characterized by her counsel as amounting to a fraud upon the court. In her affidavit, Ms Dodd deposed that another man might well have been responsible for the pregnancy (this was corroborated in an affidavit by the other man), and that this had been 'the only issue connected with her pregnancy that [she and Murphy] fought about'.[121] In their affidavits, both she and her doctor denied that he had said that the abortion would endanger her health. And finally, Ms Dodd, supported by expert evidence on her own intellectual ability and comprehension of the spoken word (she had a 90% hearing loss), was able to demonstrate that Murphy's lawyer (in her *direct* communication during service of the documents) had not explained the nature of the documents served. As a result, the ex parte order restraining Barbara Dodd from proceeding with the abortion was set aside, having been obtained by a fraud upon the court, fraud held to be related to material issues.[122]

In the abortion injunction cases, many of the judges have accepted the men's self-descriptions as 'fathers' of the 'unborn' (infant plaintiff, child). In its judgement in *Tremblay v Daigle* the Supreme Court of Canada pointedly reminded Canadians that these men are more accurately characterized as 'potential fathers'.[123] However, the answer to the question 'what makes a man a father?' seems not to lend itself to such appeals to reason. The Supreme Court may proclaim this to the 'amens' of every feminist in the country, and yet in the very real world there is fear that ideologically and culturally, the hearts and minds of many Canadians seem to be with the men, the 'fathers' who are losing to selfish women and their feminist allies.[124]

Feminist sociologist Barbara Katz Rothman[125] argues that North American society, and its legal system, have privileged biological paternity over social fathering, where pregnancy is seen as something a man 'does' to a woman, by planting 'his' seed in her, where she has 'his' children. Rothman urges a rethinking of fathering, one which de-emphasizes the 'genetic connection' and re-emphasizes the social relationship. I remain unconvinced that a man can 'forge' a relationship with a foetus, or that he can have his own 'experience' of abortion.[126] The foetus is intimately connected to and constructed within the woman's body; it can only be intimately connected to and constructed within the imagination of the man. Despite his early (and undeniably pivotal) contribution to a woman's pregnancy, it can never be his pregnancy. His relationship with the foetus, if there is to be one, is inevitably mediated by the pregnant woman, and increasingly as well by law.

The resistance we witness to the recent judicial pronouncements inhibiting men may illustrate what Michael Mandel has characterized as understandable resistance to the undemocratic nature of the 'judicial fiat'.[127] And yet, the champions of the resistance in this instance (for example, REAL Women of Canada) are themselves less than committed to the democratic process, much less the 'rule of law'. It is clear that they will continue to work in, against, and outside the law to restrict women's access to abortion.

The abortion injunction cases and anti-feminist response remind us of the urgency of Smart's challenge to take up alternative, extra-legal strategies to defend and extend women's reproductive freedom. Women may have won in court, but the real struggle continues, and real victories remain to be won.

Clawbacks: The Provinces Respond

Perhaps the most striking response to the *Morgentaler* decision is to be found in the provincial governments' reactions to the spectre of decriminalized abortion in combination with the promise of Dr Morgentaler to establish clinics in every province. As others have noted,[128] the Supreme Court's decision was less than facilitative of women's access to abortion. The Court had simply struck down one form of legal prohibition. The provincial governments of Quebec and Ontario indicated that they would continue to insure abortions under provincial medical insurance plans. However, several provinces quickly set to work erecting local barriers to access.

It is worth remembering that the 1969 reform had also been the subject of political agitation and legal challenge in some provincial legislatures prior to 1988. The nature of these early provincial initiatives, and their ultimate fate, both foreshadowed the post-Morgentaler activity and brought into sharp relief a tremendous contradiction. One concrete example will illustrate. In 1985, an anti-choice Conservative backbencher in the Saskatchewan legislature introduced a private member's bill that would have required a Therapeutic Abortion Committee to secure the 'informed consent' of the patient and spousal or parental consent.[129] In addition, the bill would have imposed a 48-hour waiting period after consent had been given before the procedure could be performed.[130] In a surprise move, the provincial cabinet referred the bill to the Court of Appeal following second reading. The Saskatchewan Court of Appeal ruled that the proposed legislation was *ultra vires* the province, as it was criminal law, and hence within federal jurisdiction.[131] Otherwise, the Conservative majority in the provincial legislature would have passed this bill, which at least temporarily would have become provincial law. This early Saskatchewan case foreshadowed the debate that ensued in the aftermath of the *Morgentaler* decision. It also illuminated an interesting paradox: the criminal denotation of abortion inhibited some forms of provincial restrictions.

Following the Supreme Court's decision in January 1988, no premier moved more quickly than did Bill Vander Zalm of British Columbia. Vander Zalm announced that BC would not pay the costs of abortions; although he pledged that nobody would be permitted to die, he insisted, 'rape and incest are not life threatening. . . . We will not be funding abortions.'[132] While Vander Zalm's brash, unilateral initiative did not withstand judicial scrutiny,[133] other provinces, like Alberta, worked more quietly to ensure that decriminalization did not mean liberalization.[134] Alberta had already experimented with 'de-insuring' certain medical services. In 1987, tubal ligation, mid-tubal reconstruction, vasectomy, and gastroplasty procedures had been de-insured by the provincial government.[135] Following the *Morgentaler* decision, the Alberta Minister of Health announced that provincial health insurance would pay only for abortions approved by hospital therapeutic abortion committees.[136] The province subsequently modified its position and issued regulations which allowed an abortion to be insured if the doctor performing it had first secured a second opinion. Beyond this, Ian Urquhart suggests that the modest fee allowed under Alberta health insurance for therapeutic abortions has operated as a financial disincentive to abortion, and he concludes:

> in the aftermath of Morgentaler, the Alberta government has used the province's health insurance program as a vehicle for preserving the essence of the situation existing prior to Court's decision. Tying health insurance coverage to the performance of abortions in approved hospitals only after a second opinion has been offered, as well as retaining the modest fee schedule, combine to restrict access to this procedure, especially for women of modest means.[137]

The fate of a similar initiative by the New Brunswick government is of interest. In the spring of 1989, Dr Morgentaler once again found himself in court; on this occasion he was a plaintiff, and the government of New Brunswick was the defendant. Morgentaler was trying to extract his fees from the New Brunswick medicare system for abortions performed on three New Brunswick women in his Montreal clinic in the spring of 1988. The provincial government had declined to reimburse him, citing provincial policy that had been issued following the Supreme Court's decision: New Brunswick defined an 'entitled service' as one for which two physicians had certified its medical necessity, and the procedure had to be performed by a specialist in an approved hospital.[138] These criteria applied to abortions performed outside the province of New Brunswick as well. As in the *BC Civil Liberties* case, the Court essentially found that the New Brunswick government had acted precipitously; the 'policy' had not been formally adopted as a regulation under the provincial legislation. As there was no statutory basis for the requirements that the province had attempted to impose, Dr Morgentaler obtained the court order he was seeking, a declaration that the policy of the government of New Brunswick was invalid with respect to abortions performed outside the province of New Brunswick.[139] Despite the absence of a statutory basis for the policy, the court did not extend the declaration to abortions performed within New Brunswick. As a result of this decision, New Brunswick doctors and New Brunswick women unable to leave the province continued to be caught by the policy.

No government resisted the implications of Dr Morgentaler's Supreme Court victory more tenaciously than did John Buchanan's Conservative government in Nova Scotia. Just as the Nova Scotia government defied the Supreme Court ruling, so too did Dr Morgentaler defy in characteristic fashion the Nova Scotia legislation. In the spring of 1989, the provincial Minister of Health announced in the legislature that 'it is not the policy of this government to endorse or support in any way the provision of [abortion] services through free-standing clinics'[140] when he introduced the bill that would eventually become the Medical Services Act S.N.S., c. 9 and regulations under it. The stated purpose of the Act set out in s. 2 was: 'to prohibit the privatization of the provision of certain medical services in order to maintain a single high-quality health-care delivery system for all Nova Scotias [sic]'.[141]

A number of medical services were required under the Act to be performed in an approved hospital: arthoscopy, colonoscopy, upper gastro-intestinal endoscopy, abortion, lithotripsy, liposuction, nuclear medicine, installation or removal of intraocular lenses, and electromyography.[142] The Medical Services Act provided that there would be no reimbursement to any person who performed or received a designated medical service in contravention of the Act, and (S.6) that anyone who contravened the Act was guilty of an offence and liable upon summary conviction to a fine of not less than $10,000.00 and not more than $50,000.00.

Dr Morgentaler defied the Act and was charged after he performed abortions at his Halifax clinic. He was ordered by the Supreme Court of Nova Scotia not to perform abortions until the charges against him were heard.[143] Following his trial in the spring of 1990, the charges against him were dismissed by Provincial Court Judge Kennedy on the ground that the Nova Scotia legislation was really criminal law, and hence beyond the legislative jurisdiction of the province.[144]

The Crown's appeal to the Nova Scotia Court of Appeal was

unsuccessful. Freeman J.A. framed the question before the court:

> The question is not whether Nova Scotia possesses legislative powers to pass a law in the form of the Medical Services Act. It clearly could have done so, even though it dealt with abortion. The question is whether the province properly used those powers and created a law within the provincial competence, or whether it improperly attempted to use federal powers to pass a law that, regardless of its form, is actually a criminal law. Only if it bears the unmistakable imprint of criminal law must it be struck down.[145]

It was Morgentaler's position that the Act and Regulation were an incursion by a province into the field of criminal law, that it was 'criminal law in the guise of hospital law'.[146] The Crown's position was the Act was 'about privatization'[147]—essentially an attempt by the Conservatives to defend medicare against the incursions of the private sector. Freeman agreed that, 'examined uncritically and within its own four corners', the Medical Services Act appeared to be no more than a piece of legislation dealing with provincial hospitals.[148] However, a more critical and contextual examination of the Act, its purpose and effect, its nature and character, led the majority of the Court of Appeal to conclude that it was virtually identical to the Criminal Code provisions that had been struck down in *Morgentaler*.[149] Despite the apparent breadth and neutrality of the provisions, the Court found that the real focus of the legislation was Henry Morgentaler and its primary thrust was to prohibit his abortion clinics. Even the fines provided in the Act had been 'tailored to the [provincial] Department of Health's estimate of his resources'.[150]

Once again Morgentaler had successfully challenged a piece of abortion legislation, this time 'defending' the federal criminal law power. The irony of this position, necessitated as it was by the clawback of the province and the exigencies of litigation, should not be lost. Perhaps more than anything else, it illustrates the inevitable compromises that engagement with the legal process involves. The constraints imposed by the litigation and judicial processes lead to legal victories that are unreconcilable politically. The constraints go further, because the political imagination inevitably yields the pragmatism of the legal shrug: What else could be argued? How else could he win?

The indeterminacy of the *Morgentaler* decision was not inevitable. The Canadian feminist and pro-choice movement made history, but not under conditions of their own choosing. The cynicism and mean-spiritedness of assorted conservative governments, and their commitment to erosion of even the modest social programs in place, meant that the legal victory of Morgentaler was just that, and no more. The struggle for choice, for change, had to continue. Once again, Canadian women found they could claim 'no easy victories'.[151]

Conclusion

The entrenchment of medical control of abortion has been identified as fundamentally implicated in ensuring the continued subordination of women.[152] For its part, the pro-life movement argues that there is no medical justification for abortion and is more than a little suspicious of what it sees as 'medical opportunists' who profit from a 'murderous industry' and who are in effect accomplices of women in abortion.[153] Thus the merits of medical determination are explicitly challenged by both feminists, who have identified the moral arbitration embedded in medical practice, and right-to-life advocates.

Although I have argued elsewhere that both the criminalization of abortion and the implications of the therapeutic exception had to be understood and challenged, I have also argued that the notion of abortion as a medical matter has facilitated the formal erosion of one form of patriarchal authority. The Morgentaler decision pushes this issue a bit further, because women have pointed to the spirit and letter of the Canada Health Act to legitimate demands for state-funded access to abortion as a health-care service. To be colloquial, it may be that we have been released for the moment from the 'criminal' frying pan only to be burned by the 'health-care' fire. Nevertheless, as we consider the litany of struggles to resist the recriminalization of abortion, it will continue to be critical for feminists, activists and academics together, to explore and expand the social right to health care envisioned by the early advocates of comprehensive health care.

An important, related question is whether all law is necessarily bad. Put another way, it is certainly critically important in my view for feminists to resist *any* recriminalization of abortion at *any* stage of pregnancy. However, it is now worth considering whether a positive, affirmative right to abortion ought to be advocated, either by way of amendment to the federal Canada Health Act and/or provincial health legislation. The absence of criminal law did not guarantee *ipso facto* a *right* of access to safe abortion, as the developments after January 1988 illustrate. Indeed, the tone and language of the Supreme Court judgements invited some of the ensuing provincial responses: to wit, 'if it's a private matter, we don't have to pay for it.' The creation of a positive, legally enforceable right through the health-care system might render more public, and perhaps more political, the legitimate rights and desires of Canadian women.

It is one of the great paradoxes in the Canadian context that the issue of women's reproductive freedom, including access to abortion, was long dominated by two men of opposing points of view: Henry Morgentaler and Joseph Borowski. Moreover, as Rosalind Petchesky has brilliantly illuminated, the imagery of the foetal personhood campaign attempts to render women invisible.[154] But women have not acquiesced to invisibility, as Chantal Daigle demonstrated in the summer of 1989 when she resisted her ex-lover, the pro-life movement, her lawyer, and the courts. Chantal Daigle reminded us that women's individual and collective struggles for choice and self-determination may have been constrained, but have never been wholly confined nor determined by the legal and judicial processes.

So too, the struggle for decriminalization and for safe, universally accessible abortion is both an individual and collective one. One is not possible without the other.

Appendix A

The Criminal Code, 1882, 55-56 Victoria, C. 29, ss. 272, 273

s. 272 Every one is guilty of an indictable offence and liable to imprisonment for life who, with intent to procure the miscarriage of any woman, whether she is or is not with child, unlawfully administers to her or causes to be taken by her any drug or other noxious thing, or unlawfully uses any instrument or other means whatsoever with the like intent. R.S.C., c. 162, s. 47

s. 273 Every woman is guilty of an indictable offence and liable to seven years' imprisonment who, whether with child or not, unlawfully administers to herself or permits to be administered to her any drug or other noxious thing, or unlawfully uses on herself or permits to be used on her any instrument or other means whatsoever with intent to procure miscarriage. R.S.C., c. s. 47.

Criminal Code R.S.C. 1985, c. c-46.

s. 287 (1) Every one who, with intent to procure the miscarriage of a female person, whether or not she is pregnant, uses any means for the purpose of carrying out his intention is guilty of an indictable offence and liable to imprisonment for life.

(2) Every female person who, being pregnant, with intent to procure her own miscarriage, uses any means or permits any means to be used for the purpose of carrying out her intention is guilty of an indictable offence and liable to imprisonment for a term not exceeding two years.

(3) In this section, 'means' includes
(a) the administration of a drug or other noxious thing;
(b) the use of an instrument; and
(c) manipulation of any kind.

(4) Subsections (1) and (2) do not apply to
(a) a qualified medical practitioner, other than a member of a therapeutic abortion committee for any hospital, who in good faith uses in an accredited or approved hospital any means for the purpose of

carrying out his intention to procure the miscarriage of a female person, or

(b) a female person who, being pregnant, permits a qualified medical practitioner to use in an accredited or approved hospital any means for the purpose of carrying out her intention to procure her own miscarriage, if, before the use of those means, the therapeutic abortion committee for that accredited or approved hospital, by a majority of the members of the committee and at a meeting of the committee at which the case of the female person has been reviewed,

(c) has by certificate in writing stated that in its opinion the continuation of the pregnancy of the female person would or would be likely to endanger her life or health, and

(d) has caused a copy of that certificate to be given to the qualified medical practitioner.

(5) The Minister of Health of a province may by order

(a) require a therapeutic abortion committee for any hospital in that province, or any member thereof, to furnish him with a copy of any certificate described in paragraph (4) (c) issued by that committee, together with such other information relating to the circumstances surrounding the issue of that certificate as he may require, or

(b) require a medical practitioner who, in that province, has procured the miscarriage of any female person named in a certificate described in paragraph (4) (c), to furnish him with a copy of that certificate, together with such other information relating to the procuring of the miscarriage as he may require.

(6) For the purposes of subsections (4) and (5) and this subsection

'accredited hospital' means a hospital accredited by the Canadian Council on Hospital Accreditation in which diagnostic services and medical, surgical and obstetrical treatment are provided;

'approved hospital' means a hospital in a province approved for the purposes of this section by the Minister of Health of that province;

'board' means the board of governors, management of directors, or the trustees, commission or other person or group of persons having the control and management of an accredited or approved hospital;

'Minister of Health' means

(a) in the Province of Ontario, Quebec, New Brunswick, Prince Edward Island, Manitoba, and Newfoundland, the Minister of Health.

(b) in the Provinces of Nova Scotia and Saskatchewan, the Minister of Public Health, and

(c) in the Province of British Columbia, the Minister of Health Services and Hospital Insurance,

(d) in the Province of Alberta, the Minister of Hospitals and Medical Care,

(e) in the Yukon Territory and the Northwest Territories, the Minister of National Health and Welfare;

'qualified medical practitioner' means a person entitled to engage in the practice of medicine under the laws of the province in which the hospital referred to in subsection (4) is situated;

'therapeutic abortion committee' for any hospital means a committee, comprised of not less than three members each of whom is a qualified medical practitioner, appointed by the board of that hospital for the purpose of considering and determining questions relating to terminations of pregnancy within that hospital.

(7) Nothing in subsection (4) shall be construed as making unnecessary the obtaining of any authorization or consent that is or may be required, otherwise than under this Act, before any means are used for the purpose of carrying out an intention to procure the miscarriage of a female person.

Supplying noxious things.

s. 288. Every one who unlawfully supplies or procures a drug or other noxious thing or an instrument or thing, knowing that it is intended to be used or employed to procure the miscarriage of a female person, whether or not she is pregnant, is guilty of an indictable offence and liable to imprisonment for a term not exceeding two years.

2nd Session, 34th Parliament 38 Elizabeth 11, 1989
THE HOUSE OF COMMONS OF CANADA BILL C-43
An Act respecting abortion

Her Majesty, by and with the advice and consent of the Senate and House of Commons of Canada, enacts as follows:

1. Sections 287 and 288 of the Criminal Code are repealed and the following substituted therefor:

'287. (1) Every *person who induces an abortion on a female person* is guilty of an indictable offence and liable to imprisonment for *a term not exceeding two* years, unless the abortion is induced by or under the direction of a medical practitioner who is of the opinion that, if the abortion were not induced, the health or life of the female person would be likely to be threatened.

(2) For the purposes of this section, 'health' includes, for greater certainty, physical, mental and psychological health;

'medical practitioner', in respect of an abortion induced in a province, means a person who is entitled to practise medicine under the laws of that province; 'opinion' means an opinion formed using generally accepted standards of the medical profession.

(3) For the purposes of this section and section 288, inducing an abortion does not include using a drug, device or other means on a female person that is likely to prevent implantation of a fertilized ovum.

288. Every one who unlawfully supplies or procures a drug or other noxious thing or an instrument or thing, knowing that it is intended to be used or employed to *induce an abortion on* a female person, is guilty of an indictable offence and liable to imprisonment for a term not exceeding two years.'

(2) This Act shall come into force on a day to be fixed by order of the Governor in Council.

Appendix B

Speakers in the 'Sense of the House' debate, July 1988

NUMBER	MEMBER
3	Marion Dewar, NDP
4	Gus Mitges, P.C.
5	Keith Penner, Lib.
6	John Reimer, P.C.
9	John Oostrom, P.C.
10	Lise Bourgault, P.C.
12	Sinclair Stevens, P.C.
14	Benno Friesen, P.C.
15	Gordon Towers, P.C.
16	Don Boudria, P.C.
20	Jim Jepson, P.C.
22	Ricardo Lopez, P.C.
23	Gaston Isabelle, Lib.
24	Gabrielle Bertrand, P.C.
25	Audrey McLaughlin, NDP
26	Alan Redway, P.C.
27	Sergio Marchi, Lib.
28	Rob Nicholson, P.C.
29	Dan Heap, NDP
30	Barbara McDougall, P.C.
31	Lawrence O'Neil, P.C.
32	Gordon Henderson, P.C.
33	Reginald Stackhouse, P.C.
34	Nelson Riis, NDP
35	Bill Gottselig, P.C.
37	Vince Dantzer, P.C.
38	Jake Epp, P.C.
40	Ken James, P.C.
42	Paul Gagnon, P.C.
43	Moe Mantha, P.C.
44	Roland de Corneille, Lib.
45	David Kilgour, P.C.
46	Lloyd Axworthy, Lib.
47	Bob Brisco, P.C.
49	Steven Langdon, NDP
51	Len Hopkins, Lib.
52	Girve Fretz, P.C.
53	Mike Cassidy, NDP
54	Gordon Taylor, P.C.
56	J. Forrestal, P.C.
57	Anthony Roman, Ind.
58	Bob Pennock, P.C.
59	Barry Turner, Lib.
61	Charles Marin, P.C.
63	John Gormley, P.C.
64	Aurèle Gervais, P.C.
67	Chuck Cook, P.C.
68	Lee Clark, P.C.
69	Bill Vankoughnet, P.C.
70	Allan Pieetz, P.C.
71	Marc Ferland
72	Jack Shields, P.C.
73	Jim Caldwell,P.C.
74	Bill Attewell, P.C.

Notes

Chapter One

[1]As with so many deeply controversial areas of politics, the choice of labels for participants is a difficult one. In Canada, for example, the label 'separatist' is an epithet and 'independentiste', despite its lack of a comfortable English equivalent, is the preferred term by those who advocate a new status for Quebec. Similarly in the abortion debate, labels are very important. In this book, we have chosen the convention of labelling each group by its chosen name. While we may think that 'pro-life' is a misleading term for a group singularly unconcerned about the quality of life of either babies or women forced to carry them, this is the label that we will use. The other side will be referred to as 'pro-choice'. No pro-choice supporter is 'pro-abortion' (an inappropriate label used by Robert Campbell and Leslie Pal, *The Real Worlds of Canadian Politics* [Peterborough: Broadview, 1991], Chapter 1) because they do not consider abortion a desirable, but simply a necessary, act. Pro-choice people are pro-abortion rights, of course, but that lengthy label is inconvenient. It is worth noting, however, that the term pro-abortion rights is the correct one to use until the mid-1970s when the 'pro-choice' label was deliberately adopted for purposes of self-designation by those who previously had no other name for themselves.

[2]This formulation is similar to that developed for class actors in Janine Brodie and Jane Jenson, *Crisis, Challenge and Change: Party and Class in Canada Revisited* (Ottawa: Carleton University Press, 1988): Chapter 1.

[3]Jane Jenson, 'Gender and Reproduction: Or, Babies and the State', *Studies in Political Economy* 20, Spring 1986 and 'Paradigms and Political Discourse: Protective Legislation in France and the United States Before 1914', *Canadian Journal of Political Science* 2, June 1989.

[4]Chris Weedon, *Feminist Practice and Poststructuralist Theory* (Oxford: Basil Blackwell, 1987): 92, 97.

[5]Zillah Eisenstein, *The Female Body and the Law* (Los Angeles: University of California Press, 1988): 10.

[6]Jane Jenson, 'All the World's a Stage: Ideas, Spaces and Times in Canadian Political Economy', *Studies in Political Economy* 36, Fall 1991.

[7]Rosalind Pollack Petchesky, *Abortion and Woman's Choice: The State, Sexuality, and Reproductive Freedom* (Boston: Northeastern Press, 1984): 67.

[8]Petchesky, *Abortion and Woman's Choice*; Linda Gordon, *Woman's Body, Woman's Right: A Social History of Birth Control in America* (Middlesex: Penguin Books, 1977); Angus McLaren and Arlene Tigar McLaren, *The Bedroom and the State: the Changing Practices and Politics of Contraception and Abortion in Canada* (Toronto: McClelland and Stewart, 1986); Barbara Brookes, *Abortion in England 1900-1967* (London: Croom Helm, 1988); Shelley A.M. Gavigan, 'On "bringing on the menses": The Criminal Liability of Women and the Therapeutic Exception in Canadian Abortion Law', *Canadian Journal of Women and the Law* 2 (1986): 279.

[9]See Shelley Gavigan, 'The Criminal Prohibition As It Relates to Human Reproduction: The Genesis of the Statutory Prohibition of Abortion', *Journal of Legal History* 4 (1984): 20-43.

[10]Ibid.

[11]Gavigan, 'On "bringing on the menses".'

[12]McLaren and McLaren, *The Bedroom and the State*: Chapter 2.

[13]Mollie Dunsmuir, *Abortion: Constitutional and Legal Developments* (Ottawa: Library of Parliament, 1989): 7.

[14]Law Reform Commission of Canada, *Crimes Against the Foetus (Working Paper 58)* (Ottawa: Supply & Services, 1989): 7.

[15]See Rosalind Pollack Petchesky, 'Foetal Images: The Power of Visual Culture in the Politics of Reproduction', in *Reproductive Technologies: Gender, Motherhood, and Medicine*, Michelle Stanworth, ed. (Minneapolis: University of Minnesota Press, 1987).

[16]Petchesky, *Abortion and Woman's Choice*: 263.

Chapter Two

[1]Madam Justice Bertha Wilson, in her separate and individual opinion, indicated that she considered that the Charter did grant women the right to unfettered access in the early weeks of a pregnancy.

[2]Michael Cuneo describes the stand-off in this way: 'Thus, by the early 1970s both sides had staked out a polemical ground which has remained

irreconcilably frozen until the present. Pro-life supporters, convinced that abortion under almost any circumstance is an unjustified taking of human life, have argued that the 1969 legislation is too lenient and the "thin edge of the wedge" for a more widespread societal disrespect for the sanctity of life. . . . The pro-choice side, in contrast, has argued that legal restrictions on the availability of abortion serve to perpetuate a traditional pattern of female biological enslavement and socio-cultural subservience.' (*Catholics against the Church: Anti-Abortion Protest in Toronto 1969-1985*, Toronto: University of Toronto Press, 1989: 5.)

[3]For a more detailed discussion of the theoretical points made in the next paragraphs see Jane Jenson, 'Gender and Reproduction: or, Babies and the State', *Studies in Political Economy* 20 (1986): 7-9 and Jane Jenson, 'Paradigms and Political Discourse: Protective Legislation in France and the United States Before 1914', *Canadian Journal of Political Science* 22,2 (June 1989).

[4]For details about how hospitals gain accreditation and approval see Margaret A. Somerville, 'Reflections on Canadian Abortion Law: Evacuation and Destruction—Two Separate Issues', *University of Toronto Law Journal* 31 (1981): 4, footnote 8. For the definition see Appendix A.

[5]In countries where abortion remained strictly illegal until the 1970s, reform of the law was often the demand around which feminists rallied and which provided the practical politics which most contributed to the formation of their collective identity. Politics focused on reproductive rights in this way provided a powerful push for a radicalized movement and the glue for its sense of solidarity. In countries like Canada, the US and UK, where abortion reform was achieved without feminist mobilization, liberal feminism, promoting a less clear gender-based identity and solidarity, was often a leading fraction of second-wave feminism.

[6]For a discussion of the commonality of experiences of other countries of Western Europe and the US see Mary Ann Glendon, *Abortion and Divorce in Western Law* (Cambridge: Cambridge University Press, 1987): Chapter 1.

[7]This alliance reflected an important change from the first years of the twentieth century, when doctors and social reformers were leaders of the campaign against 'race suicide' or against what was termed 'malthusianism'. Confronted with a declining birth rate, commercially available and widely advertised abortificants, and many women whose own moral code included the belief that abortion (or, as they called it, 'being put regular') was acceptable until quickening (the third month of pregnancy), doctors and social reformers reacted. They were highly critical of white,

anglo-saxon, married women's efforts to control family size, seeing this as the way to let the foreign-born dominate Canadian society. They were appalled by the notion that women might choose to remain childless, even if married. The idea of women choosing to be sexually active and unmarried was even more horrific to many of them. And they experienced the commercial system of distribution of products as well as reliance on traditional folk methods for controlling pregnancy as a threat to their professional position. Thus, doctors were actively involved in the various pre-1914 movements to encourage motherhood and large families among the 'better races'. On Canada see Angus McLaren and Arlene T. McLaren, *The Bedroom and the State: The Changing Practices and Politics of Contraception and Abortion in Canada, 1880-1980* (Toronto: McClelland and Stewart, 1986): Chapters 1 and 2.

[8]As an excellent example of such a rationale for reform see Wendell W. Watters, *Compulsory Parenthood: The Truth About Abortion* (Toronto: McClelland and Stewart, 1976). On the activities of International Planned Parenthood see Sandra Whitworth, 'Planned Parenthood and the New Right: Onslaught or Opportunity?', *Studies in Political Economy* 35 (1991).

[9]The composition of this leadership of the family planning movement reflected a shift from the pre-Depression decades. The Canadian movement at that time was primarily a left-leaning one, with support coming from leftists in parties, social movements (like the Women's International League for Peace and Freedom), and the trade unions. Also important was an anarchist left—the Malthusians—who had a libertarian view of sexuality and sought contraceptive reform as part of women's liberation. Maternal feminists, in contrast, were wary of advocating contraception. By the 1930s, however, the movement had shifted in the direction of family planning, advocated by middle-class reformers less for their own class than for poor, unemployed, working-class and especially Catholic families. For a description of this shift, and the important role played by doctors and Protestant clergymen in changing public opinion, see McLaren and McLaren, *The Bedroom and the State*: Chapters 3 and 4, and especially 119-21.

[10]Campbell and Pal, *The Real Worlds of Canadian Politics*: 171.

[11]McLaren and McLaren, *The Bedroom and the State*: Figure 2, 48 and 50-51.

[12]Contraception for 'family planning' did not meet the needs of single women, especially young women, but reformers rarely addressed the situation of this category of women in their calls for reform of laws regulating abortion or contraception.

[13]For a description of the *Chatelaine* article see Campbell and Pal, *The Real Worlds of Canadian Politics*: 171-2. For an analysis of similar use of exemplary and symbolic cases see the Bobigny trial described in Jane Jenson, 'Changing Discourse, Changing Agenda: Political Rights and Reproductive Rights in France', in Mary Katzenstein and Carol Mueller, *New Theoretical Perspectives from the Women's Movements of Europe and North America* (Phildelphia, PA: Temple University Press, 1987).

[14]Jane Jenson, ' "Different" but not "exceptional": Canada's Permeable Fordism', *Canadian Review of Sociology and Anthropology*, 26, 1 (1989): 78-9.

[15]The NDP did play a role in pressing for reform of the legislation controlling contraception when some of its MPs pointed out the profound contradiction of Canada supporting family planning for Third World countries but refusing to make it legal at home. McLaren and McLaren, *The Bedroom and the State*, 134.

[16]The most active religious leaders were from the United and Anglican churches. Fundamentalist Protestants did not intervene on the side of abortion reform. As will become clear below, the Catholic Church did not support abortion reform, but its own internal complications in the 1960s meant that it was a relatively inactive participant at this crucial moment.

[17]For a description of this 1892 reform see Campbell and Pal, *The Real Worlds of Canadian Politics*: 169.

[18]For details about the influence of *Bourne* in Britain see Karen Greenwood and Lucy King, 'Contraception and Abortion' in Cambridge Women's Studies Group (eds), *Women in Society* (London: Virago, 1981). On Canada and the *Bourne* case see K.W. Cheung, *Essays on Abortion* (Windsor: University of Windsor, 1977). There was some dispute about whether the *Bourne* decision applied completely in Canada, especially after the 1953-54 revision of the Criminal Code. See Monique Hébert, 'Abortion: Legal Aspects', Library of Parliament, 13 February 1987: 3.

[19]Cheung, *Essays*: 24-25.

[20]Many of these abortions were clearly illegal because licensed doctors did not perform them and therefore the practitioner could not claim the protection of the *Bourne* decision. For statistics see Alphonse de Valk, *Morality and Law in Canadian Politics: The Abortion Controversy* (Dorval, Que.: Palm, 1974).

[21]As Hébert writes in 'Legal Aspects': 1, the reform only 'rectified an unbearable situation for the medical profession'.

[22]The history of abortion reform in the USA resembled that of Canada in many ways until the late 1960s. Then, however, the issue was taken up by the American women's movement, and inserted into a discourse of individual rights, which resulted in the numerous court cases which *Roe v Wade* eventually addressed, later than the Canadian reform. For details, see Kristin Luker, *Abortion and the Politics of Motherhood* (Berkeley, CA: University of California Press, 1984): Chapters 4 and 5. See also Rosalind Petchesky, *Abortion and Woman's Choice: The State, Sexuality, and Reproductive Freedom* (NY: Longman, 1984).

[23]Quoted in de Valk, *Morality and Law*: 17.

[24]Evidence Presented to the Parliamentary Committee on Health and Welfare, 31 October 1967: 102.

[25]Evidence . . .: 109, 112, 113.

[26]This discussion of 'deformities' took place in a context in which a good deal of public attention—although not much in the Parliamentary Committee—focused on the experience women had after they took the drug thalidomide. Once the risk of deformities associated with taking the drug in the early stages of pregnancy became known, a number of women who had taken it tried to obtain abortions.

[27]Evidence . . .: 111.

[28]Only two MPs rejected the pervasive discourse to name in a positive way the recipients of abortions as 'women'. Indeed, Stanley Knowles of the NDP went out of his way to point out that women were be judged by male doctors. Both he and Warren Allmand couched their arguments in a concern for 'women'. See Evidence to the Parliamentary Committee: 112, 109.

[29]Indeed, the CMA opposed the notion of Termination Boards as unwieldy mechanisms that would slow things down by judicializing a process in which time was of the essence. Evidence to the Parliamentary Committee: 98.

[30]de Valk, *Morality and Law*: 26. See also 11-24.

[31]de Valk, *Morality and Law*: 10.

[32]The United Church position evolved quickly. By 1971 it supported abortion on demand, de Valk (*Morality and Law*: 10). On the Anglicans see 19-20.

[33]For a description of the conflicts within the Anglican Church as well as the positions adopted by its mainstream and by the United Church see Cuneo, *Catholics Against the Church:* 14.

[34]de Valk, *Morality and Law*: 22.

[35]Sandra Burt, 'Women's Issues and the Women's Movement in Canada Since 1970', in Alan Cairns and Cynthia Williams (eds), *The Politics of Gender, Ethnicity and Language in Canada*, vol. 34 of the Reports of the Royal Commission on the Economic Union and Development Prospects for Canada (Toronto: University of Toronto, 1985): 135.

[36]It is interesting and important to note that in a recent history of the mainstream Canadian feminist movement, the description of the 1960s includes consideration of Planned Parenthood's actions to overturn the ban on contraceptives but no mention of any actions on abortion reform. While the National Council of Women obviously did present such briefs, that part of their activity did not remain a vital part of the organization's historical memory. See Penney Kome, *Women of Influence: Canadian Women and Politics* (Toronto: Doubleday, 1985): Chapter 6.

[37]Lise Gotell, 'Women, the State and Abortion Policy in Canada', BA honours essay, Carleton University, 1985, 43. The Humanists of Canada, whose position the Parliamentary Committee did discuss at length, had also argued for 'abortion on request'.

[38]This analysis of the hesitancies and reluctance of the Catholics is taken from de Valk, *Morality and Law*: Chapter VIII. He was very critical of his own Church's failure to act promptly and effectively as opposition in the 1960s. For a recent review of that Church's position on abortion in these years, see Cuneo, *Catholics Against the Church.*

[39]For a complete report of the Parliamentary hearings, see de Valk, *Morality and Law*, Chapters V-IX. For details of the CMA's position see Eleanor W. Pelrine, *Abortion in Canada* (Toronto: New Press, 1971): 30-33.

[40]For a summary of the three bills see Campbell and Pal, *The Real Worlds of Canadian Politics*: Inset I, 174.

[41]MacInnis' bill differed from the CMA resolution by requiring the certification of necessity by two doctors.

[42]It is interesting to note that Herridge's proposals, with their language of need and notion that poor and working-class women would need abortions more than richer and middle-class women, shared some perspectives of the discourse surrounding reform of the regulation of contraception in the interwar years. At that time, reformers directed their attention primarily to the situation of the poor, unemployed, less educated, etc. Nevertheless, whereas the interwar position was one of paternalism towards the poor, the Herridge proposal—as the law in the UK—had arisen in the context of

a more empowering discourse of postwar social democracy. Doctors were to decide, to be sure, but women were not blamed for their condition. Rather they were viewed positively for seeking greater control over their own situations, in alliance with appropriate experts, of course.

[43]*Hansard*, 24 January 1967: 4791.

[44]See MacInnis' speech 27 January 1969, *Hansard* 4844-6. See also David Lewis (23 January 1969: 4758-9) who made the argument that the reform did not go far enough and that social concerns as well as foetal deformity should be acceptable grounds for legal abortions. Lewis also used a medicalized discourse, more than a sexual one, in supporting legalization of homosexual acts between consenting adults. For him homosexuality was a 'deviationism obviously . . . due to certain psychological and other factors'. He recommended compassion.

[45]Cuneo, *Catholics Against the Church*: 4.

[46]*Hansard*, 28 April 1969: 8060.

[47]See Glendon, *Abortion and Divorce*, Appendix.

[48]The French state requires a 'period of reflection', between the initial request for an abortion and the procedure. While for a number of years it refused to reimburse abortions under the medical insurance provisions of the Social Security system, this restriction was dropped in 1981.

[49]Obviously most Catholic hospitals did this from the beginning, but other unaffiliated hospitals too chose not to establish Committees when there were disputes among the staff or under pressure from minorities in the community.

[50]Canada, *Report of the Committee on the Operation of the Abortion Law (The Badgley Report)* (Ottawa: Supply and Services, 1977): 140-1.

[51]Watters, *Compulsory Parenthood*: 127-31.

[52]Larry Collins, 'The Politics of Abortion: Trends in Canadian Fertility Policy', *Atlantis* 7,2 (1982): 16-17.

[53]Canada, *Badgley Report*: 20.

[54]For example, hospital committees might require one or all of the following: prior consultation with one, two, or three doctors, a review of the applicant's social and economic situation, a residency requirement, tests for congenital deformities, consent of a spouse or partner, a time limit on gestation, interview of the patient by the hospital committee. None of these—with the exception of a consultation with one doctor—were

required by the 1969 abortion law. Canada, *Badgley Report*: 20; 29-30. See also, Susan A. McDaniel, 'Implementation of Abortion Policy in Canada as a Women's Issue', *Atlantis* 10,2 (1985): 78.

[55]Watters, *Compulsory Parenthood*, 128-9.

[56]For a detailed recounting of Dr Morgentaler's long experience with the criminal justice system see Campbell and Pal, *The Real Worlds of Canadian Politics*, 181-97. In order to explain the politics of abortion in Canada, that book devotes most of its attention to Morgentaler and the courts.

[57]There are complicated representational dimensions to the actions of Dr Morgentaler which cannot be explored or dealt with in detail here. For example, Campbell and Pal (*The Real Worlds of Canadian Politics*: 182-3) cite—seemingly approvingly—Morgentaler's own interpretation of his Holocaust experience as having left him with a sense of impotence and they quote him as saying: 'I came to the conclusion that, under some circumstances, it is imperative to defy authority—necessary for my self-esteem, to prove my manhood in direct conflict'. That the defiance of authority, for Morgentaler, involved both his defence of and control over women's bodies would seem to require further analysis.

[58]Somerville, *Reflections*: 10.

[59]Shelley Gavigan, 'Women, Law and Patriarchal Relations: Perspectives in Sociology of Law' in Neil Boyd (ed.) *The Social Dimensions of Law* (Scarborough: Prentice-Hall, 1986).

[60]He was acquitted by a jury and then the jury decision was overturned by a court of appeal without a re-trial. This had never happened in Canadian legal history. In addition, he was tried several times for similar offences, and had to endure the trials, despite gaining acquittals from all his juries. See Watters, *Compulsory Parenthood*: Chapter 9.

[61]Quoted in Kate Alderdice (ed.), *Women's Liberation in Canada* (Toronto: Pathfinder, 1975): 11.

[62]McLaren and McLaren, *The Bedroom and the State*: 9.

[63]Gavigan, 'Women, Law'. Or, as Hébert puts it in 'Legal Aspects': 6, 'Parliament completely replaced judicial control after the fact by medical control before the fact'.

[64]Gavigan, 'Women, Law'.

[65]Karen Dubinsky, 'Lament for a 'Patriarchy Lost': Anti-Feminism, Anti-Abortion and R.E.A.L. Women in Canada', *Feminist Perspectives féministes* (Ottawa: Criaw, 1985): 25 and *passim*.

[66]Gavigan, 'Women, Law'; Hébert, 'Legal Aspects': 9.

[67]McDaniel, 'Implementation': 80.

[68]For examples, see the descriptions of the anti-choice efforts directed against the Vancouver General in *Canadian Forum* 62 (1983): 37 and in Kathleen McDonnell, *Not an Easy Choice: A Feminist Examines Abortion* (Boston: South End, 1984): 82-83.

[69]Gotell, 'Women, the State and Abortion Policy'.

[70]The Toronto *Globe and Mail*, 30 January 1987.

[71]Kathleen McDonnell, 'Claim No Easy Victories: The Fight for Reproductive Rights', in M. Fitzgerald *et al.*, *Still Ain't Satisfied: Canadian Feminism Today* (Toronto: The Women's Press, 1982): 33. According to Nancy Adamson *et al.*, *Feminist Organizing for Change: The Contemporary Women's Movement in Canada* (Toronto: Oxford, 1989): 7, the division of labour was the following: 'Radical feminists focused on violence against women as their main issue, while socialist feminists concentrated on various aspects of women's work, and liberal feminists continued to lobby the government for legal changes.'

[72]For an interesting history of the links between radical student politics and the development of abortion and birth control politics, leading to the establishment of the Montreal Women's Centre, see Donna Cherniak and Allen Feingold, 'Birth Control Handbook', in *Women Unite! An Anthology of the Canadian Women's Movement* (Toronto: Canadian Women's Educational Press, 1972): 109-13. The League for Socialist Action also defined the abortion campaign as a way of striking at the heart of capitalism and its oppression of women. For the League, 'this struggle will remain the central confrontation between the oppressor of women and the supporters of the feminist struggle for the next period.' Quoted in Alderdice, *Women's Liberation*: 12. For the best overview of the contemporay women's movement and abortion politics within it see Adamson *et al.*, *Organizing for Change*: Chapter 2.

[73]*Canadian Forum* 50 (1970): 157; *Women Unite!*: 9, 31ff.

[74]For example, the Voice of Women (VOW) began as a peace group in the early 1960s but it also joined the birth control campaign which was gaining ground at that time. Cerise Morris, 'Determination and Thoroughness: The Movement for a Royal Commission on the Status of Women in Canada', *Atlantis* 5,2 (1980): 7. The Quebec Federation came out in 1975 for the complete decriminalization of abortion. Before that its position had been one of legalization, but still within the Criminal Code.

[75]See Adamson *et al.*, *Organizing for Change*: 45-46.

[76]The importance of the Caravan for some groups is described in this quote from the Saskatoon Women's Liberation group: 'In Canada the abortion caravan was a catalyst for the movement, generating new groups and increasing women's awareness of their collective strength.' Cited in Adamson *et al.*, *Organizing for Change*: 46.

[77]This description is from Adamson *et al.*, *Organizing for Change*: 48-9.

[78]Cited in Adamson *et al.*, *Organizing for Change*: 48.

[79]Adamson *et al.*, *Organizing for Change*: 50, describes the Toronto experience in the first years of the 1970s.

[80]Adamson *et al.*, *Organizing for Change*: 65.

[81]CARAL changed its name in 1980 to the Canadian Abortion Rights Action League.

[82]Diane Lamoureux, *Fragments et collages: Essai sur le féminisme québécois* (Montreal: Remue-Menage, 1986): 64.

[83]Lamoureux, *Fragments et collages*: 64.

[84]Adamson *et al.*, *Organizing for Change*: 54, 65. Indeed, even the Abortion Caravan had not succeeded in overcoming a major split within the women's movement throughout the 1970s, that between Quebec and anglophone Canada. Emerging out of the liberationist politics of the late 1960s in Quebec, the movement identified completely with the national struggle. For example, the Front de libération des femmes (FLF), which was close to the FLQ, did not participate in the demonstrations in Ottawa because of the legitimacy granted the federal government by such acts. By 1975 the women's movement had emerged from the shadow of Marxism and nationalism and adopted the positions of radical feminism while, as is described below, reasserting the struggle for access to abortion.

[85]The weight, or 'centre of gravity' of various women's movement were important for outcomes in several policy areas. In France for example, where the weightiest part of the movement was a revolutionary feminism which demanded women's right to control their own bodies, based on their collective difference from men, the movement successfully overwhelmed any tendencies of reformers to resort to an advocacy of abortion in order to address social problems or equal rights arguments. See Jane Jenson, 'Representations of Difference: The French Women's Movement', *New Left Review* 180 (1989).

[86]Morris, 'Determination and Thoroughness', 11ff; Lynn McDonald, 'The Evolution of the Women's Movement in Canada', *Branching Out*, 1 (1979): 39-43. For a description of all wings of the Canadian movement, as well as a discussion of liberal feminism as the centre of gravity, see Adamson *et al.*, *Organizing for Change*: Chapter 2; 190-1.

[87]CACSW, *10 Years Later* (Ottawa: CACSW, 1979): 5. Similarly, when commissioning a feminist review of selected criminal law issues, CACWS did not select abortion, despite the intensity of recent legal challenges.

[88]Burt, 'Women's Issues': 138-9.

[89]Burt, 'Women's Issues': 137.

[90]Burt, 'Women's Issues': 149; Kome, *Women of Influence*: 88.

[91]For a parallel analysis of the effects of the RCSW on legal studies, see Susan Boyd and Elizabeth Sheehy, 'Canadian Feminist Perspectives on Law', *Journal of Law and Society* 13,3 (1986): 283-320.

[92]Morris, 'Determination and Thoroughness': 11 and *passim*; Burt, 'Women's Issues': 116.

[93]Commissioner Elsie Gregory MacGill wanted an even more liberal statement, while Commissioners Jacques Henripin and Doris Ogilvie considered the recommendations to go too far. See Canada, *The Report of the Royal Commission on the Status of Women* (Ottawa: 1970): 287-8; 429; 422-3.

[94]The costs of Morgentaler's defences were often raised by pro-choice activists, despite the relative lack of attention to pro-choice themes in his legal arguments. Gotell, 'Women, the State': 77.

[95]Lise Gotell, ' "A Helluva Lot to Lose but Not a Helluva a Lot to Win": Canadian Women and Equality Rights, 1980-81', MA research paper, York University (1986): 66-7.

[96]McDonnell, *Not an Easy Choice*: 19.

[97]Lamoureux, *Fragments et collages*: 65-6.

[98]*Cayenne: A Socialist Feminist Bulletin*, 2,2-3 (1986): 25-44 describes the 1986 experience, but the matter had surfaced as early as 1978. See Adamson *et al.*, *Organizing for Change*: 171.

[99]As early as 1965, nearly 75% of the public supported therapeutic abortions when the health of the woman was threatened. In the mid-1970s almost two-thirds of those polled would leave the decision solely to the

woman and her doctor. M. Boyd and D. Gillieson, 'Canadian Attitudes on Abortion: Results of the Gallup Poll', *Canadian Population Studies* 2 (1975): 55-6. By 1982, the Gallup Poll found that 75% of Canadians would leave the decision up to women alone. *Canadian Forum* 62 (1983): 42.

[100]Kome, *Women of Influence*: 149, 180.

[101]Adamson *et al.*, *Organizing for Change*: 79-80. Of course the NDP was also divided as the actions of the NDP provincial governments sometimes indicated. The Manitoba NDP brought Dr Morgentaler to trial. McDonnell, *Not An Easy Choice*: 87-79.

[102]*Canadian Forum* 59 (1979): 20.

[103]Kome, *Women of Influence*: 174; 186-8.

[104]Coalition for Life was the lobby group of Campaign Life which collected 1,000,000 signatures in 1975 presented to Parliament to demand restrictions on abortions. Gotell, 'Women, the State': 79.

[105]A Private Members Bill tabled in 1986 proposed to amend the Constitution Act of 1982 to give a human foetus full protection under the Charter of Rights. In addition, three other bills were introduced—two to widen access and one to limit it. Hébert, 'Legal Aspects': 16-17.

Chapter Three

[1]*Globe and Mail*, 29 January 1988: A7.

[2]S. Rogers, 'The Future of Abortion in Canada: A Legal Viewpoint', in C. Overall, ed., *The Future of Human Reproduction* (Toronto: Women's Press, 1989): 200.

[3]C. Condit, *Decoding Abortion Rhetoric: Communicating Social Change* (Chicago: University of Illinois Press, 1990): 96.

[4]R. Campbell and L. Pal, *The Real Worlds of Canadian Politics* (Peterborough: Broadview Press, 1989): 204.

[5]As quoted in L. Gotell, 'Women, the State and Abortion Policy in Canada', BA honours essay, Carleton University, 1985: 88.

[6]CROP poll, *Toronto Star*, 29 January 1988: A13.

[7]Gallup Poll, Press Release, Canadian Abortion Rights Action League, 19 April 1988.

[8]I would like to thank my colleague at York, Thelma McCormack, for this observation.

[9]See B. Kay, R. Lambert, S. Brown and J. Curtis, 'Single-Issue Interest Groups and the Canadian Electorate: The Case of Abortion in 1988' (unpublished paper).

[10]See Canada, *Report of the Committee on the Operation of the Abortion Law* (Ottawa: Ministry of Supply and Services, 1977).

[11]L. Gotell, 'The Canadian Women's Movement, Equality Rights and the Charter', *Feminist Perspectives* 16, Canadian Research Institute for the Advancement of Women, 1990.

[12]J. Borowski, *Globe and Mail*, 29 January 1988: A1.

[13]*Toronto Star*, 29 January 1988: A13.

[14]Norma Scarborough, *Globe and Mail*, 9 February: A4.

[15]*Globe and Mail*, 29 January 1988: A4.

[16]*Globe and Mail*, 30 January 1988: A12.

[17]*Globe and Mail*, 29 January 1988: A7.

[18]*Globe and Mail*, 10 February 1988: A1.

[19]In 1987, BC had 7.9 abortions per 100 live births or 11,476 abortions performed in hospitals. Health Division: Vital Statistics and Disease Registration Section, Statistics Canada, 1987.

[20]*Globe and Mail*, 8 February 1988: A1.

[21]*Globe and Mail*, 3 February 1988: A1.

[22]There was an obvious hypocrisy here which was not lost on the pro-choice movement. MPs were being allowed to exercise their consciences but Canadian women were not.

[23]*Hansard*, Monday, 30 May 1988: 38.

[24]*Globe and Mail*, 21 May 1988: A1.

[25]*Globe and Mail*, 19 May 1988: A1.

[26]Interview with a Member of Parliament.

[27]Condit, *Decoding Abortion Rhetoric*: 8.

[28]Ibid.: 4-8.

[29]K. Luker, *Abortion and the Politics of Motherhood* (Los Angeles: University of California Press, 1984): 158.

[30]See, for example, C. MacKinnon, *Feminism Unmodified: Discourses on Life and Law* (Boston: Harvard University Press, 1987): 94; Luker: 193.

[31]E. Ketting and P. van Praag, 'The Marginal Relevance of Legislation Relating to Induced Abortion', in J. Lovenduski and J. Outshorn (eds) *The New Politics of Abortion* (Beverly Hills: Sage, 1986): 155.

[32]R. Petchesky, *Abortion and Woman's Choice: The State, Sexuality and Reproductive Freedom* (Boston: Northeastern Press, 1985): 2.

[33]Luker: 182-8.

[34]See Reg Whitaker, 'Rights in a "Free and Democratic Society": Abortion,' in David Shugarman and Reg Whitaker (eds) *Federalism and the Political Community* (Peterborough: Broadview Press, 1989): 327-48.

[35]Petchesky, p. 2; B. Cossman, 'The Discourse of Abortion: Self, Morality and Gender', Paper presented at the Annual Meeting of the Canadian Political Science Association, Hamilton, Ontario, June, 1987: 18.

[36]Cossman: 13.

[37]G. Willis, 'Mario Cuomo's Trouble With Abortion', *New York Review of Books*, 28 June 1990: 13; J. Elshtain, 'Reflections on Abortion, Values and the Family', in S. Callahan and D. Callahan, eds, *Abortion: Understanding Differences* (New York: Plenum Press, 1984): 58.

[38]C. Smart, *Feminism and the Power of Law* (London: Routledge, 1989): 143.

[39]For a description of the importance of the backstreet narrative during the 1960s, see Condit: Chapter 2.

[40]R. Petchesky, 'Fetal Images: The Power of Visual Culture in the Politics of Reproduction', reprinted in M. Stanworth (ed.) *Reproductive Technologies: Gender, Motherhood and Medicine* (University of Minnesota Press, 1987).

[41]C. Weedon, *Feminist Practice and Poststructuralist Theory* (London: Basil Blackwell, 1987): 99.

[42]Petchesky, 'Fetal Images': 65.

[43]Such was recently the case in Great Britain (April 1990) where the period when women are allowed choice was reduced from 28 to 24 weeks.

[44]Petchesky, 'Fetal Images', *passim.*

[45]K. Pollit, 'Fetal Rights: A New Assault on Feminism', *The Nation*, 26 March 1990: 414.

[46]Smart: 148.

[47]Ibid.: 95.

[48]Ibid.: 148.

[49]Petchesky; *Abortion*: 340.

[50]Whitaker, 'Rights in a Free . . .': 327-32.

[51]See Smart: 148.

[52]*Globe and Mail*, 29 July 1988.

[53]Kay *et al.*: 8-10.

[54]*Globe and Mail*, 23 November 1988: A16. In the spring of 1990 Thomas Wappel contested the Liberal party leadership as a pro-life candidate and gained 6% of the convention delegates on the first ballot.

[55]*Globe and Mail*, 28 January 1989: A13.

[56]*Globe and Mail*, 15 April 1989: A9.

[57]*Globe and Mail*, 4 November 1989: A8.

[58]*Maclean's*, 31 July 1989: 17.

[59]*Globe and Mail*, 4 March 1989: A8.

[60]Rev. Kenneth Campbell, Campaign Life, *Globe and Mail*, 16 January 1989: A11.

[61]*Globe and Mail*, 4 July 1989: A1.

[62]*Globe and Mail*, 25 July 1989: A8.

[63]*Globe and Mail*, 5 July 1989: A1.

[64]Interview with OCAC organizer.

[65]M. Purcel, Campaign Life Coalition, *Globe and Mail*, 12 July 1989: A1.

[66]*Globe and Mail*, 12 July 1989: A1.

[67]*Globe and Mail*, 27 July 1989: A12.

[68]*Globe and Mail*, 26, 27 July 1989: A1. In October 1990 Tremblay was charged with assaulting his new girlfriend and in the winter of 1991 he was brought to court for striking his elderly landlady.

[69]*Globe and Mail*, 27 July 1989: A10.

[70]*Globe and Mail*, 28 July 1989: A1.

[71]*Globe and Mail*, 27 July 1989: A10.

[72]*Globe and Mail*, 4 November 1989: A8.

[73]This section holds that everyone has a right to life, liberty and security of the person.

[74]Campbell and Pal: 188, 197.

[75]*Globe and Mail*, 10 March 1898: A12.

[76]*Tremblay v Daigle* [1989] SCR 21533.

[77]*Globe and Mail*, 4 November 1989: A8.

[78]Ketting and van Praag: 158-9.

[79]*Hansard*, 6 November 1989: 5593-5.

[80]*Globe and Mail*, 4 November 1989: A1, A8.

[81]The paper contacted 288 of the 293 MPs and found that 127 were opposed to the bill and 105 were in favour. The government required 147 votes to pass the bill in Second Reading. *The Sunday Star*, 26 November 1989.

[82]*Globe and Mail*, 29 November 1989: A1.

[83]All of the quotations from the committee hearings are taken either from the committee's transcripts or from a summary of the deliberations provided by the Library of Parliament. See M. Dunsmuir, *Summary of Evidence*, Prepared for the House of Commons Legislative Committee on Bill C-43, Library of Parliament, 11 May 1990.

[84]Among these were the National Action Committee and the Canadian Advisory Council on the Status of Women. *Summary of Evidence*, Library of Parliament, 11 May 1990: 13.

[85]*Globe and Mail*, 4 November 1989: A1.

[86]*Globe and Mail*, 28 February 1990: A1.

[87]*Toronto Star*, 14 May 1990: A17.

[88]Globe and Mail, 23 May 1990: A9.

[89]Ibid.

[90]*Toronto Star*, 26 May 1990: A1.

[91]*Globe and Mail*, 25 May 1990: A3.

[92] *Globe and Mail*, 29 May 1990: A4.

[93] Housing Minister Alan Redway. *Globe and Mail*, 23 May 1990: A2.

[94] *Victoria Times Colonist*, 30 May 1990.

[95] *Globe and Mail*, 16 June 1990: D2.

[96] Ibid.

[97] *Toronto Star*, 22 May 1990: A1.

[98] *Toronto Star*, 23 August 1990: A10.

[99] *Toronto Star*, 7 December 1990: A1.

[100] *Globe and Mail*, 16 October 1990: A18.

[101] Ibid.

[102] *Toronto Star*, 7 December 1990: A5.

[103] *Toronto Star*, 19 January 1991: A3.

[104] *Toronto Star*, 15 January 1991.

[105] *Toronto Star*, 19 January 1991: A11.

[106] Provincial Court of Nova Scotia, *Her Majesty the Queen v Henry Morgentaler*, Decision: 18.

[107] *Globe and Mail*, 20 October 1990: A1.

[108] *Toronto Star*, 7 December 1991: A1.

[109] *Toronto Star*, 24 January 1991: A13.

[110] *Toronto Star*, 17 January 1991: A1.

[111] In September 1990, the government used an obscure provision in the BNA to appoint eight new Conservative Senators in a desperate and successful attempt to pass the GST through the Upper Chamber.

[112] *Toronto Star*, 17 November 1990: A8.

[113] *Toronto Star*, 22 January 1991: A9.

[114] *Toronto Star*, 31 January 1991: A6.

[115] *Toronto Star*, 1 February 1991: A1.

Chapter Four

[1] [1988], 1 S.C.R. 30; (1988) 82 N.R.1; 44 D.L.R. (4th) 385 (S.C.C.).

[2]See Marlene Gerber Fried, 'Operation Oppress You: Fighting Back for Reproductive Freedom', *Radical America* 22 (1988, published June 1989): 7-13.

[3]In March 1989, the Vancouver courts were brimming with Operation Rescue activists resisting and challenging the law and defying court orders. See, e.g., Larry Still, 'Lawyers Say Abortion Foes Won't Apologize to Court', *Vancouver Sun* 2 March 1989: A-3; Phil Needham, 'Protesters Get Terms Suspended; Obey the law or face prison, judge warns anti-abortionists', *Vancouver Sun* 6 March 1989: A-1; William Boei, 'More Abortion Foes Expected to Face Jail', *Vancouver Sun* 8 March 1989: A-3; Neal Hall, 'Abortion Foes' Records to Stick 3 Years', *Vancouver Sun* 8 March 1989: A-11.

[4]Some of the scholarly critiques take up the specific problems posed by the Charter of Rights and Freedoms; others examine the role of law more generally. See Judy Fudge, 'The Public/Private Distinction: The Possibilities of and Limits to the Use of Charter Litigation to Further Feminist Struggles', *Osgoode Hall Law Journal* 25 (1987): 485-554; Judy Fudge, 'The Privatization of the Costs of Social Reproduction: Some Recent Charter Cases', *Canadian Journal of Women and the Law* 3 (1989): 246-55; Harry Glasbeek and Michael Mandel, 'The Legalization of Politics in Advanced Capitalism: The Canadian Charter of Rights and Freedoms', *Socialist Studies* 2 (1984): 84-124, who argue (at 100) that the Charter rights are really only 'rights against laws'; Michael Mandel, *The Charter of Rights and the Legalization of Politics in Canada* (Toronto: Wall & Simpson, 1989) who argues that the deleterious effect of the Charter is compounded by the undemocratic nature of litigation and adjudication. Susan B. Boyd and Amy Bartholomew, 'Toward a Political Economy of Law' in *The New Canadian Political Economy*, Wallace Clement and Glen Williams (eds) (Kingston: McGill-Queen's University Press, 1989), 212-39, argue that the law is nonetheless an important site of struggle, as do Stephen Brickey and Elizabeth Comack, 'The Role of Law in Social Transformation: Is a Jurisprudence of Insurgency Possible?' *Canadian Journal of Law & Society* 2 (1987): 97-119; see Judy Fudge's response, 'What Do We Mean by Law and Social Transformation', *Canadian Journal of Law & Society* 5 (1990): 47-69. See also Carol Smart, *Feminism and the Power of Law* (London: Routledge, 1989).

[5]Smart, idem at 143.

[6]Idem at 141.

[7]Idem at 4.

[8]Idem at 5.

[9]Idem at 99.

[10]See e.g. Gwen Brodsky and Shelagh Day, *Canadian Charter Equality Rights for Women: One Step Forward or Two Steps Back?* (Ottawa: Canadian Advisory Council on the Status of Women, 1989); Judy Fudge, 'The Privatization of the Costs of Social Reproduction', and Judy Fudge, 'The Public/Private Distinction'.

[11]Fudge, 'The Privatization of the Costs of Social Reproduction', at 250.

[12]In the new era of Charter litigation, this is almost the forgotten issue in Canadian constitutional law. For an illustration of the continuing relevance, indeed importance, of a clear understanding of the nature of the division of powers for the abortion issue, see Ian T. Urquhart, 'Federalism, Ideology, and Charter Review: Alberta's Response to Morgentaler', *Canadian Journal of Law and Society* 4 (1989): 157-73.

[13]In *Tremblay v Daigle*, [1989] 2 S.C.R. 530 the Supreme Court of Canada held that in the absence of governing legislation, the Charter did not apply in the 'private' dispute between Mr Tremblay and Ms Daigle.

[14]In an early case involving an application by a husband to prevent his wife's therapeutic abortion, *Re Medhurst and Medhurst et al.* (1984), 38 R.F.L. 225, 9 D.L.R. (4th) 252 (Ont. H. Ct.) Reid J. held at 233 that a 'husband has a direct interest in the issue of the compliance with the law. . . . I cannot think of anyone more entitled to the court's protection of that interest than a husband.' At a subsequent rehearing, Krever J. was less convinced than Reid J. that Mr Medhurst had the requisite legal status to bring the application for an injunction: *Re Medhurst and Medhurst et al.* (1984), 45 O.R. (2d) 575 at 577.

[15]In the immediate aftermath of the *Morgentaler* decision William Vander Zalm, Social Credit Premier of British Columbia, tried unsuccessfully to deny medicare coverage for non-therapeutic abortions: see *BC Civil Liberties Association v British Columbia* (1988), 24 B.C.L.R. 189 (B.C.S.C.). It was over this issue that Kim Campbell, current federal Minister of Justice and champion of Bill C-43, then a member of the provincial Social Credit caucus in the BC legislature, split with Vander Zalm: see Stevie Cameron, 'Defiant Socred Backbencher Believes Vander Zalm out of Step', *The Globe and Mail* 10 March 1988: A-2.

[16]In June 1989, the provincial government in Nova Scotia introduced the *Medical Services Act*, S.N.S. 1989, c. 9 and regulations under it, to prevent Dr Henry Morgentaler from performing abortions in his freestanding

clinic in Halifax. See 'Morgentaler defies N.S. abortion law', *Globe and Mail* 3 November 1989: A-5; *Nova Scotia (Attorney General) v Morgentaler* (N.S.S.C. Tr. Div., November 6, 1989) where the application by the province for an interim injunction to prevent Dr Morgentaler from continuing to operate his abortion clinic was granted, and to continue in effect until his trial on charges of performing abortions in contravention of the provincial Medical Services Act. This legislation was declared *ultra vires* of the province as it was held to be criminal law by Kennedy J. in *R. v Morgentaler* [1990] N.S.J. No. 252. An appeal by the Crown was dismissed by the Nova Scotia Court of Appeal on 5 July 1991: *R. v Morgentaler* [1991] N.S.J. No. 312.

[17]See also Mandel, *The Charter of Rights*, at 292-7.

[18]In this section I rely and build upon my earlier work, Shelley A.M. Gavigan, 'Law, Gender and Ideology', in *Legal Theory Meets Legal Practice*, Anne F. Bayefsky, ed. (Edmonton: Academic Printing and Publishing, 1988), which in turn drew upon the earlier work of Alan Hunt, 'The Ideology of Law: Advances and Problems in Recent Applications of the Concept of Ideology to the Analysis of Law', *Law and Society Review* 19 (1985): 11-37, Douglas Hay, 'Property, Authority and Criminal Law', in *Albion's Fatal Tree: Crime and Society in Eighteenth Century England*, Douglas Hay *et al.* (eds) (New York: Pantheon, 1975), Roger Cotterrell, *The Sociology of Law: An Introduction* (London: Butterworths, 1984).

[19]See, e.g., Alan Hunt, 'The Ideology of Law', and Stuart Hall, 'Reformism and the Legislation of Consent', in *Permissiveness and Control: The Fate of the Sixties Legislation*, National Deviancy Conference, ed. (London: Macmillan, 1979).

[20]Socio-legal studies are centrally concerned with the influence of ideas but as Roger Cotterrell once argued, the task is to understand the origins of ideas in social practices and social conditions despite the fact that many ideas about law and society seem timeless and self-evident. For Cotterrell, ideologies are 'systems or currents of generally accepted ideas about society and its character, about rights and responsibilities, law, morality, religion and politics and numerous other matters [which] provide certainty and security, the basis of beliefs and guides for conduct': *The Sociology of Law* at 121.

Moreover, in his landmark work on eighteenth-century criminal law as an ideological system, 'Property, Authority and Criminal Law,' Douglas Hay has drawn two important lessons about the nature of ideologies: 'An ideology endures not by being wholly enforced and rigidly defined. Its effectiveness lies first in its elasticity, the fact that men are not required to make it a credo, that it seems to be a product of their own minds and their own experience. . . . The second strength of an ideology is its generality. Provided that its depths are not explored too often or by too many, it remains a reservoir of belief throughout society and flows into the gaps made by individual acts of protest' [at 55].

[21]I am indebted to Rosalind Pollack Petchesky, 'Fetal Images: The Power of Visual Culture in the Politics of Reproduction,' in *Reproductive Technologies: Gender, Motherhood and Medicine*, Michelle Stanworth, ed. (Minneapolis: University of Minnesota Press, 1987).

[22]See Kathleen McDonnell, 'Claim No Easy Victories: The Fight for Reproductive Rights', in Maureen Fitzgerald *et al.* (eds) *Still Ain't Satisfied: Canadian Feminism Today* (Toronto: The Women's Press: 1982), 33. See also Jenson, this volume.

[23]Anne Collins has documented one such effort in Ontario. A group of women law students prepared a plan for a women's health clinic, which they proposed that the Minister of Health adopt as the therapeutic abortion provisions of the Criminal Code, as he was empowered to do by the Code. They were turned down twice by the Ontario Health Minister. See Anne Collins, *The Big Evasion: Abortion, The Issue That Won't Go Away* (Toronto: Lester & Orpen Dennys, 1985) at 74.

[24]*Morgentaler et al. v The Queen* 14 C.C.C. (3d) 258, 12 D.L.R. (4th) 502, 47 O.R. (2d) 353 (Ont.H.Ct.); affirmed 16 C.C.C. (3d) 1, 14 D.L.R. (4th) 184, 48 O.R. (2d) 519 (Ont. C.A.).

[25]*Morgentaler, Smoling and Scott* (1985), 52 O.R. (2d) 353, 11 O.A.C. 81 (Ont. C.A.).

[26]Idem at 377-8.

[27]Idem at 428.

[28]*Morgentaler v the Queen* (1988) per Dickson, C.J.C. at 414.

[29]Idem per McIntyre J. at 478.

[30]Idem per Dickson C.J.C at 408-9.

[31]Idem at 402.

[32]Idem at 417.

[33]Idem per Wilson J. at 486.

[34]Idem at 491.

[35]Idem at 492.

[36]Idem at 485

[37]Idem at 489.

[38]Idem at 498.

[39]Idem at 499.

[40]Idem at 471.

[41]*Morgentaler v The Queen* (1975) 30 C.R.N.S. 209 (S.C.C.).

[42]Although these legal challenges have often been labelled 'Morgentaler challenges', it is unlikely that Dr Morgentaler alone could have mustered and maintained the campaigns without the support of the Canadian feminist movement. This is not to diminish his contribution or commitment to women's rights.

[43]See 'Foetal Personhood', this chapter.

[44]Sixteen months after the Supreme Court's decision, the Law Reform Commission of Canada issued Working Paper 58, *Crimes Against the Foetus* (Ottawa: Law Reform Commission of Canada, 1989), in which 'the foetus' (and not the more amorphous 'foetal interests' referred to in Dickson's judgement) emerged as an active and interested 'party' in criminal law reform. The Commission recommended the introduction of a new discrete offence of 'foetal injury or destruction' into Canadian criminal law. The Commission contemplated that the pregnant woman would be included in this new area of criminal liability. Lawful abortion (approved and performed by a medical practitioner, *inter alia*, to save the woman's life or to protect her against serious physical injury) would be exempted from the general crime against the foetus. See especially pp. 64-5 of the Working Paper.

[45]See, for example, Susan G. Cole, 'The Real Abortion Issue', *This Magazine*, 17 (1983): 4; Shelley Gavigan, 'Women and Abortion in Canada: What's Law Got to Do with It?' in Heather Jon Maroney and Meg Luxton (eds), *Feminism and Political Economy: Women's Work, Women's Struggles* (Toronto: Methuen, 1987); and Jenson, this volume. For a similar critique within the British context, see Victoria Greenwood and Jock Young, *Abortion in Demand* (London: Pluto, 1976).

[46]*Canada Health Act*, R.S.C. 1970, c.C-6. Section 3 provides,

> It is hereby declared that the primary objective in Canadian health care policy is to protect, promote and restore the physical and mental well-being of residents of Canada and to facilitate reasonable access to health services without financial or other barriers.

[47]The judicial characterization of abortion as a private matter predates the Charter. In *Morgentaler v The Queen* (1975) 30 C.R.N.S. 209, 257-8, Dickson J. described pro-choice advocates as 'those who would have abortion regarded in law as an act *purely personal and private*, of concern only to the woman and her physician, in which the state has no legitimate right to interfere' [emphasis added].

[48]See, e.g., *Report of the Royal Commision on the Status of Women in Canada* (Ottawa: Information Canada, 1971; Eleanor Wright Pelrine, *Abortion in Canada* (Toronto: New Star, 1971); Ontario Coalition for Abortion Clinics, 'State Power and the Struggle for Reproductiove Freedom'; Gavigan, 'Women and Abortion In Canada'.

[49]*Roe v Wade*, 410 U.S. 113 (U.S.S.C., 1973).

[50]See, e.g., *Harris v McRae*, 448 U.S. 297 (U.S.S.C., 1980). In *Maher v Roe*, 432 U.S. 464 (U.S.S.C., 1977), the US Supreme Court had upheld a Connecticut welfare regulation under which medicaid recipients received payments for childbirth-related medical expenses, but not for non-therapeutic abortions. The Court held, at 474:

> The Connecticut regulation places no obstacles—absolute or otherwise—in the pregnant woman's path to an abortion. . . . The indigency that may make it difficult—and in some cases impossible, for some women to have abortions is neither created nor in any way affected by the [law].

Webster v Reproductive Services 106 L.Ed. 2d 410, 492 U.S. 109 (U.S.S.C., 1989). Interestingly, in footnote 8 of his judgement, Rehnquist C.J. noted that there is not 'socialized medicine' in the United States and intimated that if there were, the Court would have to manoeuvre somewhat differently (or in his words, 'a different analysis might apply').

[51]See Catharine MacKinnon, 'The Male Ideology of Privacy: A Feminist Perspective on the Right to Abortion', *Radical America* 17 (1983): 23-35, and Rosalind Pollack Petchesky, *Abortion and Woman's Choice: The State, Sexuality and Reproductive Freedom* (Boston: Northeastern University Press, 1985) for American feminist analyses of this judicial erosion.

[52]Gavigan, 'Women and Abortion in Canada', 277, n. 16 and n.17.

[53]See Linda McQuaig, 'Abortion Panel Quits Over Extra-Billing Ban', *The Globe and Mail* (National), 24 February 1986: A-2. It seems that abortion and extra-billing had an intimate association: see *Report of the Committee on the Operation of the Abortion Law (the Badgley Committee)* (Ottawa: Supply & Services, 1977): 388-405. Ian Urquhart notes that in Alberta, at least one gynaecologist refused to continue to perform abortions: see his 'Federalism, Ideology and the Charter'.

[54]*Borowski v Minister of Justice of Canada and Minister of Finance of Canada* (1982), 39 N.R. 331 (S.C.C.), 343.

[55]*Borowski v Attorney General of Canada* (1984), 8 C.C.C. (3d) 392, 4 D.L.R. (4th) 112, [1984] 1 W.W.R. 15 (Sask. Q.B.).

[56](1987), 39 D.L.R. (4th) 731 (Sask. C.A.).

[57]*Borowski v Canada (Attorney General)*, [1989] 1 S.C.R. 342 (S.C.C.).

[58]The most developed scholarly position of this view in the Canadian context is Edward W. Keyserlingk, 'The Unborn Child's Right to Prenatal Care, Parts I & II', *Health Law in Canada* 3 (1983): 10-21, 30-41. In the context of litigation, see the Factums in *Borowski v Canada (Attorney General)* filed in the Supreme Court of Canada on behalf of the Appellant, Joseph Borowski (Morris C. Shumiatcher Q.C. and Bradley Hunter, Counsel), Factum of the Intervenor, The Interfaith Coalition on the Rights and Well-Being of Women and Children (Claude R. Thompson Q.C. and Robert W. Stately, Counsel), and Factum of the Intervenor, REAL Women of Canada (Angela Costigan, Counsel).

[59]See Keyserlingk: 11; Borowski Factum (1988); Morris C.Shumiatcher, 'I Set Before You Life and Death (Abortion, Borowski and the Constitution)', *University of Western Ontario Law Review* 24 (Part 2) (1986-87): 1-24.

[60]The significant cases in the area of abortion law are:

Dehler v Ottawa Civic Hospital (1979) 25 O.R.(2d) 748 (Ont.H.Ct.), per Robins J. at p. 757: 'What then is the legal position of the unborn child? Is it regarded in the eyes of the law as a person in the full legal sense? . . . While there can be no doubt that the law has long recognized foetal life and has accorded the foetus various rights, those rights have always been held contingent upon a legal personality being acquired by the foetus upon its subsequent birth alive . . .'

Medhurst v Medhurst (1984) 46 O.R.(2d)263 (Ont.H. Ct.), per Reid J. at 267: 'an unborn child is not a person.'

Borowski v Attorney-General for Canada (1987) 39 D.L.R.(4th) (Sask. C.A.), per Gerwing J.A. at 754: I am of the view that, the above analysis of the Charter, including its language and the historical aspect of the concepts of the right allegedly enshrined, suggests that it was not intended as the purpose of either s.7 or s.15 of the Charter to protect the rights of a foetus to life.'

Daigle v Tremblay [1989] 2 S.C.R. 530 (S.C.C.).

[61]This is clearly the view held in Canada by Borowski and Shumiatcher. It would appear that the Law Reform Commission of Canada in its Working Paper 58, *Crimes Against the Foetus* (Ottawa: Supply & Services, 1989) is inclined to that view in the criminal law context. See also Clarke D. Forsythe, 'Homicide of the Unborn Child: The Born Alive Rule and Other Legal Anachronisms', *Valparaiso Law Review* 21 (1987): 563-629.

[62]*Edwards v Attorney-General for Canada*, [1930] A.C. 124 (P.C.).

[63]See, e.g., Rosalind P. Petchesky, 'Fetal Images'; Barbara Katz Rothman, *Recreating Motherhood: Ideology and Technology in a Patriarchal Society* (New York: W.W. Norton & Co., 1989); Janet Gallagher, 'Prenatal Invasions and Interventions: What's Wrong With Fetal Rights', *Harvard Women's Law Journal* 10 (1987): 9-58; Janet Gallagher, 'Fetus as Patient', in Sherrill Cohen and Nadine Taub (eds) *Reproductive Laws for the 1990s* (Clifton, N.J.: Humana Press, 1989), 185-235; Sanda Rogers, 'Fetal Rights and Maternal Rights: Is There a Conflict?' *Canadian Journal of Women and the Law* 1 (1986): 456-69; Christine Overall, ' "Pluck a Fetus From Its Womb": A Critique of Current Attitudes Toward the Embryo/Fetus', *University of Western Ontario Law Review* 24 (1986-87): 1-14.

[64]As Catherine Tolton suggested, drawing upon Margaret Atwood's *The Handmaid's Tale* (Toronto: McClelland & Stewart, 1986), in her article, 'Medicolegal Implications of Constitutional Status for the Unborn: "Ambulatory Chalices" or "Priorities and Aspirations" ', *University of Toronto Faculty of Law Review* 47 (1988): 1-57.

[65]Rothman, *Recreating Motherhood.*

[66]John A. Robertson, 'Procreative Liberty and the Control of Contraception, Pregnancy and Childbirth,' *Virginia Law Review* 69 (1983): 405-64.

[67]Keyserlingk, 'The Right of the Unborn Child to Prenatal Care'.

[68]Idem at 12.

[69]Petchesky, 'Fetal Images:' 271.

[70]See, e.g., Gallagher, 'Prenatal Invasions', and Rogers, 'Fetal Rights and Maternal Rights'.

[71]See, e.g., Kristen Luker, *Abortion and the Politics of Motherhood* (Berkeley: University of California Press, 1984). As recently as 1927 a judge in a Toronto abortion case said in his charge to the jury in the trial involving a young man and a doctor charged with the abortion-induced death of the young man's fiancée:

It is true that sexual intercourse between unmarried people is not a crime according to the *Criminal Code.* But gentlemen, you may think it, as in my opinion it is, a very great sin, and it is a sin which is particularly frowned upon by women, they realising very well the limitations of their sex, any of you may agree with this, that no one is more hard on a woman who is found guilty of immoral conduct than her own sisters. So that, gentlemen, although it is not a crime—when I say it is not a crime I mean it is not punishable by the Criminal Code—it is a sin. (*R. v Brooks* (1927-28) 61 O.L.R. 147 (Ont. C.A.)

[72]See Keyserlingk, 'The Right of the Unborn Child to Prenatal Care'.

[73]Ruddick and Wilcox cited by Overall, '"Pluck a Fetus From Its Womb"', at 14.

[74]See, e.g., Rothman, *Recreating Motherhood.*

[75]'The Right of the Unborn Child to Prenatal Care, Part I': 18.

[76]*Sullivan and Lemay v The Queen* (21 March 1991, Supreme Court of Canada).

[77][1989] 2 S.C.R. 530 (S.C.C.).

[78](1990), 63 D.L.R. (4th) 515 (Ont. H. Ct.).

[79]See Stuart Hall, 'Reformism and the Legislation of Consent', in *Permissiveness and Control: The Fate of the Sixties Legislation* National Deviancy Conference, ed. (London: Macmillan, 1979): 1-43.

[80]Molly McNulty, 'Pregnancy Police: The Health Policy and Implications of Punishing Pregnant Women for Harm to Their Fetuses', *Review of Law and Social Change* 19 (1987-88): 277-300.

[81]*Fetal Images*: 264.

[82]See especially Veronika Kolder, Janet Gallagher, and Michael T. Parsons, 'Court-Ordered Obstetrical Interventions', *New England Journal of Medicine* 313 (1987): 1192-6. This article is discussed as well in Gallagher, 'Fetus as Patient'.

[83]See also Susan Alter Tateishi, 'Apprehending the Fetus *en ventre sa mère*: A Study in Judicial Sleight of Hand', *Saskatchewan Law Review* 53 (1989): 113-41.

[84]More problematic is the question of whether a child can be apprehended *before* birth. In *Re Children's Aid Society of District of Kenora* (1981), 134 D.L.R. (4th) 249 (Ont. Prov. Ct., Fam. Div.), a baby apparently suffering from fetal alcohol syndrome was apprehended four days after birth. The mother's history with the Children's Aid Society (two

other children suffered fetal alcohol syndrome at birth and all four of her children were Crown wards), her chronic alcoholism, perpetual homelessness, relationship with her common law husband ('one marked by physical violence'), and refusal to follow her doctor's instructions were relied upon by the provincial court judge to support his conclusion that 'the child was a child in need of *protection prior to birth, at birth and on May 24, 1981, being the time of apprehension, [sic] . . . by reason of the physical abuse of the child by the mother in her excessive* consumption of alcohol during pregnancy, which conduct endangered the health of J.L., by her neglecting or refusing to obtain proper remedial care or treatment for the child's health, when it was recommended by a legal qualified practitioner.'

This case was followed with knee-jerk reflex months later by Madam Justice Proudfoot in British Columbia in *Superintendent of Family and Child Service v M.(B.) and O.(D.)*, [1982] 4 W.W.R. 273, a case involving a woman on a prescribed methadone treatment program whose baby was born addicted. In 1987 a Belleville, Ontario woman's erratic behaviour, homelessness, and refusal to accept medical advice resulted in a finding that both her unborn child was in need of protection and further that she was caught by the provisions of the Mental Health Act and made subject to an order for a psychiatric assessment. Her pregnancy, her medical condition requiring medical treatment, ceased to be *hers*. The pregnancy became the fetus'. *She*, and not the fetus, was homeless. *She*, and not the fetus, was behaving erratically. *She*, and not the fetus, apparently required psychiatric examination. But the fetus, and not the woman, was of central concern to the CAS authorities: *Re Children's Aid Society of City of Belleville, Hastings County and T* (1987) 59 O.R. (2d) 204 (Ont. Prov. Ct., Fam. Div.).

In *Re 'Baby R'* (1988) 15 R.F.L. (3d) 228 , a woman's initial refusal to consent to a cesarean section delivery resulted in an order of wardship, which order was subsequently struck down by Mr Justice MacDonell of the British Columbia Supreme Court:

> I conclude that the powers of the Superintendent to apprehend are restricted to living children that have been delivered. Were it otherwise, then the state would able to confine a mother to await her delivery of the child being apprehended. . . . Such powers to interfere with the rights of women, if granted and if lawful must be done by specific legislation and anything less will not do.

While Mr Justice MacDonell's judgement was more an invitation to the legislature to enact enabling legislation than a ringing endorsement of women's right to equality, integrity and autonomy, it did represent a break in what had been an inexorable escalation of coercion in the lower courts. *Baby R* may have been an important break, for still more recently in *Re A* (1990) 28 R.F.L. (3d) 288 (Ont. Unif. Fam. Ct), Judge Steinberg of the Unified Family Court in London, Ontario, declined to follow *Belleville* and held that the Court did not have jurisdiction to order the apprehension of a 'child' prior to birth.

[85]John A. Robertson, 'Procreative Liberty,' at 438.

[86]See, especially, D. Horan, E. Grant and P. Cunningham (eds) *Abortion and the Constitution: Reversing Roe v Wade Through the Courts* (Georgetown: Georgetown University Press, 1987).

[87]Janet Gallagher, 'Fetus as Patient', at 195.

[88]See Donna Greschner's excellent analysis of the Supreme Court's decision in Chantal Daigle's case, 'Abortion and Democracy for Women: A Critique of *Tremblay v Daigle*', *McGill Law Journal* 35 (1990): 633-69.

[89]See Deborah Wilson, 'REAL Women assailed on letter attacking homosexuals, feminists', *The Globe and Mail*, 28 April 1990: A1-A2.

[90]Shelley A.M. Gavigan, 'Women, Law and Patriarchal Relations: Perspectives within the Sociology of Law', in Neil Boyd, *The Social Dimensions of Law* (Scarborough: Prentice-Hall, 1986): 101-24.

[91]*Report of the Committee on the Operation of the Abortion Law (The Badgley Report)* (Ottawa: Supply & Services, 1977), 238; 245.

[92]*Whalley v Whalley* (1981), 122 D.L.R. (3d) 717 (B.C.S.C.); *Medhurst v Medhurst* (1984), 38 R.F.L. 225; 9 D.L.R. (4th) 252 (Ont. H. Ct.).

[93]See e.g. *Paton v B.P.A.S.*, [1979] 1 Q.B. 276; S.L. Caldwell, 'Abortion: The Father's Lack of Standing,' *New Zealand Law Journal* May (1988): 165-9.

[94][1978] 2 All E.R. 987; 3 W.L.R. (Q.B.). See also *C. v S.* [1987] 1 All E.R. 1230 (Q.B.D. and C.A.); leave to appeal to House of Lords refused. This case also involved an application for an injunction made by a single man to prevent his girlfriend from proceeding with a legal abortion late in pregnancy. The man was unsuccessful, although the case was decided on other grounds.

[95]*Whalley v Whalley et al.* (1981), 122 D.L.R. (3d) 717 (B.C. Co.Ct.).

[96]*Medhurst v Medhurst et al.* (1984), 9 D.L.R. (4th) 252 (Ont. H. Ct.). For a discussion of this case see Kathleen McDonnell, *Not An Easy Choice*

(Toronto: The Women's Press, 1984): 63-4.

[97]Carol Smart, 'Power and the Politics of Child Custody', in Carol Smart and Selma Sevenhuijsen (eds) *Child Custody and the Politics of Gender* (London: Routledge, 1989).

[98]In *Medhurst*, the husband had been successful in his ex parte application to the Court, having obtained an order restraining the defendants (the hospital, doctor, and his wife) until further order of the Court from 'taking the life of the infant plaintiff, either by performing or undergoing an abortion or cesarean operation or otherwise and from committing a trespass to the person of the infant plaintiff by assault or battery or otherwise' (quoted at 226). Mrs Medhurst had to move to rescind the ex parte order. In the course of her argument on behalf of the husband, Angela Costigan advised the court that since 1973, the Ontario High Court had granted at least four orders of the type initially granted to Mr Medhurst: three were issued in Ottawa, and one in Thunder Bay. Costigan further informed the court 'that in no case was any application made to set aside any of them' (at p. 227 R.F.L.). One of these unreported cases must have been the case of Louise X, discussed in Simon Fodden, *Cases and Materials in Canadian Family Law* (Toronto: Butterworths, 1977), 6-28. It appears that in Louise X's case, the husband and wife came to an agreement after the initial restraining order was issued, and it was rescinded.

[99]Notwithstanding, in the absence of a law to enforce, the dearth of legal authority giving rise to their claims: *Mock v Brandanburg* (1988), 61 Alta. L.R. 235 (Alta. Q.B.); *Tremblay v Daigle*, [1989] 2 S.C.R. 530; *Murphy v Dodd* (1990), 63 D.L.R. (4th) 515 (Ont. H. Ct.). See Sheilah L. Martin, 'Using the Courts to Stop Abortion by Injunction: *Mock v Brandanburg*', *Canadian Journal of Women and the Law* 3 (1989-1990): 69-583. In the British context, see Ian Kennedy, 'A Husband, A Wife, and an Abortion,' in his *Treat Me Right: Essays in Medical Law and Ethics* (Oxford: Oxford University Press, 1988).

[100]As in *Murphy v Dodd*, *Tremblay v Daigle.*

[101]*Tremblay v Daigle.*

[102]*Diamond v Hirsch* (unreported decision of Hirschfield J, Man. Q.B., July 6, 1989).

[103]Chantal Daigle was not cowed by the process and explained her decision to proceed with her abortion almost on the eve of the Supreme Court's unprecedented summer hearing of her appeal:

> Every time the courts said no, I felt that they were sticking their noses into what was only my business, and that made me feel more stubborn about it.
>
> Of course I wanted the courts to rule in my favour, so that I wouldn't have to break the law. But between having a baby I didn't think was right to have and disobeying a ruling I believed was so unfair, my choice was clear.

Quoted in Alberto Manguel, 'Chantal Daigle: Chatelaine's Newsmaker of the Year', *Chatelaine* 63 (January 1990): 38-41, 113-14, at 114. In *Mock v Brandanburg*, *supra*, note 45 and *Duel v Boss*, cited in Maria Walters, 'Who Decides? The Next Abortion Issue: A Discussion of Fathers' Rights', *West Virginia Law Review* 9 (1988): 164-91, the women had already had the abortions by the time the matter was back before the court.

[104]*C v S*; referred to by Marge Berer, 'Whatever Happened to "A Woman's Right to Choose" ', *Feminist Review* 29 (1988): 24-37, 28.

[105]See 'Abortion on Trial', *Maclean's* 31 July 1989: 14-21.

[106]Of these, Chantal Daigle is the most prominent example in Canada. See also Maria Walters, 'Who Decides?'

[107]*Re Medhurst and Medhurst et al*: (1984) 45 O.R. (2d) 575 (Ont.H. Ct.). Krever J. was less convinced than his brother Reid J. that Mr Medhurst had the requisite legal status to bring the application (at 577).

[108]Idem at 233.

[109]See also *Borowski v Canada (Attorney General)* (1987), 33 C.C.C. (3d) 402 (Sask. C.A.); affirmed on other grounds [1989] 1 S.C.R. 342.

[110]*Anderson v Anderson* (unreported decision of Minn. Co. Ct., File No. 8821320, 7 July 1988) per Barnes J. at 4-5 (on file with the author).

[111]*Medhurst v Medhurst*, *supra*, note 41.

[112]*John Doe v Jane Smith* (June 15, 1988, U.S.S.C. No. A-954)

[113]Idem at 2.

[114]*Planned Parenthood of Central Missouri v Danforth* 428 U.S. 52, 49 L. Ed. 2d 788 (U.S.S.C., 1976).

[115]*Doe v Smith*, *supra*, note 61 at 2.

[116]Idem.

[117]Idem at 3.

[118](1990), 63 D.L.R. (4th) 515 (Ont. H. Ct.).

[119]Idem at 518.

[120]Idem at 20-1.

[121]Quoted at 524.

[122]At 525. Notwithstanding the fraud which lay at the heart of the ex parte application, Mr Justice Gray declined to make any order as to costs.

[123][1990] 2 S.C.R. 530 at 572.

[124]Cf. Gallup Poll results reported in 1989: 57% of Canadians are reported to believe that a woman should be allowed to have an abortion even if the man involved in the pregnancy disagrees. See 'Abortion Without Male Consent Supported by 57%, Poll Says, *Toronto Star* 24 August 1989: A-1, A-15.

[125]*Recreating Motherhood.*

[126]Cf. Arthur B. Shostak and Gary McLouth, with Lynn Seng, *Men and Abortion: Lessons, Losses and Love* (New York: Praeger, 1984).

[127]Mandel, *The Charter of Rights*, at 293.

[128]See, e.g., Mandel, *The Legalization of Politics*; Fudge, 'The Public/Private Distinction'; Sheilah L. Martin, *Women's Reproductive Health, The Canadian Charter of Rights and Freedoms and the Canada Health Act* (Background Paper Prepared for the Canadian Advisory Council on the Status of Women) (Ottawa: CACSW, 1989), at 28-30.

[129]The history of this bill is reviewed in Gavigan, 'Women and Abortion in Canada' at 263.

[130]Idem, at 263.

[131]*Reference Re: Freedom of Informed Choice (Abortions) Act (1985)* (1985), 44 Sask. R. 104 (Sask.C.A.).

[132]As quoted by John Cruikshank, 'BC Won't Pay Abortion Costs, Premier Pledges', *The Globe and Mail* 8 February 1988: A-1.

[133]*BC Civil Liberties Association v. British Columbia* (1988), 24 B.C.L.R. 189 (B.C.S.C.).

[134]See Urquhart, 'Federalism, Ideology, and Charter Review' at 161.

[135]Robert Walker, 'Deinsured Services Could Cost Alta. Patients Double,' *The Medical Post* 18 August 1987 at 2.

[136]Urquhart, 'Federalism, Ideology, and Charter Review' at 161.

[137]Idem at 163.

[138]As quoted by Stevenson J. in *Morgentaler v New Brunswick (Attorney General) et al*, (1990) 98 N.B.R. (2d) & 248 A.P.R. 45 (N.B.Q.B.) at 48.

[139]Idem at 53.

[140]The Honourable David Nantes, quoted by Freeman J.A. in *R. v Morgentaler* [1991] N.S.J. No. 312 at 36.

[141]*Medical Services Act*, S.N.S. 1989, c. 9, s. 2.

[142]N.S. Regulation 152/89.

[143]See Kevin Cox, 'Nova Scotia Court Tells Morgentaler to Stop Abortions', *The Globe and Mail* 7 November 1989: A-1.

[144]*R. v Morgentaler* [1990] N.S.J. No. 252.

[145]*R. v Morgentaler* [1991] N.S.J. No. 312 at 4-5.

[146]Per Freeman J.A. at 13.

[147]Idem at 16.

[148]Idem at 17-18.

[149]Idem at 31.

[150]Idem at 51.

[151]This phrase is drawn from Kathleen McDonnell's article of the same name, 'Claim No Easy Victories'.

[152]Ann Oakley, 'Wisewoman and Medicine Man', in Juliet Mitchell and Ann Oakley (eds), *The Rights and Wrongs of Woman* (Middlesex: Penguin, 1976); Greenwood and Young, *Abortion in Demand*; Pauline Bart, 'Seizing the Means of Reproduction: An Illegal Feminist Abortion Collective—How and Why it Worked', in *Women, Health and Reproduction*, Helen Roberts, ed. (London: Routledge & Kegan Paul, 1981); Federation of Feminist Women's Health Centers, *A New View of a Woman's Body* (New York: Simon & Shuster, 1981); Cole, 'The Real Abortion Issue': 4; K. Kaufman, 'Abortion, a Woman's Matter: An Explanation of Who Controls Abortion and How and Why They Do It',

in Rita Arditti, Renata Duelli and Shelley Minden (eds) *Test-Tube Women* (London: Routledge & Kegan Paul, 1984).

[153]See Marnie de Varent, 'Feminism and Abortion: A Few Hidden Grounds', in Ian Gentles and Eugene Fairweather (eds), *The Right to Birth: Some Christian Views on Abortion* (Toronto: Anglican Book Centre, 1976).

[154]Petchesky, 'Fetal Images': 263.

Bibliography

Adamson, Nancy, Linda Briskin, and Margaret Macphail. *Feminist Organizing for Change: The Contemporary Women's Movement in Canada.* Toronto: Oxford, 1988.

Alderdice, Kate (ed). *Women's Liberation in Canada.* Toronto: Pathfinder, 1975.

Appollo, Kevin M. 'The Biological Father's Right to Require a Pregnant Woman to Undergo Medical Treatment Necessary to Sustain Fetal Life'. *Dickinson Law Review* (1989) 94.

Arnup, Katherine. 'Mothers Just Like Others: Lesbians, Divorce, and Child Custody in Canada'. *Canadian Journal of Woman and the Law* (1989) 3.

Balisy, S.S. 'Maternal Substance Abuse: The Need to Provide Legal Protection for the Fetus'. *California Law Review* (1987) 60.

Backhouse, Constance B. 'Involuntary Motherhood: Abortion, Birth Control and the Law in Nineteenth Century Canada'. *Windsor Yearbook Access to Justice* (1983) 3.

Bala Krishan, T.R., *et al.* 'Contraceptive Use in Canada, 1984'. *Family Planning Perspectives* (1985) 17.

Barach, Elaine Hoffman, *et al.* (eds). *Embryos, Ethics and Women's Rights: Exploring the New Reproductive Technologies.* New York: Harrington Park Press, 1988.

Baron, Charles H. ' "If You Prick Us, Do We Not Bleed?": Of Shylock, Fetuses and the Concept of Person in the Law'. *Law, Medicine and Health Care* (1983) 52.

Bart, Pauline. 'Seizing the Means of Reproduction: An Illegal Feminist Abortion Collective—How and Why it Worked' in Helen Roberts (ed.) *Women, Health and Reproduction.* London: Routledge & Kegan Paul, 1981.

Berer, Marge. 'Whatever Happened to A Woman's Rights to Choose?' *Feminist Review* (1988) 29.

Bigge, Ellen. 'The Fetal Rights Controversy: A Resurfacing of Sex Discrimination in the Guise of Fetal Protection'. *UMKC Law Review* (1989) 57.

Bill C-43, An Act Respecting Abortion, 2d Sess., 38 Parl., 1989.

Boyd, M. and D. Gillieson. 'Canadian Attitudes on Abortion: Results of a Gallup Poll'. *Canadian Population Studies* (1975) 2.

Boyd, Susan. 'Child Custody, Ideologies and Employment'. *Canadian Journal of Women and the Law* (1989) 3.

_______. 'Child Custody Law and the Invisibility of Women's Work'. *Queen's Quarterly* (1989) 96.

_______ and Elizabeth Sheehy. 'Canadian Feminist Perspectives on the Law' *Journal of Law and Society* (1986) 13.

_______ and Amy Bartholomew. 'Toward a New Political Economy of Law' in Wallace Clement and Glen Williams (eds) *The New Political Economy*. Kingston: McGill-Queens University Press, 1989.

Brickley, Stephen and Elizabeth Comack. 'The Role of Law in Social Transformation: Is a Jurisprudence of Insurgency Possible?' *Canadian Journal of Law and Society* (1987) 2.

Brodsky, Gwen and Shelagh Day. *Canadian Charter Equality Rights for Women*. Ottawa: Canadian Advisory Council on the Status of Women, 1989.

Brookes, Barbara. *Abortion in England 1900-1967*. London: Croom Helm, 1988.

_______. 'Women and Reproduction c. 1860-1919' in Jane Lewis (ed.) *Labour and Love: Women's Experience of Home and Family*. Oxford: Basil Blackwell, 1986.

Burt, Sandra. 'Women's Issues and the Women's Movement in Canada Since 1970' in *The Politics of Gender, Ethnicity and Language in Canada*, Vol. 34 of the Report of the Royal Commission on the Economic Union and Development Prospects for Canada, Alan Cairns and Cynthia Williams (eds). Toronto: University of Toronto, 1985.

Burton, C.R. 'Fetal Drug or Alcohol Addiction Syndrome: A Case of Prenatal Child Abuse?' *Willamette Law Review* (1989) 25.

Caldwell, J.L. 'Abortion: The Father's Lack of Standing'. *New Zealand Law Journal* (1988) 165.

Callahan, S. and D. Callahan (eds). *Abortion: Understanding Differences*. New York: Plenum Press, 1984.

Campbell, Robert and Leslie Pal. *The Real Worlds of Canadian Politics*. Peterborough: Broadview Press, 1989.

Canada. Law Reform Commission of Canada. *Crimes Against the Fetus, Working Paper 58*. Ottawa: Supply and Services, 1989.

_______. *Report of the Committee to Investigate the Abortion Law (The Badgley Report)*. Ottawa: Supply and Services, 1977.

_______. *Report of the Royal Commission on the Status of Women in Canada*. Ottawa: Information Canada, 1970.

_______, Statistics Canada. *Therapeutic Abortions, 1986*. Ottawa: Supply and Services Canada, December 1988.

_______, Statistics Canada. *Therapeutic Abortions, 1987*. Ottawa: Supply and Services Canada, 1989.

Cayenne: A Socialist Feminist Bulletin (1986) 2.

Cheung, K.W. *Essays on Abortion*. Windsor: University of Windsor, 1977.

Chunn, Dorothy E. 'Rehabilitating Deviant Families through Family Courts: The Birth of "Socialized" Justice in Ontario, 1920-1940'. *International Journal of the Sociology of Law* (1988) 16.

Cole, Susan. 'The Real Abortion Issue'. *This Magazine* (1983) 17.

Collins, Ann. *The Big Evasion: Abortion, The Issue That Won't Go Away*. Toronto: Lester and Orpen Dennys, 1985.

Collins, Larry. 'The Politics of Abortion'. *Atlantis* (1982) 7.

Condit, Celeste Michelle. *Decoding Abortion Rhetoric: Communicating Social Change*. Urbana: University of Illinois, 1990.

Cook, R.J. 'Anti-Projection Drugs: Medical and Legal Issues'. *Family Planning Perspectives* (1989) 21.

Cossman, Brenda. 'The Precarious Unity of Feminist Theory and Practice: The Praxis of Abortion'. *University of Toronto Faculty of Law Review* (1986) 44.

Cuneo, Michael W. *Catholics Against the Church: Anti-Abortion Protest in Toronto, 1969-1985*. Toronto: University of Toronto Press, 1989.

de Valk, Alphonse. *Morality and the Law*. Dorval, Que.: Palm, 1974.

de Varent, Marnie. 'Feminism and Abortion: A Few Hidden Grounds' in Ian Gentles and Eugene Fairweather (eds) *The Right to Birth: Some*

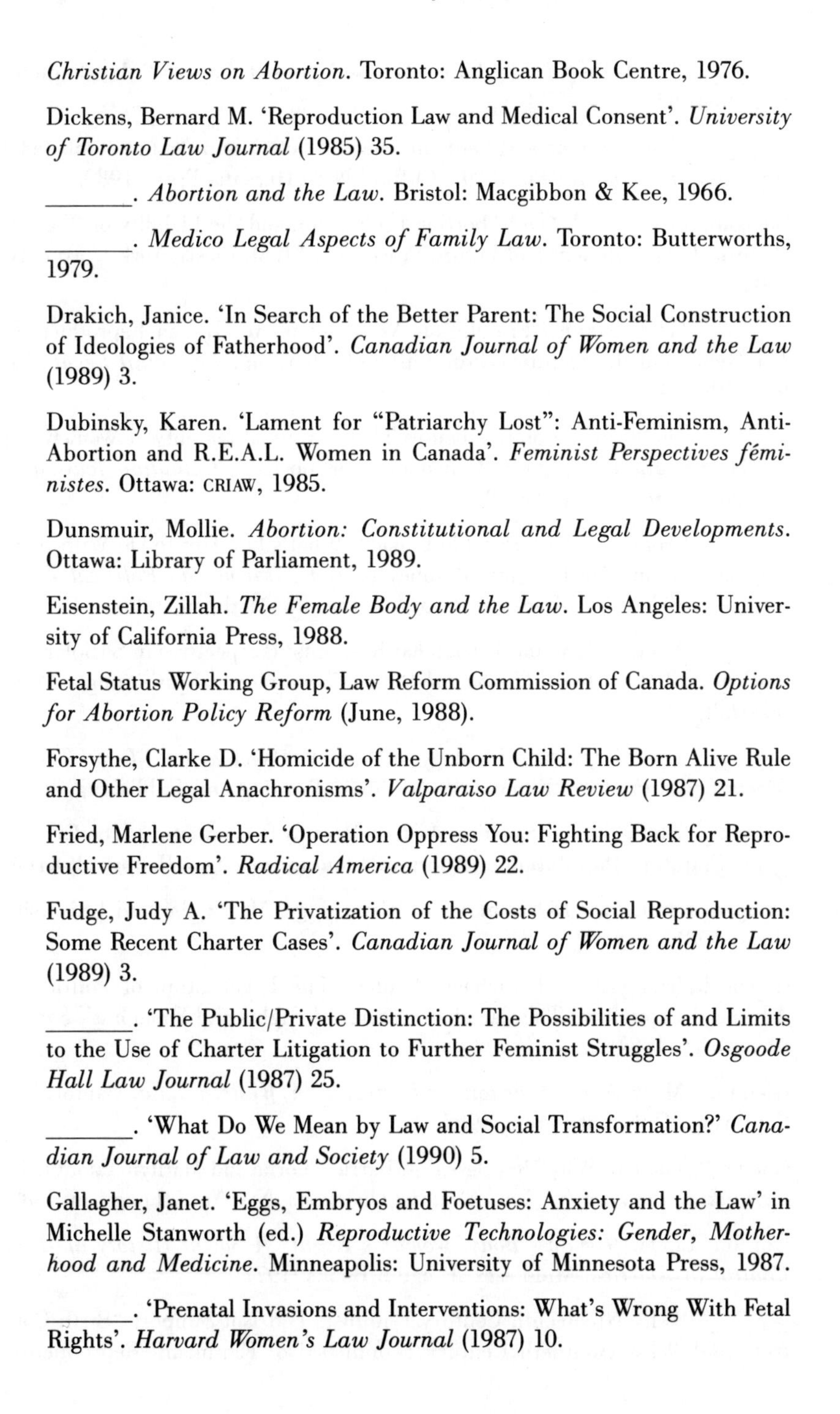

Christian Views on Abortion. Toronto: Anglican Book Centre, 1976.

Dickens, Bernard M. 'Reproduction Law and Medical Consent'. *University of Toronto Law Journal* (1985) 35.

_______. *Abortion and the Law*. Bristol: Macgibbon & Kee, 1966.

_______. *Medico Legal Aspects of Family Law*. Toronto: Butterworths, 1979.

Drakich, Janice. 'In Search of the Better Parent: The Social Construction of Ideologies of Fatherhood'. *Canadian Journal of Women and the Law* (1989) 3.

Dubinsky, Karen. 'Lament for "Patriarchy Lost": Anti-Feminism, Anti-Abortion and R.E.A.L. Women in Canada'. *Feminist Perspectives féministes*. Ottawa: CRIAW, 1985.

Dunsmuir, Mollie. *Abortion: Constitutional and Legal Developments*. Ottawa: Library of Parliament, 1989.

Eisenstein, Zillah. *The Female Body and the Law*. Los Angeles: University of California Press, 1988.

Fetal Status Working Group, Law Reform Commission of Canada. *Options for Abortion Policy Reform* (June, 1988).

Forsythe, Clarke D. 'Homicide of the Unborn Child: The Born Alive Rule and Other Legal Anachronisms'. *Valparaiso Law Review* (1987) 21.

Fried, Marlene Gerber. 'Operation Oppress You: Fighting Back for Reproductive Freedom'. *Radical America* (1989) 22.

Fudge, Judy A. 'The Privatization of the Costs of Social Reproduction: Some Recent Charter Cases'. *Canadian Journal of Women and the Law* (1989) 3.

_______. 'The Public/Private Distinction: The Possibilities of and Limits to the Use of Charter Litigation to Further Feminist Struggles'. *Osgoode Hall Law Journal* (1987) 25.

_______. 'What Do We Mean by Law and Social Transformation?' *Canadian Journal of Law and Society* (1990) 5.

Gallagher, Janet. 'Eggs, Embryos and Foetuses: Anxiety and the Law' in Michelle Stanworth (ed.) *Reproductive Technologies: Gender, Motherhood and Medicine*. Minneapolis: University of Minnesota Press, 1987.

_______. 'Prenatal Invasions and Interventions: What's Wrong With Fetal Rights'. *Harvard Women's Law Journal* (1987) 10.

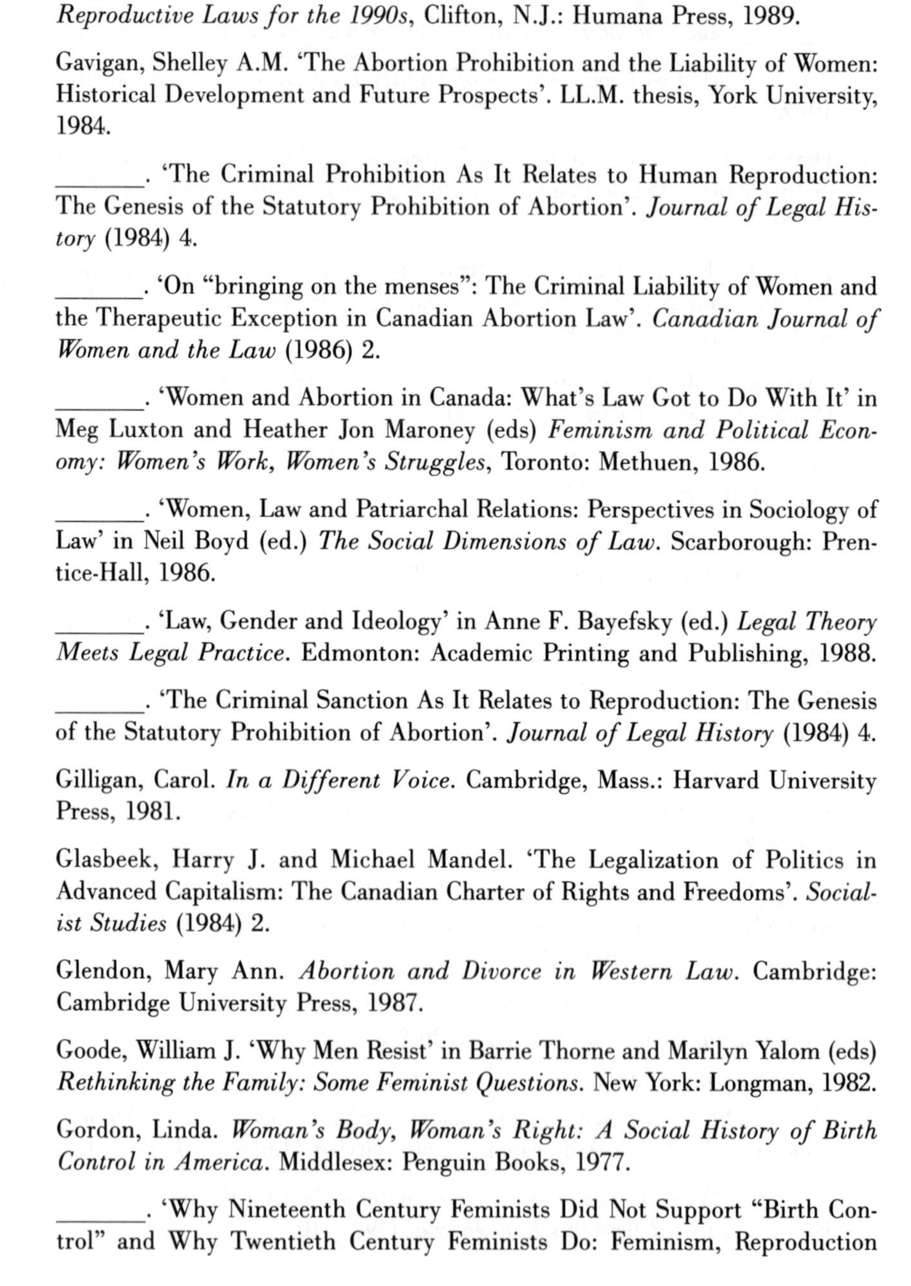

_______. 'The Fetus and the Law—Whose Life is it Anyway?' *Ms* (September, 1984) 62.

_______. 'The Fetus as a Patient' in Sherrill Cohen and Nadine Taub (eds) *Reproductive Laws for the 1990s*, Clifton, N.J.: Humana Press, 1989.

Gavigan, Shelley A.M. 'The Abortion Prohibition and the Liability of Women: Historical Development and Future Prospects'. LL.M. thesis, York University, 1984.

_______. 'The Criminal Prohibition As It Relates to Human Reproduction: The Genesis of the Statutory Prohibition of Abortion'. *Journal of Legal History* (1984) 4.

_______. 'On "bringing on the menses": The Criminal Liability of Women and the Therapeutic Exception in Canadian Abortion Law'. *Canadian Journal of Women and the Law* (1986) 2.

_______. 'Women and Abortion in Canada: What's Law Got to Do With It' in Meg Luxton and Heather Jon Maroney (eds) *Feminism and Political Economy: Women's Work, Women's Struggles*, Toronto: Methuen, 1986.

_______. 'Women, Law and Patriarchal Relations: Perspectives in Sociology of Law' in Neil Boyd (ed.) *The Social Dimensions of Law*. Scarborough: Prentice-Hall, 1986.

_______. 'Law, Gender and Ideology' in Anne F. Bayefsky (ed.) *Legal Theory Meets Legal Practice*. Edmonton: Academic Printing and Publishing, 1988.

_______. 'The Criminal Sanction As It Relates to Reproduction: The Genesis of the Statutory Prohibition of Abortion'. *Journal of Legal History* (1984) 4.

Gilligan, Carol. *In a Different Voice*. Cambridge, Mass.: Harvard University Press, 1981.

Glasbeek, Harry J. and Michael Mandel. 'The Legalization of Politics in Advanced Capitalism: The Canadian Charter of Rights and Freedoms'. *Socialist Studies* (1984) 2.

Glendon, Mary Ann. *Abortion and Divorce in Western Law*. Cambridge: Cambridge University Press, 1987.

Goode, William J. 'Why Men Resist' in Barrie Thorne and Marilyn Yalom (eds) *Rethinking the Family: Some Feminist Questions*. New York: Longman, 1982.

Gordon, Linda. *Woman's Body, Woman's Right: A Social History of Birth Control in America*. Middlesex: Penguin Books, 1977.

_______. 'Why Nineteenth Century Feminists Did Not Support "Birth Control" and Why Twentieth Century Feminists Do: Feminism, Reproduction and the Family' in Barrie Thorne and Marilyn Yalom (eds) *Rethinking the Family: Some Feminist Questions*. New York: Longman, 1982.

Gotell, Lise. 'Women, the State and Abortion Policy in Canada.' BA honours essay, Carleton University, 1985.

_______. ' "A Helluva Lot to Lose but Not a Helluva Lot to Win": Canadian Women and Equality Rights, 1980-1981'. MA research paper, York University, 1986.

Grant, Isabel. 'Forced Obstetrical Interventions: A Charter Analysis'. *University of Toronto Law Journal* (1989) 39.

Greenwood, Karen and Lucy King. 'Contraception and Abortion' in Cambridge Women Studies Group (eds.) *Women and Society*. London: Virago, 1980.

Greenwood, Victoria, and Jock Young. *Abortion in Demand*. London: Pluto, 1976.

Greschner, Donna. 'Abortion and Democracy for Women: A Critique of *Tremblay v Daigle*'. *McGill Law Journal* (1990) 35.

Harris, George W. 'Fathers and Fetuses'. *Ethics* (1986) 96.

Hartmann, Betsy. *Reproductive Rights and Wrongs: The Global Politics of Population Control and Contraceptive Choice*. New York: Harper & Row, 1987.

Hay, Douglas. 'Property, Authority and Criminal Law' in Douglas Hay *et al.* (eds) *Albion's Fatal Tree: Crime and Society in Eighteenth Century England*. London: Pantheon, 1975.

Hébert, Monique. 'Abortion: Legal Aspects'. Ottawa: Library of Parliament, 1987.

Himmelweit, Sue. 'Abortion: Individual Choice and Social Control'. *Feminist Review* (1980) 5.

_______. 'More than a "Woman's Right to Choose"?' *Feminist Review* (1988) 29.

Hindell, Keith, and Madeleine Simms. *Abortion Law Reformed*. London: Peter Owen, 1971.

Hubbard, Ruth. *The Politics of Women's Biology*. New Brunswick, N.J.: Rutgers University Press, 1990.

Hunt, Alan. *The Sociological Movement in Law*. London: Macmillan, 1978.

_______. 'The Ideology of Law: Advances and Problems in Recent Applications of the Concept of Ideology to the Analysis of Law'. *Law and Society Review* (1985) 19.

Jacobson, J.L. *The Global Politics of Abortion*. Worldwatch Paper 1987. Washington: Worldwatch Institute 1990.

Jenson, Jane. 'Representations in Crisis: The Roots of Canada's Permeable Fordism'. *Canadian Journal of Political Science* (1990) 23.

_______. 'Representations of Difference: The French Women's Movement'. *New Left Review* (1989) 180.

_______. '"Different" but not "exceptional": Canada's Permeable Fordism'. *Canadian Review of Sociology and Anthropology* (1989) 26.

_______. 'Paradigms and Political Discourse: Protective Legislation in France and the United States Before 1914'. *Canadian Journal of Political Science* (1989) 22.

_______.'Gender and Reproduction: Or, Babies and the State'. *Studies in Political Economy* (1986) 20.

_______. 'Changing Discourse, Changing Agenda: Political Rights and Reproductive Rights in France' in Mary Katzenstein and Carol Mueller (eds) *New Theoretical Perspectives from the Women's Movements of Europe and North America*. Phildelphia: Temple University Press, 1987.

Johnson, Dawn E. 'The Creation of Fetal Rights: Conflicts with Women's Constitutional Rights to Liberty, Privacy, and Equal Protection'. *Yale Law Journal* (1986) 95.

Kaufman, Michael. 'The Construction of Masculinity and the Triad of Men's Violence' in Michael Kaufman (ed.) *Beyond Patriarchy: Essays By Men on Pleasure Power and Change*. Toronto: Oxford University Press, 1987.

Kennedy, Ian. 'A Husband, A Wife, and an Abortion' in his *Treat Me Right: Essays in Medical Law and Ethics*. Oxford: Oxford University Press, 1988.

Keown, John. *Abortion, Doctors and the Law: Some Aspects of the Legal Regulation of Abortion in England from 1803-1982*. Cambridge: Cambridge University Press, 1988.

Keyserlingk, Edward. 'The Unborn Child's Right to Pre-natal Care, (Parts I & II)'. *Health Law in Canada* (1982-83) 31.

King, Patricia. 'Should Mom Be Constrained in the Best Interest of the Fetus?' *Nova Law Review* (1989) 13.

Kingdom, Elizabeth. 'Consent, Coercion and Consortium: The Sexual Politics of Sterilization'. *Journal of Law and Society* (1985) 12.

Knight, Patricia. 'Women and Abortion in Victorian and Edwardian England'. *History Workshop* (1977) 4.

Kome, Penney. *Women of Influence: Canadian Women and Politics.* Toronto: Doubleday, 1985.

Koppers, Bartha Maria. 'Modern Birth Technology and Human Rights'. *American Journal of Corporate Law* (1985) 33.

Kolder, Veronika E.B., Janet Gallagher and Michael T. Parsons. 'Court-Ordered Obstetrical Interventions'. *New England Journal of Medicine* (1987) 313.

Lamoureux, Diane. *Fragments et collages: Essai sur le féminisme québécois.* Montreal: Remue-Menage, 1986.

Law Reform Commission of Canada. *Crimes Against the Foetus.* Working Paper #58. Ottawa: Supply and Services, 1989.

Lovenduski, J. and J. Outshorn (eds). *The New Politics of Abortion.* Beverly Hills: Sage, 1986.

Luker, Kristen. *Abortion and the Politics of Motherhood.* Berkeley: University of California Press, 1984.

Luxton, Meg. 'Two Hands for the Clock: Changing Patterns in the Gender Division of Labour in the Home' in Meg Luxton, Harriet Rosenberg and Sedef Arat-Koc, *Through the Kitchen Window: The Politics of Home and Family.* Second and Enlarged Edition. Toronto: Garamond Press, 1990.

McConnell, M.C. 'Even by Common Sense Morality: Morgentaler, Borowski and the Court of Canada'. *Canadian Bar Review* (1989) 68.

McConnell, M.L. 'Capricious, Whimsical and Aborting Women: Abortion as a Medical Criminal Issue (Again)'. *Canadian Journal of Women and the Law* (1989-90) 3.

McDonald, Lynn. 'The Evolution of the Women's Movement in Canada'. *Branching Out* (1979) 6.

McDonnell, Kathleen. *Not an Easy Choice: A Feminist Re-examines Abortion.* Toronto: The Women's Press, 1984.

_______. 'Claim No Easy Victories: The Fight for Reproductive Rights' in

M. Fitzgerald *et al.* (eds) *Still Ain't Satisfied: Canadian Feminism Today*. Toronto: The Women's Press, 1982.

McIntosh, Mary. 'The State and the Oppression of Women' in Annette Kuhn and Ann Marie Wolpe (eds) *Feminism and Materialism*. London: Routledge & Kegan Paul, 1978.

_______. 'The Family, Regulation and the Public Sphere' in Gregor McLennan, David Held and Stuart Hall (eds) *State and Society in Contemporary Britain: A Critical Introduction*, Cambridge: Polity Press, 1984.

MacKinnon, Catharine A. *Feminism Unmodified*. Cambridge, Mass. Harvard University Press, 1987.

_______. *Toward a Feminist Theory of the State*. Cambridge, Mass. Harvard University Press, 1989.

McLaren, Angus. *Reproductive Rituals: The Perception Of Fertility in England From the Sixteenth Century to the Nineteenth Century*. London: Methuen, 1984.

_______. 'Birth Control and Abortion in Canada, 1870-1920' in Alison Prentice and Susan Mann Trofimenkoff (eds) *The Neglected Majority: Essays in Canadian Women's History*, Vol. 2, Toronto: McClelland & Stewart, 1987.

_______. *Birth Control in Nineteenth Century England*. London: Croom Helm, 1978.

_______. 'Women's Work and the Regulation of Family Size: The Question of Abortion in the Nineteenth Century'. *History Workshop* (1977) 4.

McLaren, Angus, and Arlene Tigar McLaren. *The Bedroom and the State: The Changing Practices and Politics of Contraception and Abortion in Canada*. Toronto: McClelland & Stewart, 1986.

McLean, S. (ed). *Legal Issues in Human Reproduction*. Aldershot: Gower, 1989.

McNulty, Molly. 'Pregnancy Police: The Health Policy and Legal Implications of Punishing Pregnant Women for Harm to Their Fetuses'. *Review of Law and Social Change* (1987-88) 19.

Mandel, Michael. *The Charter of Rights and the Legalization of Politics*. Toronto: Wall & Thompson, 1989.

Martin, Sheilah L. 'Using the Courts to Stop Abortion by Injunction: *Mock v Brandanburg*'. *Canadian Journal of Women and the Law* (1989-90) 3.

_______. 'Canada's Abortion Law and the Canadian Charter of Rights and Freedom'. *Canadian Journal of Women and the Law* (1986) 1.

_______. *Women's Reproductive Health, the Canadian Charter of Rights and Freedom and the Canada Health Act*. Ottawa: CACSW, 1989.

Mitchison, Wendy. 'Historical Attitudes Forward Women and Childbirth'. *Atlantis* (1979) 4.

National Association of Women and the Law. Response to Law Reform Commission of Canada Working Paper 58, *Crimes Against the Fetus* (Fall, 1989).

Nsiah-Jefferson, Laurie. 'Reproductive Laws, Women of Colour, and Low-Income Women' in Sherrill Cohen and Nadine Taub (eds) *Reproductive Laws for the 1990s*. Clifton, N.J.: Humana Press, 1989.

Oakley, Ann. *Women Confined: Towards a Sociology of Childbirth*. Oxford: Martin Robertson, 1980.

_______. *The Captured Womb: A History of the Medical Care of Pregnant Women*. Oxford: Basil Blackwell, 1986.

O'Brien, Mary. *Reproducing the World: Essays in Feminist Theory*. Boulder, Col.: Westview Press, 1989.

_______. *The Politics of Reproduction*. London: Routledge & Kegan Paul, 1981.

Olsen, Fran. 'The Myth of State Intervention in the Family'. *Journal of Law Reform* (1985) 18.

Ontario Law Reform Commission of Ontario. *Report on Human Artificial Reproduction and Related Matters*. Toronto: Ministry of Attorney General, 1985.

Ontario Coalition for Abortion Clinics. 'State Power and the Struggle for Reproductive Freedom: The Campaign for Free-Standing Abortion Clinics in Ontario'. *Resources for Feminist Research* (1988) 17.

Overall, Christine. ' "Pluck a Fetus From Its Womb": A Critique of Current Attitudes Toward the Embryo/Fetus'. *University of Western Ontario Law Review* (1986-87) 24.

Pelrine, Eleanor Wright. *Abortion in Canada*. Toronto: New Press, 1971.

Petchesky, Rosalind Pollack. *Abortion and Woman's Choice: The State, Sexuality and Reproductive Freedom*. Boston: Northeastern University Press, 1985.

_______. 'Fetal Images: The Power of Visual Culture in the Politics of Reproduction' in Michelle Stanworth (ed.) *Reproductive Technologies: Gender, Motherhood, and Medicine*. Minneapolis: University of Minnesota Press, 1987.

_______. 'Abortion as "Violence Against Women": A Feminist Critique'. *Radical America* (1984) 18.

Planned Parenthood Federation of Canada. *Directions for a Sexual and Reproductive Health Policy for Canada*. Ottawa: Planned Parenthood, 1989.

Powell, M. *Report on Therapeutic Abortion Services in Ontario: A Study Commissioned by the Ministry of Health (Powell Report)*. Toronto: Ministry of Health, 1987.

Report of the Social Assistance Review Committee (Transitions). Toronto: Queen's Printer, 1988.

Rhoden, Nancy K. 'The Judge in the Delivery Room: The Emergence of Court-Ordered Cesareans'. *California Law Review* (1986) 74.

Ricks, S. 'The New French Abortion Pill: The Moral Property of Women'. *Yale Journal of Law & Feminism* (1989) 1.

Roberts, Helen (ed). *Women, Health and Reproduction*. London: Routledge & Kegan Paul, 1981.

Robertson, John A. 'Procreative Liberty and the Control of Conception, Pregnancy, and Childbirth'. *Virginia Law Review* (1983) 69.

Rogers, Sanda. 'Fetal Rights and Maternal Rights: Is There A Conflict?' *Canadian Journal of Women and the Law* (1986) 1.

Rosenblum, Victor G. and Thomas J. Marzen. 'Strategies for Reversing *Roe v Wade* Through the Courts' in D. Horan, E. Grant and P. Cunningham (eds) *Abortion and the Constitution: Reversing Roe v Wade Through the Courts*. Georgetown: Georgetown University Press, 1987.

Ross, David P. and Richard Shillington. *1989 Canadian Fact Book on Poverty*. Ottawa: Canadian Council on Social Development, 1989.

Rothman, Barbara Katz. 'Motherhood: Beyond Patriarchy'. *Nova Law Review* (1989) 13.

_______. *Recreating Motherhood: Ideology and Technology in a Patriarchal Society*. New York: W.W. Norton & Co., 1989.

Rubin, E.R. *Abortion, Politics and the Courts: Roe v Wade and Its Aftermath*. New York: Greenwood, 1987.

Ryder, Bruce. 'Equality Rights and Sexual Orientation: Confronting Heterosexual Family Privilege'. *Canadian Journal of Family Law* (1990) 9.

Seward, Shirley and Kathryn McDade. *Immigrant Women in Canada: A Policy Perspective.* Ottawa: Canadian Advisory Council on the Status of Women, 1988.

Shaw, Margery W. 'Should Child Abuse Laws be Extended to Include Fetal Abuse?' in Aubrey Milunsky and George J. Annas (eds) *Genetics and the Law III.* New York: Plenum Press, 1985.

Sheehy, Elizabeth A. 'The Law of "Feticide" in the United States', unpublished manuscript, September 1987.

Shostack, Arthur B., and Gary McLouth with Lynn Seng. *Men and Abortion: Lessons, Losses and Love.* New York: Praeger, 1984.

Shumiatcher, Morris C. 'I Set Before You Life and Death (Abortion, Borowski and the Constitution)'. *University of Western Ontario Law Review* (1986-87) 24.

Singer, Peter and Deane Wells. *The Reproduction Revolution: New Ways of Making Babies.* Oxford: Oxford University Press, 1984.

Smart, Carol. *Feminism and the Power of Law.* London: Routledge, 1989.

_______. 'Power and the Politics of Child Custody' in Carol Smart and Selma Sevenhuijsen (eds) *Child Custody and the Politics of Gender.* London: Routledge, 1989.

Somerville, Margaret. 'Reflections on Canadian Abortion Law: Evacuation and Destruction—Two Separate Issues'. *University of Toronto Law Journal* (1981) 31.

Stanworth, Michelle (ed). *Gender, Motherhood, and Medicine.* Minneapolis: University of Minnesota Press, 1987.

Sumner, Colin. *Reading Ideologies: An Investigation into the Marxist Theory of Ideology and Law*, London: Academic Press, 1979.

Tateishi, Susan Alter. 'Apprehending the Fetus *en ventre sa mère*: A Study in Judicial Sleight of Hand'. *Saskatchewan Law Review* (1989) 53.

Thorne, Barrie, and Marilyn Yalom (eds). *Rethinking the Family: Some Feminist Questions.* New York: Longman, 1982

Tolton, Catherine. 'Medicolegal Implications of Constitutional Status for the Unborn: "Ambulatory Chalices" or "Priorities and Aspirations"'. *University of Toronto Law Review* (1988) 47.

Tribe, Lawrence. *Abortion: The Clash of Absolutes*. New York, W.W. Norton & Co., 1990.

Walters, Maria. 'Who Decides? The Next Abortion Issue: A Discussion of Fathers' Rights'. *West Virginia Law Review* (1988) 90.

Watters, Wendall. *Compulsory Parenthood: The Truth About Abortion*. Toronto: McClelland and Stewart, 1976.

_______, *et al.* 'Response to Edward Keyserlingk's Article'. *Health Law in Canada* (1983) 4.

Weedon, Chris. *Feminist Practice and Poststructuralist Theory*. London: Basil Blackwell, 1987.

Williams, Annette. '*In re A.C.* : Foreshadowing the Unfortunate Expansion of Court-Ordered Cesarean Sections'. *Iowa Law Review* (1988) 74.

Women's Legal Education and Action Fund (L.E.A.F.). Factum in *Joseph Borowski v The Attorney General for Canada and Women's Legal Education and Action Fund, R.E.A.L. Women of Canada, Inter-Faith Coalition on the Rights of Women and Children* (14 September 1988).

Index

Abortion: 'backstreet' abortions, 25, 31, 112; and Christian tradition, 9; deaths resulting from, 11, 22; and English criminal law, 9-10, 24, 134; and foetal rights v women's rights, 16, 17, 29, 38, 55, 59, 64, 68, 72-73, 80-87, 116, 130; infertility resulting from, 11, 22; and liberalization discourse, 19-20, 24, 26, 30, 32, 34, 36-43; medicalization of, 4-5, 8, 11, 12, 13, 17, 19-20, 21, 24, 26, 28, 30, 32, 34, 35, 36-43, 47, 54, 55, 59, 70, 98, 115-16, 120, 127; moral issues of, 16, 17, 20, 27, 28-29, 30, 40-41, 59, 67; and post-abortion syndrome, 85; principle of abortion on demand, 28, 29, 36, 44, 45, 88, 105; and rights discourse, 11, 12, 13, 17, 35, 55, 59, 70, 72; social issues of, 16, 23, 26, 27, 30, 36, 42, 55, 59, 72; and third-party interventions, 42, 91-96, 103, 106, 121, 131, 133-40; *see also entries under* Canada
Abortion Caravan (1970), 44, 47
Alberta, 66, 89, 91, 114, 141-42; and access to abortion, 111; and health insurance coverage for abortion, 142
Alberta Federation of Women United for the Family, 53
American Rights Coalition, 112
Anglican Church, *see* Churches: position of on abortion
Anti-choice movement, *see* Pro-life movement
Attorney General of British Columbia, 105
Attorney General of Canada, 96
Attorney General of Quebec, 96

Badgley Committee, Badgley Report, *see* Committee on the Operation of the Abortion Law
Beatty, Perrin, 114
Bill C-43, An Act Respecting Abortion (1991), 4, 12, 96-116; and definition of health, 98, 100-102, 105, 106; and issue of access to abortion services, 98, 99, 104, 105-107, 114; and pro-life movement, 97-98, 99, 100, 105-106, 108; and pro-choice movement, 98-99, 100, 102, 103, 105, 106-107; proposed amendments to, 108; and public hearings, 99-100; and third-party prosecution, 103, 106
Birthright, 53
Black, Dawn, 108
Borowski case, 94-95, 129
Borowski, Joseph, 94, 129, 146
Bourgault, Lise, 101
British Columbia, 65-66, 89, 105; Everywoman's Health Clinic, 90; and health insurance coverage for abortion, 141
British Columbia Civil Liberties Association, 65
British Columbia Civil Liberties case, 142
British law, 9-10, 24, 33; Act of 1837, 10; *Bourne* case, 10, 24, 31; English criminal law tradition, 9-10; Lord Ellenborough's Act, 9, 10; *Offences Against the Person Act*, 10, 24; and 'quickening' as defining beginning of life, 9, 10

Buchanan, John, 143
Burt, Sandra, 48

Campagnola, Iona, 54
Campaign Life Coalition, 54, 92, 96, 98, 105, 112
Campbell, Kim, 106, 107, 108, 110, 112, 113, 114, 115
Campbell River and District Hospital, 134
Canada: abortion issue in 1988 federal election, 88-89; and access to abortion, 25, 37, 38, 42-43, 51-52, 53, 62, 73, 89, 98, 99, 104, 105-109, 111, 114, 118, 121, 124, 125, 134, 141; and Criminal Code reform (1969), 19, 20-36, 44, 51, 53, 72, 122, 124; and decriminalization of abortion, 35, 44, 47, 61, 116, 118, 122; and individual privacy issue, 41; and legislation respecting abortion, 10, 11-12, 18-36; and parliamentary abortion debate (1988), 69-87; and proposed amendments to government resolution on abortion (1988), 86-88; and provincial responsibility in area of abortion, 60, 64, 89, 98, 105, 107, 127, 140-45; and provision of medicare funds for abortion, 121, 122, 141; and public opinion on abortion issues, 60-61, 77-78, 88, 114; rate of abortions in Canada, 22, 25; response of federal government to *Morgentaler* decision, 62-70, 86-116; *see also* Bill C-43
Canada Health Act, 65, 73, 107, 118, 145, 146
Canadian Abortion Rights Action League (CARAL), 46, 47, 50, 63, 65, 66, 96, 105, 106, 109
Canadian Advisory Council on the Status of Women, 47, 48, 66
Canadian Alliance for the Repeal of the Abortion Law, *see* Canadian Abortion Rights Action League (CARAL)
Canadian Bar Association (CBA), 25, 30, 32, 38, 40, 97; proposals to Parliamentary Committee (1967), 29-30
Canadian Civil Liberties Association (CCLA), 96
Canadian Committee on the Status of Women, 31
Canadian Congress of Catholic Bishops (CCCB), 101
Canadian Labour Congress (CLC), 102, 104
Canadian Law Reform Commission on Crimes Against the Foetus, 97
Canadian Medical Association (CMA), 25, 26-29, 30, 32, 36, 38, 66, 88, 97; response to Bill C-43, 103, 104, 105, 107; resolution on legal abortion (1967), 27, 28, 33
Canadian Physicians for Life, 96, 98, 101
Canadian Rights Coalition, 112
Canadian Women's Educational Press, 46
Centre des femmes, 46; 'Nous aurons les enfants que nous voulons', 47
Charter of Rights and Freedoms, 4, 16-17, 50, 59, 63, 95, 118, 120, 123, 124-26, 129
Chatelaine, 23
Churches, position of on abortion: Anglican Church of Canada, 30; Church of England, 30; Protestant churches, 21, 22, 30; Roman Catholic Church, 32, 53; United Church of Canada, 30
Clinics, free-standing abortion, 16, 18, 39, 51, 52-53, 58, 62-63, 89-90, 105-106, 121; *see also* Morgentaler clinics
Comité de lutte pour l'avortement et la contraception libres et gratuits, 47
Committee for the Establishment of Abortion Clinics, 122
Committee on the Operation of the Abortion Law (Badgley Committee),

37, 38-39; *Report of the Committee on the Operation of the Abortion Law (The Badgley Report)*, 37, 47, 134
Conservative party, *see* Progressive Conservative party
Costigan, Angela, 136, 139
Criminal Code of Canada, 1, 12, 20-36, 64, 87, 97, 98, 103, 106, 107, 108, 109, 113, 118, 122, 124, 127, 128, 129, 134, 137, 144; and *Offences Against the Persons Act*, 10, 24; and omnibus bill to reform (1969), 33-34, 36, 41; and 'saving' provision, 24; Section 251, 4, 11, 16, 17, 20, 34, 39, 59, 60, 63, 64, 95, 106, 124, 126; Sections 271-274, 24; *see also* Canada: and legislation respecting abortion
Crosbie, John, 60

Daigle, Chantal, 93-94, 95-96, 103, 135, 146
Democracy on Trial, 40
de Valk, Reverend Alphonse, 115
Dewar, Marion, 73, 88
Dixon, Marlene, 45
Doctors, 24-25, 26-29, 32, 39, 40, 94, 103-105, 110-14, 128; decision-making power of, 11, 17, 24-25, 27-28, 36, 41, 42, 78-79, 98, 100, 102; and definition of 'health', 24-25, 37-38; fear of legal liability of, 11, 24, 25, 34, 38, 102, 104-105, 108, 111-12, 115, 118; number of doctors performing abortions in Canada, 104, 112; professional needs of, 21, 30, 39; and response to Bill C-43, 103-105, 110-14; rights and responsibilities of, 16, 24-25, 46; *see also* Canadian Medical Association (CMA)
Dodd, Barbara, 91-93, 136, 138
Duek, Peter, 65

Epp, Jake, 64

Family planning movement, 22
Fathers' rights, *see* Abortion: third-party interventions
Fédération des Femmes du Québec, 44
Focus on the Family, 100
Foetus, rights of in abortion issue, 11, 12-13, 16, 17, 19, 29, 38, 41, 42, 54, 55, 59, 63, 64, 66, 68, 70, 72-73, 76, 79, 80-81, 85, 93, 95, 116, 129, 130-33, 146
France, abortion laws in, 37
Fudge, Judy, 120

Gallagher, Janet, 133
Globe and Mail, 31-32, 40
Goods and Services Tax, 110

Haidasz, Stanley, 68, 115
Herridge, H.W., 33; private member's bill, 33
Hnatyshyn, Ray, 64, 88
Hospitals: and access to abortions, 42-43, 51, 53, 62; decision-making power of, 17, 37, 38; *see also* Therapeutic Abortion Committees (TACs)
Humanist: Fellowship of Canada, 28, 29; Association of Canada, 104

International Planned Parenthood Federation (IPPF), 22, 138
International Women's Day Coalition, 52

Jewett, Pauline, 54

Keyserlingk, Edward, 130, 131, 132
Kome, Penney, 48

Lang, Otto, 38
Law Reform Commission of Canada, 88, 102, 105, 106, 114
Lepine, Marc, 133
Lewis, Doug, 99, 101, 104, 106, 107, 108
Liberal party, 5, 35, 53-54, 60, 63, 65, 69, 89, 99

Macdonald Commission, *see* Royal Commission on Economic Union

and Development Prospects for Canada
McArthur, Laura, 62
MacDonald, Flora, 54, 88
McDonald, Lynn, 54, 88
McDougall, Barbara, 63, 76, 94
MacGuigan, Mark, 34
MacInnis, Grace, 32-33, 34-35; private member's bill, 33
Maclean's, 136
Mandel, Michael, 140
Manitoba, 93, 94; and access to abortion, 111; and free-standing abortion clinics, 39, 64; and health insurance coverage for abortion, 64
Medhurst, Alexander, 134, 138
Medhurst v Medhurst, 41, 91, 134-35, 136-37, 137-38
Medical Services Act (Nova Scotia), 113, 143, 144
Mitges, Gus, 66; private member's bill, 66-67
Morgentaler clinics, 16, 39; in Halifax, 89, 113, 143; in Montreal, 89, 119, 142; in Toronto, 52-53, 58, 90, 123
Morgentaler Defence Committee, 46, 47
Morgentaler, Dr Henry, 16, 29, 39-40, 46, 47, 50, 51, 52, 89-90, 111, 113-14, 118, 123, 124, 140, 142, 143-44, 146
Morgentaler v The Queen (1988), 1, 4, 5, 12, 14, 16, 17, 18, 20, 43, 55, 58-60, 67, 89, 94, 95, 96, 97, 102, 107, 115, 116, 129, 135, 145; and its effect in making abortion a legislative issue, 16, 17, 59; legal consequences of, 118-46; political consequences of, 62-66
Mulroney, Brian, 54, 64, 67, 87, 88, 94, 99
Mulroney government, 1, 64, 65, 66-70, 95, 96-110; and attempt to bring abortion under Criminal Code (1988), 1, 62-70, 86-116
Murphy, Gregory, 92, 139
Murphy v Dodd, 91-93, 131, 136, 138

Nathanson, Dr Bernard, 67, 115
National Action Committee on the Status of Women (NAC), 48, 66, 103, 104
National Association of Women and the Law (NAWL), 102, 106, 109
National Council of Women, 31, 44, 47
New Brunswick, 62, 89; and health insurance coverage for abortion, 89, 142-43; Morgentaler's case against, 89, 118-19, 142-43
New Democratic Party (NDP), 23, 32, 35, 36, 54, 60, 63, 65, 73, 87, 99, 109; and pro-choice stance, 54, 63
Newfoundland, 43, 62, 89, 105, 114
Northwest Territories, 89
Nova Scotia, 89, 105, 113-14, 118, 143-44; and access to abortion, 110; and health insurance coverage for abortion, 114; and opposition to Halifax Morgentaler clinic, 89, 113, 143-44

Ontario, 64, 89, 109; and health insurance coverage for abortion, 64, 141
Ontario Coalition for Abortion Clinics (OCAC), 52, 55, 65, 92, 109
Ontario Court of Appeal, 118, 123
Ontario Criminal Lawyers Association, 113
Operation Rescue, 90-91, 95, 119

Parliamentary Committee on Health and Welfare (1967), 26-29, 32, 38
Parti Québécois (PQ), 51, 52
Paton v Trustees of B.P.A.S., 134
Pépin, Lucie, 88
Petchesky, Rosalind, 77, 131-32, 146
Peter Lougheed Hospital, 111
Planned Parenthood, *see* International Planned Parenthood Federation (IPPF)
Planned Parenthood v Danforth, 138
Prince Edward Island, 43, 62, 89, 105, 106

Pro-choice discourse, 55, 70, 71-77; and foetal rights, 72-73, 76, 79; and legal posture, 71; and medical rationale, 71, 72; and pragmatic rationale, 71, 73-75; and principled rationale based on rights, 59, 72, 75-77, 119; and sociological argument, 72
Pro-choice movement, 11, 12, 16, 18, 20, 40, 44, 54, 58, 60, 61, 62, 63, 64, 66, 69, 71-77, 88, 92, 94, 112-13, 118, 122, 132, 136, 145; and Bill C-43, 97, 98-99, 100, 102, 103, 105, 106-107, 108-109, 116; in the House of Commons, 66, 76; principles of, 5, 17, 19, 52, 127, 145-46; in the Senate, 114; tactics of, 44-45, 66, 109, 112-13; and women's rights, 17, 59, 70, 72
Pro-life discourse, 70, 77-86, 94, 121, 126, 130; argument for adoption in, 85-86; campaign against women in, 81-85, 130, 131; presentation of foetus in, 80-81, 132, 146; use of science in, 78-80
Pro-life movement, 4, 13, 16, 20, 43, 51, 52, 53, 58, 59, 60, 61, 62-63, 64, 69, 70, 77-86, 92, 94, 104, 121, 128-29, 135, 136, 146; and Bill C-43, 97-98, 99, 100, 105-106, 108-109, 116; and foetal rights, 16, 17, 19, 42, 54, 55, 63, 70, 73, 79, 80-81, 85, 130-33; in the House of Commons, 66, 67, 68, 69, 87, 99, 109-110; and morality of abortion, 17, 75; as percentage of Canadian public, 77-78; principles of, 5, 16, 17, 19, 42, 53, 55; in the Senate, 115; tactics of, 18, 42, 53, 54, 58, 62-63, 66, 88, 89, 90-91, 112
Progressive Conservative party, 5, 53-54, 60, 63, 66, 69, 99

Quebec, 64, 89, 109, 123; and anti-abortion discourse, 35; and Chantal Daigle case, 93-94; and free-standing abortion clinics, 39, 46, 51-52, 64, 122; and health insurance coverage for abortion, 64, 141; and pro-life groups, 93; women's movement in, 46-47, 51-52
Quebec Court of Appeal, 118, 135
Quebec Medical Association, 94

Real, Equal, Active, for Life, *see* REAL Women
REAL Women, 53, 96, 101, 133, 140
Rebick, Judy, 103
Regroupement des Centres de Santé des Femmes, 109
Report of the Royal Commission on the Status of Women (RCSW), 47, 48-50; recommendations on changes to Criminal Code, 49
Right to Life movement, *see* Pro-life movement
Right-to-Life (Toronto), 62
Robertson, John, 130, 133
Roe v Wade, 26, 37, 41, 91, 125, 127, 132, 134
Roman Catholic Church, *see* Churches: position of on abortion
Rothman, Barbara Katz, 140
Royal Commission on Economic Union and Development Prospects for Canada (1985), 48
Royal Commission on the Status of Women, 48; terms of reference, 48-49

Salvation Army, 100
Saskatchewan, 89, 105, 141; Bill 53 (The Freedom of Informed Choice in Abortion Act), 42
Saskatchewan Court of Appeal, 129, 141
Saskatchewan Reproductive Rights Coalition, 107
Scott, Dr Robert, 90, 123, 124
Senate of Canada, 4, 60, 110-112, 112, 113; and defeat of Bill C-43, 114-15
The Silent Scream, 66
Smart, Carol, 119, 120, 135, 140
Smoling, Dr Leslie, 123, 124
Social Credit party, 35

Society of Obstetricians and Gynaecologists, 112
Stanbury, Robert, 26, 27
Standing Committee on Health and Welfare (1967), 32
Student Union for Peace Action (SUPA), 43
Sullivan and LeMay case, 131
Supreme Court (British Columbia), 42, 65-66, 134
Supreme Court of Canada, 1, 4, 11-12, 16, 17, 39, 43, 55, 58, 59, 61, 64, 67, 94, 95, 97, 103, 109, 115, 123, 124, 126, 129, 135, 139, 141, 146: *see also Morgentaler v The Queen*
Supreme Court (Nova Scotia), 143
Supreme Court (Ontario), 91, 92
Supreme Court (US), 26, 37, 91, 94, 127-28, 137, 138

Therapeutic Abortion Committees (TACs), 4, 11, 12, 18, 21, 25, 27, 33, 39, 41, 98, 128, 134, 137; criteria of, 21, 28, 62; dissolution of, 69, 89; and lack of legal standards, 38; and limits on access to abortion, 37, 38, 42-43, 51, 53, 62, 125, 134, 141
Toronto Star, 99
Tremblay, Jean-Guy, 93, 138
Tremblay v Daigle, 131, 139
Trudeau, Pierre, 40
Turner, John, 35, 38, 54, 63, 87

United Church of Canada, *see* Churches, position of on abortion
United States: abortion clinics in, 63; abortion law in, 13, 41, 91, 127; and issue of individual privacy, 41; legal cases in, 91, 127-28, 132-33, 136, 137; and 'pro-family' themes, 41, 42; and public opinion concerning abortion issues, 61; *see also Roe v Wade*
Urquhart, Ian, 142

Vancouver Women's Caucus, 44
Vander Zalm, Bill, 65, 141
Victoria General Hospital, 111

Wahn, Ian, 33; private member's bill, 33
Wappel, Thomas, 89
Webster v Reproductive Health Services, 91
Wilson, Justice Bertha, 59, 125
Winnipeg Health Sciences Centre, 111
Women's College Hospital, 91, 92
Women's Legal Education and Action Fund (LEAF), 96, 102, 104, 106
Women's Liberation Group, 31; Toronto chapter, 31
Women's movement, 16, 21, 25-26, 31, 43-50, 61, 70, 72, 122; conflict within over abortion issues, 44-47, 50; and liberal feminism, 47-48, 50; and marginalization of women in abortion debate, 20, 31-32, 61; as outgrowth of student movement, 43; in Quebec, 51-52; and racial issues, 52; and radical feminism, 46, 47; reaction of to pro-life movement, 43, 51, 52; and socialist feminism, 46, 47; and Trotskyists, 45, 47; *see also* Women's rights in abortion issue
Women's rights in abortion issue, 16, 17, 36-37, 38, 59, 64, 70, 72, 116
World Health Organization, 102

YMCA, 104
Young Socialist/League for Socialist Action, 45